Happy Birthday!
All the best
in the year
ahead!
With Love,
Jan + Tim

American Pain

Also by John Temple

The Last Lawyer: The Fight to Save Death Row Inmates
Deadhouse: Life in a Coroner's Office

American Pain

How a Young Felon and His Ring of Doctors Unleashed America's Deadliest Drug Epidemic

John Temple

Guilford, Connecticut

An imprint of Rowman & Littlefield

Distributed by NATIONAL BOOK NETWORK

British Library Cataloguing in Publication Information Available

Library of Congress Cataloging-in-Publication Data Available

ISBN 978-1-4930-0738-7 (hardcover)
ISBN 978-1-4930-1959-5 (e-book)

∞™ The paper used in this publication meets the minimum requirements of American National Standard for Information Sciences—Permanence of Paper for Printed Library Materials, ANSI/NISO Z39.48-1992.

In passages containing dialogue, quotation marks were used only when the author was reasonably sure that the speaker's words were verbatim, such as exchanges taken from court testimony or captured on audio recordings. When a source recounted a conversation from memory, the author did not use quotation marks in that dialogue.

Contents

Prologue

Broward County, Florida
November 19, 2009

Red caution lights flashed, warning bells chimed. A gold Toyota Camry with Tennessee plates approached the railroad crossing. It was 8:43 a.m., the end of rush hour in Fort Lauderdale.

The crossing gate was halfway down when the Camry lurched forward and slipped under the red-and-white-striped arm. Two hundred yards down the tracks, a train engine came into view, barreling toward the Camry at 60 mph, backed by a 325-ton chain of sky-blue Tri-Rail commuter cars. Plenty of time to get across, but drivers watching from other cars couldn't believe the woman behind the wheel would risk it.

Then the Camry stopped. On the tracks.

For a few agonizing seconds, the car sat motionless as the caution lights alternated, and the warning bells sounded. The Camry driver put the car in reverse, but could back up only a few feet before running into the now-horizontal gate.

Just as the train engine hurtled into the crossing, the driver made an inexplicable decision, gunning the car forward. The engine's rail guard slammed the Camry with an unearthly rending reverberation, and the gold sedan became a toy car flung by a child, flipping through the air sixty feet down the track, swiping a small service hut and coming to rest near a cluster of palmetto.

One of the drivers behind the Camry dialed 911 and ran over to help. He knelt by a middle-aged white woman who'd been thrown from the mangled car, which was resting on its roof nearby. A few yards away, the man's fiancée attended to another bloody woman, younger, and she was praying. Other witnesses were screaming. Blood was everywhere, staining the man's pants. The woman below him gasped for breath.

He said: Everything's OK.

There was nothing he could do but simply be there as she tried to heave oxygen into her broken lungs.

He said: Ambulance is coming. Everything's gonna be OK.

And soon the paramedics did come, and the cops, and the reporters, but they were too late. Both women died beside the train tracks. A man who was in the car was still alive, and they took him to North Broward Medical Center. Crime scene investigators searched the crumpled, upside-down Camry and found an amber prescription bottle and a scattering of blue pills.

And that's when everything made sense, as it would to any cop or paramedic or reporter working in South Florida in 2009. The Tennessee plates. The driver's bad decisions. Her sluggish reactions.

Oxy.

Talking to his best friend and boss over the phone at a quarter after eight the next morning, Derik Nolan's growling voice was as full of swagger and humor as usual, and it also contained an edge of wonderment, like, *you* believe *this shit?* Something Derik still felt every day working at American Pain. Wonderment at the things he witnessed, the jams that human beings, including himself, would get themselves into while they were trying to get the thing they wanted.

"They tried to fucking weave through a railroad crossing and got hit by a fucking train yesterday," Derik said. "Two of them are dead. One of them is in critical condition."

Derik was sitting in his office at American Pain, underneath the Spartan warrior swords he'd bought and mounted on the wall after seeing the movie *300.* A few minutes earlier, a woman at one of the MRI services he used had called and told him to look at the *Sun-Sentinel.* Derik had immediately pulled the story up on his computer: two women from Tennessee killed in a train crash, another man badly injured. Derik's contact was all upset because the police had called her after finding an MRI report from her company among the wreckage, along with a bunch of pills. She'd looked up the dead women; they'd been American Pain patients.

After that initial conversation, Derik had called Chris George about the story. Chris had just turned twenty-nine, three years younger than Derik, but he was the boss.

"Did it say they were pain clinic people?" Chris asked.

"No, the story doesn't say anything about pills or American Pain. But it will tomorrow," Derik predicted.

"Oh yeah?" Chris said.

"It'll say tomorrow that there was roxies scattered throughout the car."

It wasn't good news, but, hey, add it to the list of administrative headaches that came with running the biggest oxycodone clinic in the country. Headaches like the upstart pain clinic that was getting ready to open in Jacksonville. Those crooks were trying to steal Derik's patients, calling them up in Kentucky and saying they were a new branch of American Pain. Derik was going to have to drive up there and put the fear of God into them, show them who was top dog.

Or, speaking of problems, how about the story in the *Palm Beach Post* five days earlier about a different dead patient, a guy who'd overdosed after going to a pain clinic that belonged to Chris George's twin brother, Jeff. And Jeff's dumbass quote to the reporter comparing the dead guy to his car: "If I wreck my Lamborghini, am I going to hold the Lamborghini dealership responsible?" The quote was funny, and Derik thought it made sense, but it was needlessly inflammatory, perfectly in keeping with Jeff's general attitude that everyone better get out of his way. Jeff, who was right now *suing* Chris, his own twin brother. Jeff thought Chris owed him a cut of American Pain because it had been Jeff's idea to start a pain clinic. Whereas Chris thought that because Jeff had done almost none of the work actually building or running the place, he wasn't entitled to half the profit.

Add to these problems the fact that every time Derik walked out of American Pain, the same Ford Excursion was parked across the street, with black windows and a little glass bubble thing that rose out of the roof. It was obvious the Boca Raton cops or the DEA or maybe that pesky reporter from Channel 7 had the pain clinic under surveillance, so obvious that Derik wondered why they didn't just set up a tripod and camera on the sidewalk. Derik and Chris half-seriously discussed calling a tow truck or shooting out the vehicle's windows with Derik's trusty slingshot. Once, Derik walked across the street and tried to confront whoever was in the Excursion, but the vehicle hauled ass when he approached it, and they all had a good laugh.

Chris and Derik knew they were on the feds' radar. Four of the doctors at American Pain were among the top nine physician purchasers of oxycodone in the United States, according to the DEA, which meant that together, they were a juggernaut. A buddy of Derik had been arrested a month earlier, and he'd told Derik the FBI had grilled him about American Pain, even pulling out an organization chart that included photos of Chris and Derik and everyone else, like in a mobster movie. Under Derik's photo was the tag, "Enforcer."

American Pain had made Derik rich, or it would have, if Derik had any ability to manage his money. But running American Pain consumed him. American Pain *was* drug addiction. Being inside the waiting room was like being inside the fevered skull of a junkie: conniving, scheming, desperate, desirous. It was loud in there, the babble of the zombie horde, and it stank. Ceiling fans stirred the air, but nothing could dispel the funk of 150 people who'd spent the night squeezed into the back seats of shitbox clunkers rolling south from Kentucky and West Virginia. They all wanted Derik's attention, knew he could deny them their fix. Everyone had an angle, a hustle. Derik wasn't sure how much longer he could do it. He was exhausted, depleted in every way, doing lots of pills and coke himself, just to keep going.

So, add the dead Tennessee women to the list of complications, a list that grew longer every day yet still never quite brought down American Pain. Because Derik and Chris had the law on their side. Or the lack of law.

"You gotta be an idiot to get hit by a train," Chris said, and he and Derik laughed. Because that was reality at American Pain—tragic, sure, but also funny, if your eyes were open to the absurdity of it all. And you had to see the oxy business that way, or else how would you keep doing it?

At the Drug Enforcement Administration's Miami Division office, in a large room devoted to the interception of Title III wiretaps, a federal agent was listening through headphones to the conversation between Chris George and Derik Nolan. The DEA had been running a wiretap on Chris George's cell phone for fourteen days, under the supervision of an FBI special agent named Jennifer Turner.

Turner had first heard about rogue pain clinics a year earlier. Back then, she knew next to nothing about painkillers and addiction. Since then, she'd witnessed the destructive power of oxycodone, and it awed her.

To understand oxycodone, imagine everything that makes a man or woman feel good, all the preoccupations and pastimes we are programmed to enjoy. Sex, love, food. Money, power, health. Synthesize all of that pleasure-kindling potency, and multiply by ten. Then cram it all into a pebble-sized blue pill. That's oxycodone—one of the most irresistible opioid narcotics ever cooked up in the six-thousand-year history of dope. Crush and snort a 30-milligram pill, known as an oxy 30, and feel the euphoria bloom in your limbs, the ecstatic warmth settle in the depths of your belly. It's an interlude of bliss. It's basically heroin, only synthetic and FDA-approved.

Not long ago, doctors feared the addictive power of narcotic painkillers so much that they prescribed them mostly to end-stage cancer patients or massively broken motorcyclists—patients who were going to heal or die. But since the mid-1990s, pharmaceutical giants have aggressively marketed painkillers to a wider group of patients with long-term or milder forms of pain. At the same time, the federal government has approved one massive increase after another in the quantities manufactured, even as its own officials declared prescription drug abuse a mounting epidemic.

More and more of the pills were diverted to the black market and by the eve of 2010, more people were addicted to or abusing narcotic painkillers than any illegal drug except marijuana. Far more. The number of people who regularly used prescription drugs to get high in 2009 was more than four and a half times higher than the number of people who regularly used cocaine.

And like cocaine before it, the illicit painkiller trade was dominated by one state: Florida. But the similarities between cocaine and oxycodone ended there. Oxycodone wasn't created in Colombian jungle laboratories or smuggled in suitcases or on thirty-foot "go-fast" speedboats. It was manufactured in pharmaceutical plants in St. Louis and promoted on highway billboards, and in page after page in the back of the *New Times*, a free weekly newspaper in South Florida. The bigger advertisements usually showed a woman holding her forehead and wincing, or a man's torso arched in agony. The ads blared: "CHRONIC PAIN? STOP HURTING AND START LIVING!" Then, in smaller type: "Walk-Ins Welcome. Dispensing On-Site!" Some offered coupons or specials. One clinic's ad said nothing about pain itself and simply displayed the goods: an amber prescription bottle, dozens of little blue pills tumbling out.

Florida pumped millions upon millions of doses of those narcotics—oxycodone, mostly—northward, not through a major criminal organization like the cartels of Mexico, but via thousands of individuals who streamed up and down Interstate 75 or flew from the Tri-State Airport in Huntington, West Virginia, to Miami International, on a flight nicknamed the Oxy Express. They went to the pain clinics complaining of back pain and received a massive supply of narcotics once only available to ease the agony of a Stage 4 cancer patient. A supply that could keep even the most hardcore junkie satisfied for a couple of weeks. A supply worth $6,000 to $8,000 in the coal patches and hollows of Kentucky.

Cops and reporters called these clinics "pill mills," and American Pain was the king of them all. Its doctors distributed massive quantities of oxycodone to hundreds of customers a day. The clinic had already moved three times in less than two years; its current location was a ten-thousand-square-foot suite in a strip mall in Boca Raton, next to a family restaurant. Outside, it looked like a bustling doctor's office, or the DMV. Inside, Derik Nolan's crew of heavily inked muscle-heads and ex-strippers operated the office and pharmacy, counting out pills and stashing cash in garbage bags. Under their white lab coats, the doctors carried guns.

When Chris George had opened his first clinic in February 2008, there were only a handful of other pain clinics in Broward County. But he made millions, and soon it seemed every shady operator in South Florida had witnessed George's success and wanted a piece. So by November 2009 there were 115 pain clinics in Broward alone. But American Pain had the drug wholesalers and the customer base. And American Pain was the first to advertise on billboards, to use rubber prescription stamps (so the doctors' hands wouldn't cramp from writing the same scrips over and over), to hire beautiful women to dispense the pills. Chris George and Derik Nolan developed record-keeping protocols and insisted that all patients have some sort of file, in case the DEA came calling.

Chris George was constantly expanding, trying to stay one step ahead of the evolving laws. He had two major pain clinics in South Florida, another new one starting up soon outside of Atlanta, pharmacies in Boca Raton and Orlando, all in the names of various straw owners: tens of thousands of patients, dozens of employees, eight full-time doctors, lawyers, private investigators.

American Pain—and the whole industry, really—had exploded in the year since Jennifer Turner began her investigation. There was no easy way to shut down the pill mills, or her task force would have done it months earlier. Traditional drug-enforcement strategies, such as searching patients' cars or doing buy-and-busts, had proven relatively useless against pill mills. Even if they caught a patient selling pills, it rarely led to bigger fish. The pills originated from the same source—a doctor's office—and it was next-to-impossible to prove that a doctor *knew*, beyond a reasonable doubt, that a patient was faking pain.

Turner was fighting a new crime with old laws, and she wasn't sure who would prevail.

Chris and Derik hadn't expected any of this success or trouble when they'd started the ride almost two years earlier. Before opening the clinics, they'd run construction crews in North Port and didn't know the first thing about painkillers. But they'd parlayed business skills and youthful aggression into a mega-clinic, and now oxycodone was the hottest game in Florida, in the country. They were riding a rampaging elephant; the only way to stop it was to kill it. And they didn't want to kill American Pain. Not now, not when the clinic was inhaling $100,000 a day. A *day*.

Chris and Derik had a plan they believed would solve their problems. They were going to move the flagship. They'd moved the clinic three times before, but this time they weren't just going to another office park or shopping plaza to get away from police pressure or angry neighbors. They needed a new start, one that reflected how far they'd come. The day after the train crash story in the *Sun-Sentinel*, Chris and Derik went to Lake Worth to check out a promising new location, a former bank building.

They loved it. Three floors and twenty thousand square feet, twice the size of their current space in Boca Raton and almost twenty times the size of the little bungalow they'd renovated on Oakland Park Boulevard two years earlier. A gigantic waiting room that could hold hundreds of pill-heads. Three vaults for the cash and oxy, actual bank vaults with those big round doors you walked through. A second floor for administrative offices with a catwalk for security to keep an eye on the waiting room below. And the open third floor where they could do whatever they wanted. It even had an elevator. The place would be a true headquarters, from which they would expand and seed the entire country with pain clinics. It would be a fortress.

All they had to do was talk the owner—an art-collecting millionaire CEO from Palm Beach—into letting them transform his building into a Walmart of oxycodone.

Derik didn't know much about the guy, but he liked their chances. Over the last two years, Chris and Derik had pulled off this particular sleight of hand a hundred times, helping straight citizens profit from the painkiller trade. The key was to make sure nobody thought too deeply about what they were doing. And that was the power of oxycodone, a power they understood by now. Oxycodone came in amber pill bottles, not little plastic bags, and it took the form of manufactured tablets, not powder or jagged shards. Pills *looked* legitimate. Their precise, factory-shaped contours made it easy for people to believe they weren't making money from opioid addiction, just as they made real patients believe they wouldn't become junkies.

Or maybe it came down to an even simpler truth. No matter how many pillheads died in train crashes, no matter how many times cops or TV reporters set up cameras across the street from American Pain, no matter how many politicians complained about pill mills destroying Florida, one thing remained the same: Wave enough cash in an upstanding citizen's face, and he suddenly stopped worrying about whether the money had come from an addict's pocket.

When Jennifer Turner heard Chris George talking on the wiretap about moving, she drove to Lake Worth to take a look at the new building.

It was enormous, a three-story, gleaming-white colossus that stood by itself on Dixie Highway, isolated by a buffer of 153 parking spaces. Windowless and invincible-looking, a solid block-like structure, taller than anything else in the area.

Turner imagined a sea of addicts inside the massive facility, hundreds of them lined up at customer windows, receiving their bottles of narcotics, then streaming out into the Florida sunlight to wreak havoc.

The vision haunted her. She had to stop this. But how?

Part I

1

It was late 2007 when Chris George told Derik Nolan that he was going into the pain management business with his twin brother Jeff. Derik wasn't particularly surprised. The brothers already owned a place called South Beach Rejuvenation Clinic, basically a front to sell anabolic steroids. They called it a "telemedicine" clinic, and this meant the doctors consulted with patients over e-mail or phone, writing prescriptions for pretty much whatever muscle-builder the patients wanted. They advertised the clinic in bodybuilding magazines, and Derik was a faithful customer. So it didn't sound to him like a huge leap to open another place that involved doctors and meds. The significance of it all escaped him.

Derik had met the George brothers when they were all competing to build houses in Loxahatchee in the early 2000s. Those were the boom years, when you could sell houses in Florida as fast as you could put them up, and housing prices seemed like they'd never stop rising. Derik had spent five years doing plumbing for someone else before investing in his own home construction company. Jeff's hurricane shutter business did some subcontracting for Derik, and they started hanging out.

Derik had been pretty focused on building his business in those years, but Jeff brought out his crazy streak. They were in their twenties, guys with money in their pockets, but they still enjoyed kid stuff, mixing ammonium nitrate and flash powder, making their own quarter-sticks of dynamite and tossing them out the window of Jeff's pearl-yellow Lamborghini in downtown Fort Lauderdale. Then speeding away, doubled over in laughter, hearing the *boom*, people scared shitless. Once, stopped at a streetlight, a guy pulled up next to Jeff and Derik's car. Derik was driving, Jeff eating a piece of pizza, and Jeff just reached out the open window and put the greasy, half-eaten slice of pizza on the hood of the guy's car. Why? No reason at all, except he thought it would be funny. The guy was pissed, but when he looked over at them—Jeff's neck flaring out with muscle thicker than his head, Derik sporting a multi-broken nose—he knew there was nothing he was gonna do about it. A couple of times, Jeff and Derik did worse things to people who actually had it coming to them, and Derik started developing a reputation: a guy you didn't mess with.

In 2006, the housing market started to teeter. Derik was overextended and went out of business. He took a job as a field superintendent with Majestic Homes, which was owned by Jeff George's father, moving around the state and finishing mid-stream construction jobs, closing things down. He wound up on Florida's west coast, in North Port, where Jeff's twin brother Chris was running a division of Majestic Homes with half a dozen employees.

Chris cropped his hair short and had a good-looking, clean-cut college-boy look that Derik kind of envied, a look at odds with his police record. Chris had been thirteen the first time he got arrested. He and Jeff were busted making acid bombs on the Fourth of July. They did community service and took classes in fire safety. Later years brought a string of charges: possession of alcohol, fighting, disorderly conduct, obstruction of justice, and grand theft for stealing a police motorcycle when he was nineteen, the height of his crazy period. He never spent time behind bars until 2003, after a cop caught him picking up a package of anabolic steroids ordered from Europe. The steroids were for himself, Jeff, and a couple of friends. He pleaded guilty to felony drug possession charges and was sentenced to eight months in Palm Beach County Jail. He served six, most of it on work release, working for his father as a draftsman and supervisor. When he got out, he kept working for Majestic Homes.

Most people, seeing Chris and Derik together, would have pegged Derik as the criminal. Derik stood out at the gym, in the mosh pits, on the party boats on the Gulf. Tribal tattoos curlicued down his biceps and thick forearms. Off and on, he sported a Mohawk. He had a big square frame, big square brawler's fists, and a big square head sitting right on his shoulders. His nose kind of mashed to the right. He spoke with a New York rasp, talking with his hands and his excitable, cocked, quizzical eyebrows. His walk was a swagger, his resting position a restless sprawl, thick arms flung wide, head tilted to the side. Derik called attention to himself, invited engagement, often the negative kind; certain people wanted to punch him in the face. If there was booze or coke around, and sometimes even if there wasn't, Derik was going to fight. He knew he was supposed to cycle up and down on the testosterone and stanozolol, but he loved the way they made him feel: bigger, louder, stronger than the next guy. So he took them even when he wasn't working out much. After Chris and Jeff opened South Beach Rejuvenation, Derik never paid for steroids again. He'd order whatever he wanted, and Jeff had them mailed directly to Derik's place.

Chris had settled down a bit after his jail time, or at least he didn't call as much attention to his troublemaking as Jeff did. Pretty soon, Derik considered Chris to be his best friend. Derik was three years older than the George twins, but he looked up to Chris, as much as he looked up to anyone. Derik didn't hold it against Chris that he'd grown up loaded, the son of a multi-millionaire home builder, or that Chris had an Iron Cross tattooed on his upper chest and a Nazi SS insignia on his abdomen. Likewise, Chris didn't care about Derik's dark family history, or the things he'd done. Also, Chris barely drank, which worked out well for Derik, because Derik liked to get plastered or do a line of coke and have others do the driving. Chris was a healthy guy, aside from the steroids, and would sit in the strip club or the bar or the boat and sip his diet cola as the party raged around him.

Derik was used to working long days and coming home exhausted and filthy. But working on Florida's west coast as the market was dying was easy, especially when you were best friends with the boss's son. They'd put in half a day, then take a long lunch, and work maybe a couple more hours in the afternoon. Then Chris wanted to go out to eat every night, hit the gym, then head to a strip club, find some girls. Night after night. It was an exciting life, where you might spend the morning installing windows on a mid-level McMansion in Port Charlotte, then drop everything and charter a cruiser to the Keys. Derik could keep up with Chris's pace, and they had the same stupid sense of humor.

Chris was obsessed with this girl who danced at a place called Emerald City Gentleman's Club in Port Charlotte. Her stage name was Katie, kind of a plain name for a stripper, surrounded by Jades and Fantasias and Candis. Derik thought Katie was her real name for about six months, only to find out that she was actually named Dianna, which sounded more stripper-like than her stage name. Dianna Pavnick had long jet-black hair, mischievously arched eyebrows, muscular curves, and a severe mouth. Chris couldn't stop talking about her, wanted to go to her club over and over.

Chris would say: Oh, man, Derik, we gotta go to Emerald tonight.

Derik would say: Dude, this is like four nights in a row.

The head bouncer at Emerald was Dianna's boyfriend. Derik would distract the guy by bringing in a huge stack of ones and making a scene, something that came naturally to him, and Chris would spend time with Dianna, trying to get her to go out with him. One day, the guy smacked Dianna around, and she went home with Chris that night, and they stayed together. Derik liked to say it was just a story of love at first sight at the strip club.

For a couple of months it was the three of them—Chris, Dianna, and Derik—but then Derik went to jail. Derik was a terrible driver, always getting pulled over, and the tickets had piled up until he'd had his license suspended for five years. He started paying a guy to drive him to the construction jobs he was overseeing in North Port. One day, the guy didn't show, and Derik decided to drive himself, made it a mile before getting pulled over, which ended up being a felony beef: driving with license suspended. His probation officer found out, and Derik went to jail. He'd never been behind bars, other than holding tanks. St. Lucie was the worst county jail in Florida from what the other inmates told him. Derik had no serious trouble there, maybe due to the fact that he was a sizable guy, 6'1" and 210 pounds when he was juicing. But he felt panicky the entire time and spent hours a day on the phone with his sister and his lawyer.

When he got out in January 2008, Derik had to start from scratch at thirty years old. Chris George's father fired him from Majestic Homes, and Chris just disappeared on him, wouldn't pick up the phone. Derik heard Chris and Dianna had moved back to Florida's east coast without telling him. They'd moved into Jeff's mansion in Wellington's Edge, and Chris was working with Jeff at the steroid clinic.

Derik felt a little betrayed by Chris, but he got on with his life. He started a new business, window installation, friends driving him everywhere since he had no driver's license.

So Derik was surprised when Chris got in touch a couple weeks later. Chris said he needed help, and Derik's irritation vanished. All was forgiven. Chris had that kind of hold on Derik.

Chris told Derik about his new venture. He and Jeff were going to open a chain of small pain clinics. Jeff had recently bought a second steroid clinic, and a doctor there, a guy named Mike Overstreet, had worked briefly at a pain clinic called One Stop Medical. Steroids were small potatoes, Dr. Overstreet had told Jeff. The real money was in painkillers like oxycodone.

Chris didn't even know what oxycodone was, much less how a pain clinic operated. He and Jeff ran some numbers and did a break-even analysis. The projections didn't impress Chris. He wasn't sure the business would be viable. But he told Jeff he'd give it a shot. They decided Jeff would open a clinic in West Palm Beach, and Chris would open one a little farther south, on Oakland Park Boulevard near Fort Lauderdale. They'd see how the two little clinics did, and maybe end up growing the chain.

In December, when Derik was still in jail, Chris and Dianna had gone to meet with Dr. Overstreet at his house in Fort Lauderdale. Overstreet was a nice guy, black floppy hair, thirty-eight years old, more laid-back and irreverent than Chris expected a doctor to be. Chris liked him. He showed Chris and Dianna his vintage truck and motorcycle, then took them to a shed behind the three-bedroom house and showed them empty oxycodone bottles, meds he'd ordered when he worked at One Stop Medical.

Oxycodone was a legal controlled substance, Overstreet said. Some people took it for pain relief. Others took it to get high. It was addictive, and most doctors made it difficult for patients to obtain. Those doctors drowned their patients in paperwork, drug tests, and diagnostic reports. Some did extensive physical exams, interviewed their patients at length, referred them to specialists, made them do exercises and therapies and non-pharmaceutical treatments before agreeing to medicate. Despite all the tests, no doctor could ever really be 100 percent sure whether a patient was in real pain. Only the patient knew for sure. The doctor had to make a judgment call before writing a prescription. People wanted a doctor who would take them at their word, wouldn't ask too many questions, wouldn't make it too hard to get the drugs. Dr. Overstreet wanted to open a clinic that catered to those people. Other doctors had done this, and their waiting rooms were packed. At his previous clinic, Overstreet had developed a reputation as a big writer who asked few questions. His patients called him "The Candyman."

Chris and Overstreet had struck a deal. Chris would make the initial investment, renovate the building, buy blood pressure monitors and exam tables and office supplies, manage the office, buy the pharmaceuticals. Overstreet would write the scrips and they'd split the profits, 50/50. The doctor said he didn't want the responsibilities involved with running an office, so he'd leave that stuff to Chris.

Jeff had found a little storefront on Oakland Park Boulevard that previously held a Mobile One store. A handful of other pain clinics were operating in Broward County, including two that had opened on the same street. The area was becoming known for its pain clinics, and Chris thought it made sense to open there. That's when Chris got in touch with Derik to ask if he'd help renovate the space.

Chris wasn't sure if the clinic would work out, but he was confident about his business skills. He believed no physician-run operation could compete with him. Doctors didn't understand marketing, minimizing costs, maximizing efficiencies, managing people, accounting. The basics of business. Chris had studied business and construction management. He'd gone to college for four years, two years at Palm Beach Community College and another couple at Florida International University, but he never graduated, just took classes he wanted to take and avoided the ones he thought were stupid. His father would say Chris and Jeff absorbed business principles by growing up in an entrepreneurial family, sitting at the dinner table during the years John George was building Majestic Homes, driving a backhoe as soon as their feet could reach the pedals. John George had moved to Florida as a young guy, taught shop class for a while, and he wasn't shy about mentioning the time he'd been named the Palm Beach County Teacher of the Year. John had stood out as a teacher before quitting to follow in his own father's footsteps—construction—where he *really* stood out, making millions building houses. He'd taken a huge gamble, quitting a steady job, and he made a success of it. John George divorced the boys' mother when they were eight, but he and Denice stayed on good terms most of the time, and she even worked for him for seven years.

After his prison stint on the steroid conviction, Chris went to work for his father. He moved to North Port to expand Majestic Homes's reach to the west coast of Florida. Chris built some fifty custom houses for Majestic Homes before the crash, juggling subcontractors, buyers, realtors, suppliers, and banks. By comparison, he figured, running a pain clinic would be a piece of cake.

Derik had a buddy drive him out to Oakland Park Boulevard to take a look at the future location of Chris's pain clinic. It was kind of a dump, three miles from the beach and a few doors from a dive motel and a Publix supermarket. Most of the surrounding buildings—an auto insurance agency, a bridal headpiece shop, a podiatry office—were a similar size and shape as the Mobile One storefront: single-story stucco bungalows. Four parking spaces in the front, a few more around back. The storefront was an orangey-tan with white trim. Two dilapidated columns held up the front overhang, including one that had crumbled and detached from the roof, revealing the pole underneath the stucco shell. The brown fronds of an ungroomed palm tree spilled into the parking lot.

Chris and Derik renovated the building with a couple pals, not exactly a bang-up job. Chris just wanted to get the place open. He figured it didn't much matter how it looked. So they tore all the walls down and reframed the interior, about eleven hundred square feet. There was a waiting room, a window where Dianna could greet customers, three examination rooms in the back, a little closet where the drugs would be kept. New carpet, doors, paint, the cheapest stuff they could find. A two-week job. But one of the first things Chris did was put a sign on the big white pole out front. Big red letters on a white background: Pain Clinic. And even bigger letters on the sign on the roof of the small building: South Florida Pain Clinic. Chris bought stick-on lettering for the windows:

Pain Management
Testosterone
Weight Loss
HGH
Walk Ins Welcome

Basically the offerings included everything that people desperately wanted from a doctor but usually couldn't get. Drugs to make their life more enjoyable, without the usual hassle. Dr. Overstreet believed pain meds would be the big draw, but he had experience with the muscle and weight-loss stuff from Jeff's steroid clinic, so they'd decided to throw those into the mix.

The signs worked. Pretty much every day somebody stopped by to ask about when they were opening. Oakland Park Boulevard regulars: fidgety, dirty, aggressive. Derik and Chris would be working, covered in sawdust, pencils behind their ears, and some guy would stick his head inside, inquire about their status. One night around 8:00 p.m., Derik was gluing down fresh carpeting and a guy walked in, nonchalant, or trying to act that way. He looked at Derik, who was covered with carpet glue, sweaty, dirty. The floor was half-carpeted, tools everywhere.

The guy: I need a doctor. Can I see a doctor?

Derik looked at him like he was crazy.

Derik: For real, bro, look around. Does it *look* like we're open for business?

The visitors made an impression on Derik. People were crazy for this painkiller stuff, talking themselves into believing they could find a doctor at eight o'clock at night in a place that was torn apart.

One day, Chris and Derik took a break from the renovation to try to track down a guy who owed Chris money. Driving around, they saw a pain clinic sign and decided to check the place out. Once inside, they said they were in pain, and asked if they could see a doctor. A staffer gave them forms to fill out, and then they walked out the door with the forms. Chris decided to use the same forms. Chris had Dianna cut the clinic name off the top of the forms and make copies with South Florida Pain Clinic on top. Chris figured he'd need some paperwork, to keep up appearances, look legit and everything.

A friend of Derik was helping with the renovation. He had a hard time grasping the whole concept.

He kept saying: But you guys aren't *doctors*.

Another friend, also from back home and visiting Derik at the time, couldn't believe it either. It made no sense to him that a guy who wasn't a doctor could open up a pain clinic. No way this could be aboveboard.

He said: Yo, Derik, you're gonna get thrown in jail again.

But Chris George kept telling the guys that it was all legal. As long as you had a doctor ordering the drugs and writing prescriptions, you were fine. That's how the other pain clinics in Florida did it. No one cared who *owned* the place.

Chris told Derik that once Jeff got his West Palm Beach clinic open, Jeff might give Derik a job at the patient window. Nothing great, maybe $12 an hour or so. But they had to see how it went first, whether Jeff would take enough time away from his other ventures to get the place open, and whether the clinic would attract enough customers to survive. Derik was only mildly interested. He figured Chris and Jeff might be able to turn the pain clinics into moderately successful small businesses, something along the lines of South Beach Rejuvenation, but working the patient window wasn't going to make Derik rich.

So Derik finished the renovation and went back to his construction business, thinking that was that.

Derik didn't know much about painkillers. Drugs, to him, meant weed or cocaine. He'd never messed with heroin or meth or OxyContin, didn't hang out with anybody who did what he considered hard stuff. A girlfriend a few years back had always been on the hunt for Lortabs, though, and he'd noticed in recent years that some of the guys on his construction crew were too. Further back, the aunt who'd raised him in Binghamton, New York, had been taking prescription painkillers for years, doling them out when the kids had injuries, but that seemed different to Derik.

Derik's family was hard to explain. Growing up, he lived with his aunt and uncle during the school year, then with his real father during the summers. So he had a mess of half-siblings and cousins he called his brothers and sisters. Derik didn't mind explaining why his family was so splintered, but few people ever asked for the full story of what had happened, especially if they knew something about it.

Derik was an accidental pregnancy in 1977, his parents just out of high school in Sullivan County in upstate New York. Robert Nolan and Margaret got married, and Robert built a home insulation and window installation business. They separated when Derik was still a toddler, and Margaret moved with Derik to the village of Loch Sheldrake, where she worked as a barmaid at a place called Bum & Kel's. She started seeing the tavern owner.

Derik was only four the day his mother died, but the memories appear to him in vivid visual flashes, bound together by facts he'd read or heard over the years. Derik and his father spent the day fishing. He fell asleep watching TV at his father's house. In the middle of the night, his father woke him up, said they were going to look for his mother. They drove to the bar, and it was closed. Down the road, they saw Margaret's car in the driveway of the bar owner. His father parked up the road, and carried Derik to the house. Through a front window, they saw Margaret and the bar owner in the living room, having sex.

Derik remembers his father banging through a screen door and setting him down inside.

He remembers his mother grabbing a knife from the kitchen, and his father pulling out the buck knife he'd used during the fishing trip.

He remembers his father chasing the bar owner outside.

He remembers his mother screaming: *Don't kill him, kill me!* and Derik's father replying: *Don't worry, bitch. You're next.*

He remembers his father, back inside and on top of his mother, stabbing her with the buck knife, over and over.

He remembers shaking his mother awake. She opened her eyes and looked at him, and her eyes were strange. Derik gave her another push, and blood sprayed, so he stopped shaking her.

He remembers finding his father, who was on his knees, his flannel shirt soaked in blood, the barrel of a shotgun in his mouth. Derik called to his dad, who looked at him, let out a sigh. His dad dropped the gun and picked up Derik.

He remembers hanging onto his father as he ran to the truck, Derik looking back, over his father's shoulder, the house getting smaller and smaller.

Of the next year, Derik remembers almost nothing.

Hours after the double homicide, Robert Nolan turned himself in to police. He went to trial the following summer on charges of aggravated manslaughter. He argued that he'd been driven temporarily insane by seeing Margaret and the tavern owner having sex. The jury deadlocked, causing a mistrial. In a second trial, he was acquitted. He did some outpatient therapy and then resumed his life. He remarried, this time to a woman five years younger than himself who had been named Miss Sullivan County the year before Robert killed Margaret. They moved to Freehold, New Jersey, where Robert built a concrete company and sponsored a Little League team. Robert's company thrived. The Nolans put up showy Christmas decorations and threw a pool party every summer.

Derik's aunt and uncle had taken him in during the trials, so he continued to live with them during the school years. They had a small farm, where they raised horses and chickens. Summers, he lived with his father and his new family, which included three young sons. Derik played quarterback in the fall and pole vaulted in the spring, and when he wasn't doing those sports, he was likely skipping school, hunting deer and riding four-wheelers on the farm. The day after his high school graduation party in 1995, he moved to Florida. He said he was going to college, but he just wanted out of New York. He got a job at a nightclub, went to a few classes at Palm Beach State College before quitting. He became a plumber, making good money.

But the story with his father wasn't finished. Almost three years after Derik graduated from high school, Robert Nolan's second wife served him with divorce papers. They'd been married for ten years. She said he was extremely cruel, though not physically abusive. The day after he got the divorce papers, Robert followed her into a walk-in closet and shot her point-blank with a 20-gauge shotgun. He went out behind the pool cabana, smoked a cigarette, drank a Scotch, and shot himself in the head with a .25-caliber Beretta handgun.

The story of Robert Nolan's dead wives became a cautionary tale about the persistence of domestic violence as well as the fatal flaw of the insanity defense (his first trial had taken place the same summer as would-be Reagan assassin John Hinckley Jr., was found not guilty by reason of insanity). The *New York Times* published an in-depth story about the case. So people knew about Derik's father, and Derik didn't keep it a secret. Chris George knew about it, though he and Derik never discussed it in any detail. Derik already had a reputation. People already thought he was crazy. Better, he thought, to leave a little mystery.

Derik never really explained to anybody what he thought about his father. He knew that a beast had lived inside Robert Nolan. But most of the rest of the time, he hadn't been a bad father. Derik had a temper, could kind of understand how someone could do what his father had done, snap under the pressure of family and work, especially if you saw your wife with another man. He didn't hate his dad. What good would that do? Instead, Derik directed his hate toward the cops and prosecutors who tried to put his father away.

Derik grew up, but he didn't plan for the future. He was easily influenced by friends. He liked swords and slingshots and fistfights and blowing things up. People sometimes told Derik he was basically a 6'1" child, even at thirty years old. Derik didn't mind because he knew it was true, and because he felt like acting like a kid was something everybody should try—it was fun. Still, he was smart enough, and he worked hard. He made good money as a plumber and used it to start building houses. He believed he'd found his one gift: running a business day-to-day. And then Chris George came along, and gave him a shot at the pain management racket.

When his cell phone lit up with Chris George's phone number, Derik was crossing the Royal Park Bridge on his way home from a window job on Palm Beach. It was March 2008, a couple weeks after Derik had completed the renovation of Chris's pain clinic. Even as recession loomed, the Florida dream was everywhere around him, a cluster of sparkling white boats bobbing on the intracoastal marina to his left, coral-and-white office towers and condos of downtown West Palm standing tall straight ahead.

Derik answered the call.

Chris needed a favor. South Florida Pain had opened the previous week and was already pulling in decent traffic, fifteen to twenty patients a day. But Chris's father needed him to go to the west coast for the day on Majestic Homes business. So Chris asked if Derik could keep an eye on the pain clinic while Chris was gone, make sure Dianna was safe. Because, Chris said, everyone in the place was a fucking junkie.

Chris didn't want to leave Dianna alone with those people, all the cash and pills lying around. He said Dianna would be happy to drive Derik to the clinic, since he still had no license. Two hundred bucks for the day. Easy money.

Derik pondered Chris's offer. He'd thought he was done with South Florida Pain when he'd finished the renovation. Derik was on probation, couldn't afford to get in trouble. And this sounded sketchy. He wasn't even supposed to leave Palm Beach County, and South Florida Pain was in Broward. Besides, Derik was a construction superintendent, not a security guard.

But no one had ever accused Derik of being prudent, a good decision maker. He had a hard time saying no to friends, especially Chris. When they were renovating the clinic building, Chris had explained to him how the place would work, and Derik was curious to see it in action.

So Derik told Chris he'd do it, even though he knew it was probably a bad idea.

In fact, what Derik said was this: Man, you're gonna get me locked up again.

So Derik hung out at the clinic the next day, twiddling his thumbs, helping out when he could. There wasn't much need for muscle. The patients got what they came for and went away happy. The place felt illegitimate to Derik. The exam rooms had examination tables and blood pressure cuffs and anatomical posters depicting the human spine, just enough medical stuff to be identifiable as a doctor's office—but somehow it didn't feel *real*. Derik doubted the patients ever actually lay down on the exam tables.

It was a simple operation. Dianna greeted patients through the customer window, explaining that seeing the doctor required cash or credit card up front. No health insurance. Dr. Overstreet, the clinic's sole physician, had explained that insurance companies would cause problems for pain clinics if they felt they were paying for unnecessary prescriptions. Taking insured patients wasn't worth the scrutiny. Dianna took the

$200 they charged for new patient visits, and the patient filled out the paperwork Chris and Derik had lifted from the other clinic. When it was the patient's turn to see Overstreet, Dianna hit a switch that unbolted the magnetic lock on the door between the waiting room and the exam rooms. The patient went back to the exam room, came out five or ten minutes later with a prescription in hand, usually 240 oxycodone 30 milligrams, 60 to 120 oxycodone 15 milligrams, and 60 alprazolam. Chris hadn't known how to order prescription pads, so he had called a print shop in West Palm Beach and given them Overstreet's name, address, phone, and license number, and they'd printed them up, using some kind of special prescription paper.

So the patient would give the scrip to Dianna, and she would go back to the "dispensary," a big name for the nine-by-three-and-a-half-foot closet where they kept the drugs in a gun safe they'd picked up at Costco and bolted to the floor. A laptop connected to a label printer sat on a card table. They'd copied the label format from a legit pill bottle to make sure they had all the right information on there. She'd punch in the patient's information, print a label, fix it to a pill bottle, pull the drugs from the safe, and fill the bottle. Back at the front desk, she'd take the money for the meds, usually between $400 and $700, hand over the bottle, staple the receipt to the patient's paperwork, and file it. Done.

Chris had Googled a few policies; the rest he either made up as he went along or he asked Overstreet. The doctor didn't seem worried that anybody would be checking up on them.

On the first day of business, Dr. Overstreet had brought a bunch of small bags filled with pills from his house—oxycodone, Xanax, and Valium. He'd ordered the pills when he was still working at the One Stop Medical clinic and took them when he left. The bags weren't labeled, and Overstreet didn't even seem entirely sure exactly what was inside them. Five patients showed up on Day One, and Dianna counted their pills out of the bags and put them in pill bottles.

Everyone got pills, or, if the dispensary was bare, they got a prescription. Overstreet never turned anyone away empty-handed. His only restriction seemed to be that he wouldn't prescribe more than 240 oxycodone 30-milligram pills per patient every twenty-eight days. More than 240 pills, he told Chris, and you're likely to attract police or DEA attention. Better to stay under the radar. He didn't say how he knew this.

Derik figured it couldn't be kosher for Dianna—whose previous work experience consisted primarily of dancing at Emerald City Gentleman's Club—to be operating the drug dispensary. He asked Chris about it. Didn't you have to be a pharmacist to hand out pills? Especially *these* pills? Chris said he'd asked Overstreet the same thing, and the doctor said it was OK because Dianna was under his supervision. Chris had looked up the rules, and as far as he could tell Overstreet was right. Lucky for them, Florida law allowed doctors not only to write prescriptions but also to actually *sell* the controlled substances themselves. No pharmacist needed.

In fact, a major key to the pain clinic business, Overstreet had told Chris, was dispensing the drugs in-house. That way, patients didn't have to find a pharmacy to fill their prescriptions, which wasn't always easy. Legitimate pharmacies sometimes blacklisted a pain clinic, refused to fill its scrips. They didn't like to see too many suspicious-looking patients with large narcotics prescriptions from the same place. They'd grill the patient, call the clinic. Patients hated this. If South Florida Pain Clinic wrote *and* filled the prescriptions, patients would flock there. And the clinic would get paid twice—once for the doctor's visit and once for the pills.

Overstreet's stash of pills had lasted less than a week, but by then Chris had bought more. The doctor had told Chris which drug wholesalers he'd used in the past and how to fill out the order forms, called 222 forms, that let the DEA track the flow of controlled substances. The order forms listed the supplier, the purchaser, the drugs and amounts. Before the clinic opened, Chris had called Overstreet's wholesalers and asked them about the ordering process. He was used to dealing with vendors from his days at Majestic Homes, and he was good at working the phone, asking the right questions. He sent in the forms, along with Overstreet's state medical license and DEA registration number, which allowed the doctor to prescribe controlled substances, and the drugs were shipped. The wholesalers didn't ask many questions about the office or Chris, though some said they would be sending someone to inspect the clinic. Basically, the wholesalers verified that Overstreet had an active DEA registration, and if the credit card number went through, they sent the drugs. It was unbelievably easy, like ordering a shipment of drywall.

And that was the part that blew Derik's mind the most: how this quack Overstreet could order narcotics and no one blinked an eye. He'd assumed there was someone paying attention to this stuff, that you couldn't just team up with a doctor to buy and sell pills to drug addicts. It was way too easy. But that's what they were doing, and Derik was starting to wonder if Chris was on to something.

The clinic was pulling in a few more patients every day, Chris told Derik. Five on Day One. Then seven. Twelve. Eighteen. Twenty. Word was spreading. Even better, every patient booked a follow-up appointment twenty-eight days later. After a couple of days, Chris had begun to wonder if his early volume projections were a little low. Less than two full weeks in, he knew the pain clinic was a go.

Chris wanted to make the whole process as easy as possible for the patients. The word about convenience would definitely get around. That was good business. Patients were used to doctors giving them a hard time. At South Florida Pain, they would be treated differently. Customer service was key. Overstreet said they didn't need any sort of diagnostic test—no CAT scan or MRI—on the first visit, though he thought they should start requiring them on the second visit a month later.

Chris had come to the conclusion that almost every single patient was a drug seeker. Overstreet had never really spelled this out, and it wasn't always obvious, because the patients would lie their asses off to get a fix, saying they were in agony from an old construction injury or whatever. And sometimes Chris wondered if maybe some of them *were* in pain. It was hard to tell who was injured and who was in withdrawal—both conditions gave people a panicky look. Chris didn't know what Overstreet was doing in the examination room, but the appointments took just a few minutes and nobody was asking for the other meds they offered—HGH or testosterone or weight-loss pills. These people didn't care about looking good. All they wanted was oxycodone. For all Chris knew, some of the patients might be in real pain and maybe need the drugs. But it hadn't taken him long to realize that pain sufferers weren't the target demographic. The clinic's bread-and-butter was people who took the pills to get high.

The following week, Chris asked Derik to spend another day guarding the clinic, a Friday. Derik agreed, though he already couldn't stand Overstreet. The doctor seemed arrogant, cocky, thought he was some kind of gangster. Derik saw Overstreet popping Vicodin, which he kept in the gun safe along with some Viagra and the rest of the clinic's drugs, and meeting with shady-looking people next to his Land Rover after closing time.

When it was time to split the week's cash that night, Overstreet insisted that Derik leave the room. Derik left, irritated, and when Overstreet came out, he was carrying a large stack of cash, thousands, which he pretended to conceal, but Derik could tell Overstreet wanted him to see the money. Overstreet said he was going on a trip and needed the cash. Fishing or something.

Overstreet split the money he and Chris had made in the third week of business at South Florida Pain—his half of the profits was $24,000—and flew to the Republic of Panama. He was taking a weeklong vacation, going fishing.

Overstreet had planned the trip in advance, and a doctor named Rachael Gittens had agreed to cover for him during his absence. Gittens had worked with Overstreet briefly at One Stop Medical. She was planning to work for Jeff's clinic in West Palm Beach, if he ever got it up and running.

Chris couldn't get ahold of Overstreet all week. Yes, the doctor was on vacation, but he *never* called in. No one knew where he was. Chris wondered if he had been scared off, thinking he was under investigation or something. Or maybe he just wanted to leave everything behind. Who knew?

The mystery was solved when Overstreet's wife called Jeff. She had some bad news: The doctor was not just missing. He was dead.

During his vacation in Panama, he'd somehow flipped his Jeep into a ditch. It had taken the local authorities some time to figure out who he was and get in touch with his wife. It seemed like she hadn't even known where he had gone until the consulate called saying he was dead.

So Overstreet was gone for good. A strange feeling. And bad timing. The clinic had been open only three and a half weeks, and Chris had lost his only doctor. But Chris had no intention of closing—not when the place was just beginning to show its potential.

Dr. Gittens said she was happy to just continue working at South Florida Pain; she liked it there.

Rachael Gittens was a family practice doctor who had gone to med school at the State University of New York, graduating in 1998. Despite her lack of experience in pain management, she wasn't afraid to write big prescriptions. Sometimes she wrote even higher than Overstreet had, up to 360 oxycodone 30 milligrams, a few times. The patients loved her.

Chris wanted to expand, but he had no idea how doctors found jobs. When they'd been building houses in North Port, Derik had introduced Chris to Craigslist.org, the free classified advertisements website. Very few of the other job postings on Craigslist's medical/health jobs section were for doctors—they tended to be for physician assistants, front desk staff, nurses, physical therapists. But they'd used the site to sell houses, so they figured, why not use it to hire doctors? Chris wrote and posted an advertisement, something along the lines of: "MD with DEA license needed for busy pain clinic, make up to $400 an hour."

Dr. Enock Joseph responded to the ad, and after a brief interview, Chris hired him. Dr. Joseph was an older guy, short, not much more than five feet tall. Like Gittens, he was black. Heavy cologne, glasses, thick Haitian accent. He'd gone to the State University of Haiti in the 1960s, then did an obstetrics/gynecology residency in Harlem in the 70s. Spoke French and Creole. Most importantly, Dr. Joseph had worked at a clinic named Art of Pain that paid doctors $35 per patient. Chris offered $75 per patient, and Dr. Joseph jumped at the raise.

Pretty soon, Chris realized he didn't need Overstreet. He'd already learned enough about the business to get by. The doctors were interchangeable, one as good as the next, as long as they were willing to write big numbers. Dr. Gittens sometimes took too much time with the patients, which meant they had to stay open late to accommodate the crowds, but she was an adequate replacement. Same with Dr. Joseph.

And another thing. Chris paid the new doctors $75 a patient, which was half what the clinic charged for a doctor's visit. Meanwhile, he kept the money he made from selling the meds, offering the docs a $1,000 weekly fee for the use of their DEA registrations, which allowed him to order the drugs. All in all, a much better deal than the 50/50 split on total profits that he'd had with Overstreet.

As the weeks went by, more and more of the patients came from out of state, especially hill-country states like Kentucky and Tennessee, where authorities had cracked down on narcotic painkillers. They were white country people, mostly, and they stood out in South Florida in their pasty winter skin and camouflage baseball caps, scrawny as crack fiends or spilling out of their T-shirts and cutoff jeans shorts. They usually drove down in groups, and they looked and smelled like people who had spent a long time in a car, with their rumpled clothes and sour breath. Some looked sick, sweaty, like they had the flu.

The new doctors liked having Derik around. Things seemed to run better, and he made them feel safe.

One night, Dianna drove Derik home and asked him if he would come on board full-time. The place was growing. They needed him.

Derik wasn't sure. He'd always made good money in construction, but he wasn't sure whether he could make ends meet going solo. He still didn't have a driver's license, and getting to worksites was tough.

Dianna said: Don't worry about the money. We'll give you whatever you want.

So Derik started working every day at South Florida Pain. Chris paid him $1,000 a week to start out. Derik was good with the patients. He came up with ways of dealing with the constant overflowing parking lot, kept order in the waiting room, developed systems for the paperwork. He figured it was a short-term gig. He'd make a little money and return to construction when he got his driver's license back.

At first, Derik kept mixing up the name of the primary drug they were selling. Dr. Overstreet had told Chris to order generic versions of Roxicodone instead of the better-known but more expensive OxyContin. They were basically the same drug—oxycodone—but Overstreet also believed OxyContin prescriptions were more closely monitored than the generics. Plus, a lot of recreational users seemed to prefer roxies, especially the little blue ones made by Mallinckrodt, which were supposed to be easiest to crush, dissolve, and inject. Derik kept calling them RoxiContins, which apparently didn't exist, and the others busted his chops about it.

In those early days, everything was loose and easy, and everything was funny. Dianna brought her wiener dog, Moe, to the clinic each day, because they usually stayed open late. When Derik got a phone call from someone he didn't want to talk to, he'd say that the caller needed to talk to the clinic's office manager, Moe, but he was sorry, Moe wasn't available right at that moment. Or he'd put Moe's name on paperwork. Derik and Chris flew remote control helicopters in the parking lot, and zapped each other with stun guns. Derik kept the fridge in a back room stocked with cold Bud Lights. When the lines in the waiting room got too long and people were getting impatient, Derik would buy a meal for the whole room. The toilet at South Florida Pain was always out of order, so they'd put up a sign directing patients to use the restrooms at C.C.'s Fish Camp across the street. Two hours later, when that bathroom was destroyed, they'd put up a new sign telling people to go to McDonald's to relieve themselves. People would drive by and see the long lines outside and think the Christian radio station in the bungalow next door was doing a giveaway promotion. Parking was a problem from the get-go. They rented four extra spots from the podiatrist to their east, but that wasn't enough. Patients parked in neighboring businesses' lots, wherever they could find a spot. It was chaos, and the most fun place Derik had ever worked.

Neighbors complained, of course. They rarely came over to the clinic, but they did call the cops from time to time. The neighborhood was an odd mix, Derik thought. The clinic sat just inside the border of Wilton Manors, which had gentrified little ranch houses and a significant gay population. But Oakland Park Boulevard itself was more blacks and street people. With either crowd, the white hill folk coming to South Florida Pain stood out.

Chris and Derik learned that certain patients were more valuable than others because they would organize and bankroll entire groups. Cops and druggies called these people "sponsors." One woman in the neighborhood would go down the street to a free HIV clinic and round up patients, usually homeless people. She'd haul them to the clinic and hand each of them enough money to pay for the doctor's visit and the pills. Derik would greet the woman in the waiting room, and she would tell him: I got ten new ones for you today, Derik. Best of all, they didn't even have to offer a group discount for her people. When everyone was done, she'd would just collect the patients' pills and pay them each $200. Everybody won: the clinic, the woman, her "patients." It was crazy.

Derik threw himself into recruiting patients and sponsors. He was at a bar or casino or strip club most nights, knew lots of people. When he ran into acquaintances or met someone new, he told them to stop by the clinic. Over the last decade, he'd worked with hundreds of contractors and subcontractors. Many were out of work now and weren't opposed to earning some money by becoming a patient at South Florida Pain and then selling their pills. They began coming in droves, dozens of them, many from Loxahatchee, where Derik had spent years. The clinic staff called them the Loxahatchee Crew.

The customers kept coming. Thirty a day. Fifty. They opened earlier and earlier, and even at 6:00 a.m. there'd be a line snaking down the street. They'd roll up and the patients would be roaming the neighborhood, causing havoc, but as soon as they saw Derik or Chris or Dianna, they'd snap to attention like dogs looking for a treat, run to grab their places in line. The line got longer every day, and the sight of it each morning amazed Derik. At the end of business hours, there'd still be dozens in the waiting room. Chris didn't want to turn anyone away, so they never seemed to close up shop before 8:00 p.m. Overstreet had sometimes spent ten or fifteen minutes with patients, but the visits kept shrinking until the new doctors were spending just enough time with the patients to fill out the paperwork.

Derik controlled whether patients got to see the doctors, and he was learning how to turn that power into cash. If the patients wanted special treatment, it came at a price. Patients who'd driven all the way from Kentucky often didn't want to spend three or four hours waiting to see the doctor, so they'd offer Derik $50 or $100 to be moved to the front of the line. The longer the lines, the more patients were willing to pay. Fifty bucks here, $100 there—it added up to an additional grand or two a week in Derik's pocket. Before long, he was making more from these payoffs than he was from his base salary.

Nine o'clock one night, Derik was outside smoking a cigarette. It was one of those warm South Florida nights when the bathwater air almost dripped with possibility. Inside, the waiting room was still packed, more patients hanging out in the parking lot, more money to be made. Derik had just ordered pizza for everybody. He was feeling good, magnanimous.

A truck went by, a guy checking out the action, how busy the clinic was that late at night.

The guy yelled: Gimme some roxies, dude!

And roared away. Like Derik was a king, the guy who had everything, the guy making the decisions. Figuring out who got what.

Chris and Derik laughed about it the rest of the night.

⁓

Every so often, a patient went away unhappy.

One day, an out-of-state patient submitted a forged medical record, and Derik kicked the guy out. A few minutes later, Derik was catching a smoke in the parking lot, and several things happened, one right after another. A smacking sound on the asphalt of the parking lot a couple feet to Derik's left, followed by a crack of gunfire from somewhere nearby. Without thinking, Derik was moving toward the building. Another bullet rapped the stucco wall behind him, shoulder height, way too close. Derik crouched behind the big plastic garbage can and saw a battered blue pickup swerve out of CC's Fish Camp parking lot across the street. Derik realized the garbage can wasn't going to protect him. He stood up and moved toward the door. The truck sped away—no more gunfire.

Derik went inside, jumpy with adrenaline, laughing his loud laugh. He told Chris and Dianna what had happened. After a while he went back outside. The slug had knocked a little stucco and paint off the wall, but the building wasn't in great shape anyway, and the bullet hole was barely noticeable. A couple of patients were standing by their cars, and they gaped at Derik.

One asked: Was someone just *shooting* at you?

Derik just laughed it off and went back to work.

⁓

Derik and Chris tried to shield the doctors from incidents like that. And they never had a frank conversation with Gittens or Joseph about what was really happening at South Florida Pain, what the patients were doing with the pills. Why broach the subject? It might make the doctors feel uncomfortable or guilty, and that was the last thing they needed.

Derik couldn't tell what the doctors thought about the clinic and its customers. Gittens and Joseph were fast, yet still more cautious than Overstreet, who would write for basically anybody over eighteen. The new doctors sometimes turned down patients who were incoherent or had obvious needle tracks from shooting up. But it was difficult to say no to a desperate addict who would beg or threaten. So they'd just leave the room and tell Derik, and he'd bounce the patient, no problem.

Dr. Gittens made a big deal of these ejections, pitching a little fit, as if she was shocked and disappointed that one of her patients was using the drugs for the wrong reasons. She told Chris that she believed that some of the patients were lying to her, and it troubled her that they all asked for oxycodone. Derik didn't buy it. He believed her scenes served a psychological purpose: to justify her actions to herself, to prove she was still a good doctor, despite the fact that she was churning out oxycodone prescriptions all day long for $75 a patient.

Dr. Joseph was a little different, Derik believed. He rejected fewer patients than Gittens. And when a major problem did arise with a patient, Derik noticed that he didn't make trouble. He would simply instruct Derik to refund the patient. He seemed to just want the problems to go away.

You'd have to be an idiot, Derik believed, to not figure out that virtually every patient was either using or selling the drugs, often both. Or else why would the majority of them drive across four states to get legal medications? Why were they so desperate? Why were so many of them nodding out in the waiting room?

Derik believed the doctors *had* to know the score.

Dr. Gittens told Chris the clinic needed to beef up its diagnostic procedures, or at least its paperwork. She wanted the clinic to require patients to bring in MRI reports, something South Florida Pain could put in its patient files. Something to show they weren't just writing scrips based on the patients' word that they were in pain.

Chris understood. It was asking for trouble to have no real diagnostic paperwork in the patient file. What if the Florida Department of Health showed up? Or, God forbid, the DEA?

But procedure and paperwork created a problem on the customer-relations side of things. The entire business philosophy of South Florida Pain, the thing that gave them an edge, was customer service, making it easy for patients to get what they wanted. Chris didn't want to tell every patient, including walk-ins who had just driven fifteen hours across four states, that they had to go get an MRI before seeing the doctor. Dr. Overstreet had referred some patients to an MRI service, but only every once in a while. That diagnostic company took three days to turn around the MRI reports, which wasn't going to work for most of South Florida Pain's out-of-state patients. So Chris and Derik would give the patients one free pass but told them they *had* to bring an MRI to their next visit, twenty-eight days later, which gave them time to get it done at home. Of course, being junkies, they usually didn't do it. So they'd give the patients *another* month, but say that this was the last time, they absolutely had to bring an MRI report to their next appointment.

Derik discovered there was competition in the MRI world. Half a dozen MRI services were fighting for South Florida Pain business, representatives visiting the clinic, handing out leaflets. Certain companies were willing to kick back fees to Derik in exchange for referring patients to them. Before long, Derik was making a grand or two a week just from the MRI companies.

One guy said he could match the prices of the company the clinic was currently using, but he would turn around the reports in twenty-four hours, which would make things much more convenient for South Florida Pain's out-of-state patients. The interesting thing about this company was that its MRI machine was located inside an eighteen-wheeler trailer, and the unmarked trailer was parked behind a strip club called Goldfinger Gentlemen's Club, a place up in Lake Park that Derik had never patronized. A line of people stood and sat in the strip club parking lot all day and night, holding red medical folders, waiting their turn to pay two or three hundred bucks to climb up into the trailer and onto the MRI machine inside.

Most of the reports noted some slight abnormality or other finding, and Derik noticed something funny. Say a patient had complained of neck problems early on, but then the MRI of the neck region showed nothing out of the ordinary. The patient would just get a couple more body regions scanned until some protrusion or compression or extrusion was discovered, maybe in the lower spine this time. Then the patient would return to South Florida Pain, *now* complaining of lower back pain. Derik never saw the doctors make an issue of this shifting pain, as long as the paperwork was in order.

Every once in a while, though, they'd see something they couldn't ignore. One day, a guy came in, maybe thirty years old: dreadlocks, sagging black shorts, and a wife-beater. Derik took his $200 and made a copy of his MRI report, sent the guy back to Dr. Joseph.

A little while later, Dr. Joseph called Derik to the examination room, pointed to the MRI report. He looked upset.

Dr. Joseph said: Please read the conclusions, Derik.

Derik read the report aloud, all the way to the part where it noted a tear in the uterine wall. Dr. Joseph pointed at the patient.

Dr. Joseph: Does he *look* like he has a uterus?

Derik looked closer at the report and could tell the patient had duplicated his name over whoever's report it actually was. The birth date on the report didn't match the guy's ID. Worse, on the gender line the guy had just left the "F."

Derik apologized to Dr. Joseph and kicked the patient out. The guy had the nerve to argue with him over his $200 fee, which Derik refused to give back, on principle. He didn't want word getting out that if you got ejected from South Florida Pain they'd just give your money back. Derik threatened to call the cops, have the guy arrested for prescription fraud. The guy left, then came back later with some friends. Dr. Joseph heard the commotion, came out and told Derik to give the guy his $200 back. So Derik did, and that was that.

Hey, Derik thought, *I'm* not the one who went to medical school. I'm learning as I go here.

And it was hard work. At any moment in a typical day, a million things were happening. Patients waiting in a long line out the door. Multiple phone lines ringing. A toilet overflowing because a patient had tried to flush a bottle of Mountain Dew. The patients were desperate and strung out, eagerly peppering Derik with flecks of spit when they finally reached the customer window. Or just standing there in a stupid opiate haze, drawling in that distinctive guttural oxycodone register, as if the drug had dulled their voice boxes along with everything else.

Derik called them zombies. Dumb and slow, but you had to watch your back around them. If one crushed a pill and nodded off, another would try to steal his meds. Or they'd start making side deals with each other and a fight would break out. They would lie to each other or rip each other off, if they thought they could get more pills. Or a guy would see someone he knew from back home in Kentucky and flare up over some old beef. One day, Derik saw two guys staring each other down and intervened: turned out, both were carrying guns.

And the parking lot! Everything you could imagine took place in that little lot, steps away from the cars on Oakland Park Boulevard. Pill-sick patients sweating, trembling, vomiting, peeing on the palm tree, trading pills for cash. A couple months in, Derik caught a guy shooting up around the side of the bungalow. The guy ran off, dropping an insulin needle. After that, patients shooting up became a regular occurrence. Chris bought a vending machine and a forty-two-inch flat-screen TV for the waiting room, trying to keep the patients from going outside and causing havoc, but it didn't really work.

Derik also began paying a homeless guy who hung around the clinic, to keep an eye on the parking lot, and to call him when necessary. Everyone on Oakland Park Boulevard knew the vagrant, who slept at a nearby coin laundry, a gaunt and sickly-looking guy who was also funny and game in his cowboy hat and boots. One of those people whose age you couldn't tell—could have been thirty, could have been fifty. Derik and Chris liked their new parking-lot sentry, kept him around like a stray dog, feeding him and paying him to run errands. The homeless man wasn't really able to handle parking-lot problems himself, because no one took him seriously, but he could at least report them to Derik.

Derik was learning that even crafty and experienced addicts could be counted on to screw up. Derik gave these incidents a name: "junkie stunts." Some would take prescriptions from multiple doctors to the same legit pharmacy and get busted for doctor shopping. Others would slam a pill right before their appointments and nod out in the waiting room, and Gittens would kick them out for being high. And they'd all come to Derik, begging for a second chance. He'd give an offender a stern talking-to, and then suggest a solution: *Come back tomorrow, see the other doctor.* He reasoned that since the drugs were all they cared about, they'd clean up their acts to preserve their access to the clinic.

At the end of a day of dealing with the zombies, Derik went home more exhausted than he had been after pouring concrete for a house foundation. He needed help. He just couldn't handle it by himself anymore. In most situations, Derik was a friendly guy, but it didn't take much to make him twitchy. A patient would irritate him, and he'd start flinging his big arms around, eyebrows jumping, voice getting unnaturally loud. He couldn't quell it.

So he hired his roommate, who'd helped him with the office renovation, to cover the front window. They'd known each other since kindergarten up north. Derik had told him stories about South Florida Pain, but his roommate didn't believe them, scoffed at the description of the hillbillies who drove fourteen hours for oxycodone, the doctors who wrote scrip after scrip all day, the lines out the door. It was a sweet feeling when his friend started working there and told Derik: I can't believe you were telling the truth.

It hadn't taken Chris long to realize that South Florida Pain had more potential than his other business, South Beach Rejuvenation. More people wanted painkillers than steroids, and the buying power of addicts was greater than Chris had ever imagined.

Jeff was paying attention to Chris's success too. He hadn't managed to open his own clinic in West Palm yet, and after South Florida Pain started making buckets of money, Chris and Derik knew he was going to cause trouble. Jeff and Chris argued about it a few times, and then Jeff brought a couple of his pals to South Florida Pain one day, barged in past Derik and into Chris's office. There was lots of yelling, and at one point Jeff grabbed a pair of needle-nose pliers and waved them at Chris. When Jeff and his buddies left, things were different between the twins. A couple of months later, Jeff sued Chris over the ownership of the pain clinic.

Jeff and Chris had clashed plenty of times growing up, of course, but they'd never had a serious falling out. This time felt different. Chris stopped speaking to Jeff altogether, and Derik followed Chris's lead out of loyalty.

Meanwhile, Chris and Derik grew closer. Chris started introducing Derik as his brother.

Chris took what he knew from the home-building trade and applied it to pain management, starting with marketing. Chris believed he was the first pain clinic to advertise by billboard, and it was the single best return on investment he made. He bought billboards for southbound drivers on I-95 and the Turnpike, all the way from the Georgia/Florida line to Fort Lauderdale. The billboards were straightforward; just huge block-letter words—Pain Clinic—a phone number, a half mile east off exit 31. Later, he added one of the doctor's names.

He wasn't the first to advertise in the local free weeklies, the *New Times* and *City Link*. Those publications called him, asking if he wanted to place ads in their back pages, which was where people went to find strip clubs and escorts. There were already a sprinkling of pain clinic ads. Chris bought advertising in both papers and on the Internet and offered promotions in print and online Yellow Pages, up and down the eastern half of the United States. He hired a search engine optimization expert to make sure that South Florida Pain's website popped up early in pain clinic searches. When people searched keywords like "pain medication," "oxycodone," or "pain clinic," a link to South Florida Pain's website came up on the first page, often within the top five links.

The clinic website contained stock photos of doctors in white jackets who appeared to be conducting experiments. The doctors in the pictures were in sleek laboratories, not a crumbling yellow bungalow in a sketchy stretch of South Florida. The text and format of the website was cut-and-pasted from other pain clinic sites, and Chris had inadvertently neglected to remove a different clinic's name from one section of text.

Derik looked at the website only once and thought it was over-the-top and not quite believable, like something a kid would put together, trying to pass himself off as a businessman. It mentioned a bunch of official-sounding organizations—the International Association for the Study of Pain, the National Institute of Health, the American Medical Association, the American Pain Society—and said that millions of Americans suffered from chronic pain and couldn't get help. One confusing line: "The majority of people suffering with chronic pain have been living with their pain for over 5 years, almost 6 days a week." No explanation of what was going on on the seventh day of the week. The "Education" page had a lot of words that sounded made-up, like "radiculopathy" and "herpetic" and "splanching," stuff Chris and Derik knew nothing about.

Chris spent a lot of time in his office on the phone, looking for drugs. Keeping the clinic flush with oxycodone meant additional profits. Wholesalers charged between 33 cents and $1.25 per 30-milligram oxycodone pill, prices that fluctuated with supply and demand. Chris usually charged about $2 per pill.

The clinic grew more popular as word got around that South Florida Pain almost always had Mallinckrodt-made "blues" in stock. For patients, this meant one-stop shopping and no hassling with pharmacists who might question the flood of oxycodone scrips pouring out of South Florida Pain.

But as the number of patients grew, it became harder to keep the dispensary stocked all the time. Usually, the maximum amount an individual drug wholesaler would allow Chris to order was five thousand pills per doctor per week. Occasionally, one would agree to send ten thousand pills at one time, or to send five hundred every day, which Chris assumed they did to avoid large individual shipments. But the standard weekly shipment was five thousand per doctor. If the doctors prescribed two hundred pills per patient on average, one order would meet the needs of approximately twenty-five customers, which would get them through maybe half a day. So Chris needed multiple wholesalers.

First he looked into major wholesalers, national suppliers like Cardinal Health and McKesson and AmerisourceBergen. But the big guys had too many regulations, including a requirement that individual drug orders had to include at least 50 percent non-controlled substances. So Chris began looking at smaller wholesalers. He researched the companies on the Internet and called one after another, filling out application forms for credit lines. Over the next few months, Chris developed a roster of half a dozen wholesalers that he used regularly.

One day that spring of 2008, Derik was smoking a cigarette in the clinic parking lot, when a car pulled in. Blue Nissan Sentra, late 90s model. Windows rolled down, rap music pulsing. Good old-school stuff. The guy behind the wheel was black, which put Derik on alert. There were plenty of black guys on Oakland Park Boulevard, but they weren't customers of South Florida Pain Clinic. Most of their customers were white hillbillies. What was this guy doing here?

The guy got out, baseball cap tilted to the left, gold chain around his neck, friendly as he could be.

He said: What's up, man? I got this package for you.

The guy said he was from a local company that sold drugs wholesale. Derik knew Chris had placed a big order the previous day, but he still didn't quite believe this guy worked for a drug wholesaler. Most of the drug shipments came by UPS or another delivery service. What company would trust this dude to deliver a load of narcotics? Drugs worth about $20,000 retail, maybe $200,000 on the street? Pulling up in his ten-year-old blue Sentra, blaring his Tupac?

But there were the boxes, two of them, sitting there on the Sentra's front passenger seat. Derik thought they should have been in some kind of bulletproof briefcase, chained to the guy's wrist.

Derik told the guy to follow him. The guy grabbed the boxes, headed inside, through the waiting room, patients watching. Walking with a little swagger, thousands of pills inside the box shaking along with his rhythmic stride: *chica-CHICA, chica-CHICA.*

And that's when it really hit home for Derik, what they had here. They had a license to deal drugs. No one was watching. He'd thought the pain clinic was a short-term gig, a way to get back on his feet after his jail stretch, but he'd been wrong. This was where he was meant to be. He and Chris were going to be rich.

It couldn't be this easy, could it?

2

On the west coast of Florida, a pharmacist named Larry Golbom was pondering the same question as Derik Nolan: How had it become so easy to obtain and prescribe heavy-duty narcotics in the United States?

On a balmy Sunday in early May 2008, Golbom left his home in Clearwater, Florida, and drove over the long Courtney Campbell Causeway. The skies were blue and cloudless, and Old Tampa Bay glittered in the sun, but Golbom's stomach was in knots. He was always nervous before going on the air, and this had been an especially discouraging week at the major-chain drugstore where he worked. In the past few days, he'd refused to fill huge narcotic prescriptions from three doctors he'd never heard of. One customer was nineteen years old and could barely speak. He had a prescription for 240 oxycodone 30s from a pain clinic in Tampa. Another was in his twenties, and looked fit enough to run in a track meet. He wanted oxycodone and muscle relaxant. Golbom had reported the doctors to the state board of pharmacy, but he wasn't holding his breath for a response.

After reaching Tampa, Golbom pulled into a nondescript office park just off Tampa International Airport, long tresses of Spanish moss trailing from the pin oaks that surrounded it. The building was the home of WGUL-AM, a local talk-radio station owned by Salem Broadcasting. Once a week, Golbom paid Salem $125 so he could talk about legal narcotics on the air. He'd been doing the one-hour show—called Prescription Addiction Radio—for a year and a half, since the fall of 2006. Golbom had no idea how many people were listening.

Inside, Golbom entered a beige studio, just four walls and a desk, a few computer monitors and microphones. No personal items adorned the studio, no workspace toys or ornaments. The studio was nobody's permanent home, just space rented by the hour.

Tonight, Golbom pulled on bulky headphones and kicked off the show by playing a few lines of a 2002 rap song that described the pleasures of OxyContin, Lortabs, and Percocets. Then the sound engineer faded the song away, and Golbom spoke close into the microphone, his insistent nasal drone in distinct contrast with the Memphis rapper's drawl.

"Again, folks, in case you missed it, that's the lyrics of the song, 'Oxy-Cotton' by Lil Wyte. That song's actually been around for a little while. There's no question that since the introduction of OxyContin, our country's been experiencing what I refer to as the new opium epidemic of the twenty-first century. The active ingredient of oxycodone is interchangeable with heroin, and I think more and more people are beginning to understand that we have a huge medical hoax going on."

Golbom believed he'd been an unwitting part of the hoax until the day, five years earlier, when he'd discovered that his teenage son had bought oxycodone pills from a local woman. Golbom had reported the woman's doctor to the Florida Board of Medicine. The subsequent investigation revealed that the patient was a textbook drug seeker. She'd altered prescriptions. She'd been charged with possession of a controlled substance. She'd claimed more than once that her medications had been stolen. She'd claimed to need drugs early so she could go on trips. Despite all these red flags, the doctor had continued to prescribe the woman high doses of opioids.

In 2006, the doctor settled his case. He was fined $12,500, plus administrative costs, and was ordered to do seventy-five hours of community service and complete two courses. He retained his medical license, continued practicing.

To Golbom, it felt like nothing had been accomplished.

But in the meantime, he'd educated himself about opioids. In fact, the drugs had become his obsession. He'd founded the radio show and talked on-air to hundreds of people about the resurgence of opium in America—public officials, experts, addicts and their relatives. He'd read medical texts and histories of past temperance movements. He'd delved deep into obscure corners of the Federal Register to find statistics about oxycodone production. He'd searched newspaper archives for information about pharmaceutical companies.

He couldn't believe he hadn't figured out sooner what was going on. He'd spent more than twenty-five years as a pharmacist, meaning he had lived through an entire sea change in narcotics prescribing practices and never questioned it. Or even realized it.

It embarrassed Golbom, and it made him angry. If he'd been fooled, along with most other pharmacists and doctors, what chance did the average person have?

Through his research, Golbom discovered that humans have known about the wondrous substance inside opium poppies since before the dawn of recorded time. It's not hard to extract. Just before the plant's seed pod ripens, scratch its smooth, blue-green skin and catch the tears of whitish milk that leak out. Dried until it's a sticky yellow residue, opium contains the elemental ingredients for the vast array of illegal and legal opioid narcotics made today, from heroin to oxycodone.

Opioids subdue pain. They work beautifully, blocking electrical and chemical signals before they can leap the synapse from one nerve cell to the next. In six thousand years, we've never found another painkiller that works as well. They don't cure anything; they simply mute sensations. They also change the way the brain perceives the nerve signals. Suddenly, pain doesn't cause as much panic or stress. It becomes tolerable.

But opioids produce a number of additional effects. They slow the pump of heart and lungs. Bowels grow sluggish too, causing constipation. They galvanize the brain's pleasure centers, causing joy.

Another thing about opioids: Nerve cells become desensitized to them more quickly than any other group of drugs. Higher and higher doses are necessary to produce the same impact.

They're also addictive. Severely. Profoundly. And quickly. Withdrawal symptoms can be detected at the cellular level after a single dose of morphine. Administer opioids long enough, and the patient will become physically and psychologically dependent, terrified that the supply will be cut off, willing to go great lengths to forestall the nibbling panic of early withdrawal. That dread is felt more frequently as the body builds a tolerance to the drug, always needing more. Long-term users become physically dependent. Addicts go a step further and crave the drug psychologically, love the euphoria and seek more of it.

American doctors have known about the dark side of opioids for a long time, at least since hundreds of thousands of Civil War veterans became morphine addicts after that drug was administered liberally to wounded soldiers. Around the turn of the previous century, opium and other narcotics were available in a number of snake-oil elixirs, including baby-soothing formulas. Over time, the medical establishment came to the firm conclusion that heavy-duty narcotics were best prescribed sparingly, to patients in such bad shape that the risk of addiction seemed a laughably minor menace, such as cancer patients with tumors gnawing at their bones, or to someone in agony in a controlled, hospital environment. Almost by definition, opioids were not considered to be acceptable treatments for long-term chronic pain, because long-term use meant dependence. Doctors generally agreed you didn't simply send people home with a big supply of the stuff and hope for the best.

It was often hard to tell who was in pain. Pain is personal, subjective. It is influenced by mood, psychology, upbringing. It's cultural too. The Irish were less likely to voice pain than the Italians, according to a 1950s study at a veterans hospital in San Francisco. Pain had a randomness, an arbitrary nature that didn't sit well with doctors, who were, after all, scientists looking for something to measure.

Over the decades, pharmaceutical companies developed and released an ever-expanding lineup of narcotics of different strains and mixtures and strengths. Vicodin, a mix of hydrocodone and acetaminophen. Percocet, oxycodone and acetaminophen. Fentanyl, usually administered through a skin patch. MS Contin, a long-acting morphine formulation. Sometimes researchers thought they'd found one that didn't get you high, but there was an army of junkie scientists out there who would burn and dissolve and combine until they unlocked the narcotic trove. Then word would get around. Mix pentazocine with this drugstore antihistamine and you've got yourself a nice speedball. Or take a time-release morphine tablet, painstakingly peel off the outer coating, then crush, dissolve, and inject. There was always a way.

So the pharmaceutical companies kept the dosages small and typically cut their products with acetaminophen or aspirin, which discouraged addicts from ingesting massive doses. And doctors were trained to regard painkillers as a last resort. Which meant that many patients lived in pain. Too many, according to a new generation of doctors that began to emerge in the 1980s. Pain management specialists saw patients in agony, desperate for a cure and often unable to get medicine that would give them relief. Pain was real, they said, and it was destroying lives. These specialists began to wonder if physicians had become *too* reluctant to use the painkilling power of opioids.

By the early 1990s, as some doctors were reconsidering their approach to pain, a smallish, family-owned pharmaceutical company called Purdue Pharma was looking for ways to grow its customer base. Purdue was best known for an extended-release morphine drug called MS Contin. Unlike traditional morphine, which wore off within a few hours, these pills dissolved slowly and allowed cancer patients to sleep through the night. But Purdue's patent on the formulation would expire soon, which meant that cheaper generic versions would soon be eating into its market share. The company was developing a new drug, an oxycodone pill it would call OxyContin.

Like MS Contin, OxyContin was a controlled-release pill. Swallowed, the dose broke down slowly in the digestive system, doling itself out over twelve hours. This meant Purdue could pack much more oxycodone into each pill. Percocets contained doses of 5 or 10 milligrams of oxycodone. By contrast, OxyContin came in doses of 10 milligrams, 15 milligrams, 20 milligrams, 30 milligrams, 40 milligrams, 80 milligrams, and even the whopping 160-milligram horse pill, a midnight-blue oblong pebble nearly an inch long. The other thing was that OxyContin was pure. It wasn't cut with acetaminophen or aspirin. The only active ingredient in the pill was oxycodone.

Purdue didn't want simply to provide an alternative to MS Contin. That drug was used primarily to ease the suffering of cancer patients, a limited pool of consumers who typically either died or got better. Purdue wanted OxyContin to be prescribed to a much broader array of patients and for a longer period of time. The untapped marketplace was chronic pain, which could mean anything from backaches to arthritis to the crippling agony of trigeminal neuralgia. If Purdue could persuade a portion of that vast and varied market to take OxyContin, the drug would be a blockbuster.

To accomplish this, Purdue had to do no less than undertake a massive, multi-pronged hearts-and-minds campaign to change the way American doctors and the public felt about prescription narcotics. The company needed to train people to think of opioids as benign liberators, as long as they came in pill form and with a prescription.

Purdue leaders borrowed a page from the advertising industry: problem-solution marketing. They would market and publicize the problem of untreated pain. Then they'd promote the solution: OxyContin.

Over the following decade, Purdue Pharma created or funded a vast network of mouthpieces to promote and justify the use of heavy-duty narcotics to ease all kinds of pain. The company's primary hurdle was to convince prescribers that their pain patients would not become addicted to OxyContin, even if they took heavy doses of it for a long period of time. This was no easy task, since it directly contradicted thousands of years of human experience with opiates.

The company found and cultivated "key opinion leaders," usually doctors who were already promoting the idea that pain was undertreated and that narcotics should be more liberally prescribed. Researchers like Dr. J. David Haddox, who helped coin the term "pseudoaddiction."

Pseudoaddicts, Haddox said, were pain patients who displayed common drug-seeking behaviors: demanding specific drugs, hoarding drugs, seeking early refills, taking higher doses than prescribed. Pseudoaddiction *looked* a lot like addiction, Haddox said, but it wasn't addiction. Those patients simply needed more pills. The counterintuitive concept was based on a case study of a single cancer patient, and it hadn't been backed up by rigorous studies. Nevertheless, Purdue seized upon the new word—pseudoaddiction—and liberally sprinkled it throughout educational materials. The company also hired Haddox and made him a top executive.

Purdue poured millions of dollars into organizations like the American Academy of Pain Medicine, the American Pain Society, and the American Pain Foundation, and those organizations backed or promoted the work of pro-opioid researchers. Some researchers dug up obscure and largely inapplicable nuggets of scientific data that seemed to support a pro-opioid hypothesis, then published and republished that data. One Purdue-funded study claimed that "psychological dependence or addiction is low" for chronic pain patients on narcotics. The Purdue study cited a single article from the prestigious *New England Journal of Medicine*. It didn't mention that the "article" was a letter to the editor, published in 1980, and that its conclusions were based on a simple review of the charts of hospitalized patients, not a scientific study of long-term narcotic use.

But the idea was out there, published in a scientific journal: Fewer than 1 percent of pain patients would develop addictions.

Armed with this seemingly legitimate number, Purdue got to work.

Suddenly, in the late 1990s, news stories about pain began to appear. Profiles of chronic pain sufferers who couldn't get narcotic prescriptions due to doctors' fears of addiction. Trend pieces about the prevalence of pain and its undertreatment. Purdue officials themselves were rarely mentioned, but the stories were peppered with quotes from Purdue-backed consultants and researchers and doctors. The stories created the general impression that tens of millions of Americans were suffering in needless pain.

Many of the stories were planted by groups like the American Pain Foundation. The foundation claimed to be a patient advocacy organization, but 90 percent of its money came from the drug industry, including big grants from Purdue. The foundation acted as a front for Purdue and other drugmakers, advancing pro-opioid policies in ways that the companies themselves could not. The foundation funded pain management web talk shows, published policy guides that plugged narcotics, and marshaled pain patients to send angry e-mails to reporters, prompting news stories about the stigma they had faced when seeking medication. It was a smart move, Golbom believed, because it created the impression that anyone who questioned the escalating use of prescription narcotics lacked empathy for people in pain. Only a heartless clod wanted to deny people in pain the medications they said they couldn't live without.

Similar stories originated from new "grassroots" regional pain advocacy organizations that had sprung up, such as the Appalachian Pain Foundation, based in Huntington, West Virginia, which received a $20,000 grant from Purdue shortly after it formed in 2000.* The foundation arranged a series of meetings in Kentucky and West Virginia to spread the word among local doctors that opioids were underutilized even in their pill-swamped communities. The doctor who co-chaired the foundation said the Purdue grant had no effect on the foundation's work. Years later, he lost his medical license after airport officials found oxycodone and hydrocodone bottles with other people's names on them among his luggage. A subsequent investigation revealed that a number of his patients had died of overdoses.

Purdue targeted the doctors who controlled the prescription pads. Most physicians had received maybe an hour or two of pain management training way back in med school. They needed a re-education in painkillers, and Purdue supplied it with the largest narcotics marketing campaign ever.

* Both the American Pain Foundation and the Appalachian Pain Foundation have since shut down.

Between 1996 and 2002, Purdue funded more than twenty thousand pain-related educational programs, almost ten a day, seven days a week. During the same years, Purdue conducted more than forty national pain management training conferences at resorts in Boca Raton and Scottsdale, paying the travel costs for more than five thousand physicians who attended. More than twenty-five hundred physicians were on Purdue's speaker bureau list. They went home with plush toys, fishing hats, CDs, and pens, all branded with the OxyContin logo. A favorite freebie was the heat-sensitive OxyContin mug that bore the words: "The one to start with . . . ." When filled with hot coffee, the rest of the slogan materialized: "The one to stay with."

The educational seminars made the most of the unfounded statistic that "fewer than one percent" of patients would develop addictions. One continuing medical education program sponsored by Purdue promoted opioid therapy as the only solution for chronic conditions such as back pain. The program contained a role-playing exercise in which a patient admits he is taking twice as many pills as he's supposed to. An authoritative narrator cautions the doctor not to jump to the conclusion that the patient is addicted, even if he seems desperate. The role play ends with the doctor prescribing a high-dose opioid.

Purdue doubled its sales force during those years, from 318 to 767 pharmaceutical reps. In the trade, the reps are called detailers, and they're typically good-looking, gregarious, and well-dressed. They remember the names of the clinic receptionists and secretaries and nurses. Purdue expected each drug rep to develop a list of 105 to 140 physicians within a specific sales region and call each one every three or four weeks. And they didn't target only oncologists and pain management specialists. They went after family doctors and general practitioners, a broader and less painkiller-savvy prescriber. Purdue paid its reps better than most drugmakers paid theirs—by 2001, an average salary of $55,000 and an average bonus of $71,500. Purdue spent a half-billion dollars on the one-on-one sales strategy between 1996 and 2001.

Purdue drug reps also had another tool: OxyContin coupons. Free samples were a common way to promote a new medication, but the DEA didn't allow it with controlled substances like OxyContin. So in 1998 and 1999, Purdue bypassed this rule by giving each rep twenty-five coupons for a free thirty-day supply of the drug. In 2000 and 2001, as OxyContin's reputation grew, the company cut the free trials to seven days. Reps gave the coupons to doctors, who passed them on to patients. The freebies cost Purdue $4 million a year, but in the narcotics business, it was a good long-term strategy.

Purdue drilled its reps on two selling points. One, OxyContin was the first narcotic that wouldn't hook patients. And two, fewer than 1 percent of pain-management patients get addicted anyway.

Purdue's army of drug reps reminded Golbom of the salesmen a century earlier who peddled patent medicines like Hamlin's Wizard Oil or Hostetter's Celebrated Stomach Bitters, men who assured their customers that a bottle of snake oil would cure everything from arthritis to kidney disease.

⁂

The heart-and-minds campaign worked, beyond even Purdue's expectations. Within a few years, OxyContin became a major pharmaceutical hit, one of the top-twenty brand-name medications in the United States. By 2002, six years after its release, Purdue was selling almost $1.5 billion of the drug each year—eight times the volume the company had projected. The single drug represented 80 percent of Purdue's net sales. It was the biggest-selling brand-name controlled substance on the market.

The once sleepy drugmaker was now a powerhouse, and it wasn't about to concede that its star product had a major flaw.

OxyContin's warning label instructed users not to crush or dissolve the pills because the entire narcotic load would be released at once. In other words, do not powderize the pill . . . unless you want to get ecstatically, euphorically high. Abusers paid attention and realized how ridiculously easy it was to beat the pill's timed-release formulation. Just crush it, and they'd get the whole thing at once. They could wrap it in foil and grind it between their molars, or take a hammer to it. Still, after ingesting it that way for a time, the knife-edge of joy became just a bit blunted. So abusers would try snorting it to get it to the bloodstream faster, boost the rush. And when that dulled, they could mix the powder with water, draw it into a needle, and shoot it straight into the vessel.

People began dying with OxyContin in their bloodstreams. At first, around the year 2000, the overdose reports were haphazard and anecdotal, a few dozen deaths tallied by a worried medical examiner in Virginia or a few hundred reported by a DEA researcher. News reports detailed a wave of OxyContin abuse that originated in rural areas with a tradition of pill dependency, such as western Virginia, eastern Maine, and Kentucky.

Purdue pushed back against the evidence. Just because oxycodone was found in a corpse's bloodstream didn't mean it came from an OxyContin pill, company spokesmen said. And if there were other drugs or alcohol involved, as was often the case, how could you definitively blame oxycodone?

But deaths involving prescription narcotics continued to mount, until the trend was impossible to dismiss. Overdose deaths involving prescription opioids quadrupled between 1999 and 2007, from about three thousand to twelve thousand per year. By contrast, cocaine killed about six thousand users in 2007, heroin about two thousand. Prescription narcotics were now killing more Americans than all illegal drugs combined.

In fact, while the heroin years of the 1970s and the crack crisis of the 1980s had produced a frenzy of publicity, those outbreaks had barely nudged the overall drug death rate. The unintentional drug overdose death rate had hovered between one and two annual deaths per one hundred thousand citizens during the heydays of those drugs. By 2007, the overdose rate had shot up to about nine deaths per one hundred thousand, almost entirely due to opioid-related deaths. Pills were far deadlier than crack or heroin, but they didn't create the same national hysteria.

There was a reason for this lack of outrage. Golbom noticed that almost every story about the increasing devastation quoted a pain management doctor or "expert" from one of the industry fronts like the American Pain Foundation. There was always a paragraph about the "undertreatment of pain," with the implication that even more opioids were needed to solve the problem. Purdue had created a truth, backed up by a body of seemingly legitimate research and publication, and few seemed to question the underlying premise that OxyContin was an effective drug for chronic pain, safe "when taken as prescribed."

It took Golbom time to fully comprehend the implications of Purdue's strategy, but once he did, he realized its brilliance. The company was selling an addictive drug that it said would not addict you as long as it was *taken as prescribed.* Then, when the drug did addict someone, and they began taking too much of it, or hoarding it to take all at once, or trying to obtain multiple prescriptions or early refills—then, that person was no longer taking it *as prescribed.* That person became one of the outcasts, an addict, and therefore the "safe when taken as prescribed" dictum remained valid. Purdue seemed to regard those folks as a tragedy of their own making. But the company affirmed that its responsibility was not to addicts who were abusing the drug, but to the untold millions of pain sufferers who needed it.

Golbom wondered how many addicts had begun taking OxyContin under the care of a doctor. He came to realize that there was very little difference between heroin and opioid narcotics. Heroin had been stigmatized as a bottom-of-the-barrel drug, the destination of the dirtiest of street junkies. Whereas, "pain pills" had been systematically sanitized in the public's mind. Even in the flood of news stories about oxycodone deaths, reporters and experts referred to prescription narcotics as if they were, at worst, a gateway to the hard stuff. As a pharmacist, Golbom could determine only two clear advantages OxyContin had over heroin as a recreational drug. One, OxyContin was legal. Two, it was pharmaceutical-grade—you knew exactly what was in it, unlike a bag of heroin bought on the street. Other than that, oxycodone addiction and heroin addiction were *the same thing.*

Nevertheless, Purdue had inflated the market for opioids, and other pharmaceutical companies rushed to meet the demand. They copied Purdue's OxyContin marketing techniques. They re-educated doctors about narcotics, hired "key opinion leaders" to promote the drugs, funded pro-opioid medical education courses, funneled money to seemingly independent patient advocacy groups, and professional societies. And the companies developed one new opioid narcotic after another, hailing each as a breakthrough.

Cephalon promoted its berry-flavored narcotic lollipop Actiq for migraines, sickle-cell pain, and injuries, despite the fact that the FDA had approved its use only for cancer pain.

Janssen Pharmaceuticals, Inc. promoted the narcotic Ultracet for everyday chronic pain, distributing posters to doctor's offices that showed people in active professions with the breezy tagline "Pain doesn't fit into their schedules."

Endo, maker of Opana, Percocet, and Percodan, distributed a patient education publication that said withdrawal symptoms and increased tolerance to narcotics are not the same as addiction. "Addicts take opioids for other reasons, such as unbearable emotional problems."*

The overall impact of the lollipops and posters and authoritative assurances was to create the impression that prescription opioids were like any other class of drugs—a life-enhancer like the erectile dysfunction pills or acid reflux tablets advertised on TV.

The tactic of distinguishing between addiction and physical dependence was key to many of the feel-good campaigns. On their drug labels, the companies were required by the FDA to acknowledge that opioids are addictive narcotics that could kill. But the companies often left that information out of patient education materials. Brochures and websites often mentioned only the least scary side effects of the drugs, usually leading with constipation, which no doubt seemed a small price to pay for pain relief. The drug companies also highlighted drowsiness, confusion, nausea, and dizziness, among other mild complaints. And the side effects would probably go away in a couple of days, they assured.

Janssen sponsored a multimedia patient education campaign called "Let's Talk Pain," which warned that strict regulatory control had made

* The promotional efforts of Endo, Janssen, and Cephalon are alleged in the pending lawsuit, *The People of the State of California v. Purdue Pharma L.P. et al.*

doctors fearful to prescribe opioids, leaving patients to suffer in pain: "This prescribing environment is one of many barriers that may contribute to the under treatment of pain, a serious problem in the United States."

Despite the competition, Purdue continued to be the face of the opioid gold rush because it had introduced the first blockbuster narcotic. In response to the bad press, Purdue eventually did make a number of concessions. The company put additional warnings about addiction in its information about OxyContin. It stopped making the much-sought-after 160-milligram mega-pill. It began reporting physicians it believed might be diverting drugs.

Hundreds of lawsuits were filed against Purdue, mostly personal-injury claims from small-town plaintiffs claiming they'd been hurt by the drug, and the drugmaker was committed to winning them all. No trials, few settlements. Purdue hired big-gun corporate defense law firms in Atlanta and New York and spent $3 million a month in legal bills. The company beat back almost every lawsuit, including a number of class-action cases.

When Purdue finally lost a big one in 2007, it was a criminal case, not civil. The charge was led by a US attorney named John Brownlee, whose district in Roanoke, Virginia, had been devastated by pharmaceutical painkillers. Brownlee had prosecuted street dealers and doctors and finally decided to investigate the top of the narcotics chain. The company pleaded guilty to federal criminal charges that it had lied about the drug's risk of addiction. Three top executives paid $34.5 million in fines and the company paid $600 million, one of the largest such fines ever paid by a pharmaceutical company.

Golbom and a group of activists traveled to Virginia for the sentencing, and Golbom spoke at a rally outside the courthouse. Golbom let loose. A photographer snapped a picture of him mid-cry, his face contorted in anger, chopping a hand through the air. The anger was real, but his outbursts on the radio and at the rally were not quite genuine. His natural state was quieter, more analytical. But he was experimenting, willing to do anything to strike a chord.

Golbom didn't want to do away with opioids. Morphine was a godsend for someone with pancreatic cancer, someone hospitalized for trauma. But over the long run, he increasingly believed, few people seemed to get better on the stuff. He didn't even want new laws; he just wanted people to better understand what they were taking.

And to Golbom, the federal government's approach to the opioid crisis was contradictory.

On one hand, there was plenty of concern and action. The feds had gone after Purdue, and the Centers for Disease Control and Prevention had published report after report on painkiller deaths. Lawmakers held hearings and railed about oxycodone crime and addiction in their districts. The DEA stepped up its investigations of doctors whose patients had died after receiving huge prescriptions.

On the other hand, the government was ultimately responsible for the flood of narcotics. The FDA signed off on one new opioid formulation after another—patches, lollipops, and pills, pills, pills. Many observers questioned why the FDA was so compliant with the pain industry. What escaped most people's attention was that the pharmaceutical companies had an even more dependable ally in, ironically, the Drug Enforcement Administration.

One of the DEA's most important and least recognized duties is to decide how much of each controlled substance can be manufactured. If the DEA decides that the amount of oxycodone being made exceeds the "medical, scientific, research, and industrial needs of the United States," it can reduce the drug's production, simply cut it down by denying pharmaceutical companies' annual requests to manufacture more of the drugs.

Instead, year after year, the DEA had signed off on hikes in the manufacturing quotas of all popular prescription narcotics. Golbom dug up the numbers. And they were stunning.

In 1993, three years before OxyContin came out, the DEA allowed pharmaceutical companies to manufacture 3,520 kilograms of oxycodone.

In 2007, the DEA signed off on the production of seventy thousand kilograms of oxycodone.

Almost twenty times the amount manufactured just fourteen years earlier.

Twenty times.

Less than four tons compared to seventy-seven tons.

And it wasn't just oxycodone. Between 1996 and 2007, the DEA had nearly quadrupled the production of hydrocodone, allowed manufacturers to produce almost ten times the amount of fentanyl, and hiked the quota of hydromorphone by four and a half times.

Despite its impact on public health, the quota-setting process was conducted in secret. Each pharmaceutical company applied to make a certain amount of a given controlled substance each year, but the DEA wouldn't reveal how many pills each wanted to produce. That was considered to be a trade secret. Then, the companies and the DEA had negotiation meetings, the content of which was restricted from the public record. The DEA then set quotas based on "expected need." Essentially, the only information the DEA revealed each year was the total amounts of each drug requested by the entire industry and the total amounts the DEA allowed them to produce. The DEA said it would be unfair to the pharmaceutical companies to reveal how many pills the individual companies wanted to manufacture.

Amid the uproar over painkillers and all the strategies invoked to curb abuse and overprescription, few officials or politicians seemed to consider simply reducing the supply. The idea had been brought up seriously only one time, in 2001, when the country was first becoming aware of OxyContin abuse. The DEA had asked Purdue to restrict OxyContin prescribing to physicians trained in pain management, and Purdue balked. In response, during a congressional subcommittee hearing, DEA administrator Donnie R. Marshall said he was considering "rolling back those quotas to 1996 levels." The pain industry said this would be a disaster, that prices would skyrocket and pain patients would suffer. Purdue didn't budge, and the quota-cut idea vanished when new administrators came in.

Cutting back the quotas wasn't a radical idea. In fact, the DEA had combated drug waves by reducing quotas before. In the 1970s, when speed pills were popular, the DEA cut the quota of amphetamines by 90 percent, and the illicit market dried up. A decade later, sedative-hypnotics like Quaaludes swept across the country, and the DEA cut the quota of the ingredient methaqualone by 74 percent, which effectively erased the problem.

Now, prescription narcotics were killing far more people than speed or sedatives, but the government was signing off on large increases in the supply each year. It baffled previous DEA administrators like Gene Haislip, former head of the DEA's Office of Diversion Control. Haislip had been in charge during the methaqualone quota reduction. It hadn't been easy to buck the pharmaceutical industry, but, as he told a reporter shortly before his death: "You've got to have some kind of principles."

Golbom had come to the conclusion that a $7 billion industry had been built on marketing and bad science.

By 2008, the United States was awash in prescription narcotics, enough for every American adult to pop a 5-milligram Vicodin every four hours for nearly a month. According to the International Narcotics Control Board, the US had consumed 83 percent of the global supply of oxycodone in 2007. And *99 percent* of the world's hydrocodone. No one believed that the US was in that much more pain than the rest of the world.

Golbom could see how it had happened. It wasn't the 1970s or the 1980s any more. Pharmaceuticals were the most profitable industry in the country, and the pharmaceutical lobby was by far the biggest in Washington.*

* In her 2004 book, *The Truth About the Drug Companies*, former *New England Journal of Medicine* editor Marcia Angell reported that in 2001, the top ten American pharmaceutical companies took in an average net return on sales of 18.5 percent. In 2002 alone, 675 pharma lobbyists spent more than $91 million.

He'd never considered himself prone to conspiracy theories. But now he had his own pet belief that he couldn't stop thinking about. He'd been an unwitting tool of the conspiracy for years, until it had infiltrated his home. When he came across an advertisement for radio time—"You, too, can be on the radio!"—he decided to take the leap. To Golbom, prescription narcotics seemed like a natural topic for a talk radio show. By now, just about everyone knew someone who had a problem with pain pills.

Golbom spent three weeks writing his first hour of radio. He wrote out every word of the early shows. His stomach churned every week when he walked into the station. To protect his job and his son, he called himself "Larry G" on air. And he never explained in any depth why he'd begun investigating controlled substances. His personal story didn't matter. He also wouldn't reveal his employer. He needed his pharmacy job.

Each week he interviewed different drug experts, legislators, recovering addicts. There were always fresh topics to discuss—a suspicious new pain clinic in town, a new narcotic coming out, new legislation. His network of listeners kept track of trends and reported back to him.

On the July 6, 2008, show, Golbom reported a strange new phenomenon. A pain clinic in Pinellas Park seemed to be serving customers primarily from out of state. Golbom told his listeners what his source had seen.

"One car had a Louisiana license plate. Another car had a New Jersey license plate. This individual saw cash going back and forth, and they saw the deal get done. And here's what so frightening, folks: We are now becoming the suppliers for people around the country."

Golbom wasn't the only one who'd noticed this trend. That same summer, in Fort Lauderdale, a television news reporter named Carmel Cafiero got a tip about pain clinics that serviced out-of-state patients.

Cafiero was an anomaly in the South Florida TV news scene, a pixie-cut redheaded grandmother among younger blown-out blondes and brunettes. She was in her early sixties and had worked for WSVN-TV Channel 7 since 1973, producing a weekly investigative segment called "Carmel on the Case." She specialized in "jump-outs"—on-camera ambushes of pimps, bad cops, crooked businessmen—after she'd gotten the goods on them. She found joy in her job at the family-owned Fox affiliate, and it showed in her big blue eyes and her *hee-hee-hee* chortle.

Cafiero's source said the biggest pain clinic around was located on Oakland Park Boulevard, so she and a cameraman, Anthony Pineda, drove out to take a look. The clinic was in a small bungalow, lots of people loitering outside. Cafiero and Pineda parked across the street and settled in to watch. The patients waited in a ragged line. Many went shirtless. They all seemed to drink Mountain Dew and smoke cigarettes. There was a guy riding an old bike around the parking lot. He appeared to be the security guard. He also looked like a street bum.

Carmel thought: *Whoa, what* is *this place?*

She could have put together a story right away, collected some interviews with neighboring businesses and plugged the package into the weekly "Carmel on the Case" lineup. But she didn't want to do that. She had a feeling about this strange little clinic. Something big was going on here. She was going to sit on this one for a while, do some digging.

For the next three months, every time Cafiero and Pineda were between assignments in Broward, they'd go to South Florida Pain and shoot video. They used the station's unmarked silver Dodge Caravan. Pineda had an uncanny ability to pick which pain clinic patient was most likely to do something interesting on camera. The cameraman would park next to the target's car, and he and Cafiero would move to the rear of the van and draw the curtains behind the front seat. Pineda would shoot through the van's dark-tinted windows. They got video of patients shooting up, trading cash for pills, leaving children in their cars.

Cafiero also dug into state corporate records and identified the clinic manager as a Christopher P. George of Wellington, Florida. She interviewed local police and the Broward sheriff's office. She found statistics about drug-dispensing doctors in the state of Florida. The picture began to come together.

Pretty soon, Cafiero would be ready for her jump-out on this Christopher P. George character.

3

To Derik Nolan, the whole thing felt like the biggest practical joke ever. Two assholes like Chris and himself could just open a pain clinic, and nobody could do anything about it. Derik figured they were getting away with it because the basic transaction that was taking place—a patient getting a prescription from a licensed doctor—was legal. Whatever the patients did with the pills after leaving the clinic, that was on them.

Same with the doctors. They might be violating the law inside their offices, not following diagnostic guidelines or something. But Chris and Derik weren't doctors—neither of them even had a college degree—so what they didn't know couldn't hurt them. How could they be held responsible for the way people with medical degrees prescribed medicine?

Besides, they weren't going to quit just as they were starting to make real money. Chris had grown up rich, and Derik had enjoyed some flush years. When Derik was nineteen, making good money as a plumber, he'd bought a $60,000 Mustang Cobra convertible and had his own house. Later, he'd owned his own companies, pulled down six figures in the good years. But this was different. They'd tapped into something big and rich and desperate here, something that made people line up around the block at 6:00 a.m. every morning. The clinic accepted credit cards, but almost nobody paid that way. Cash poured into the clinic so fast that they'd given up on using their register. No cash register could take in $20,000 to $30,000 a day. It took too long to push all those buttons and ring someone up, and the cash drawer was too small. They had to empty it too often, and it was taking time away from processing the patients. So Derik had just grabbed a couple of nine-gallon garbage cans, the kind you see in bathrooms, and stuck one under the customer window. When it filled up, he'd cart it back to Chris's office to be counted and stick the empty one under the window.

Every day seemed like a miracle. Every day they were amazed by the things they saw. Every day they realized that this thing was bigger than what they'd thought it was just the day before. Oxycodone was growing out of control, like black mold in a Florida bathroom, and they'd suddenly become a major supplier for a half-dozen states.

By summer 2008, they were seeing one hundred patients a day. The little bungalow couldn't handle that amount of traffic. As the days had grown hotter, they discovered that the two old air-conditioning units cut into the waiting-room walls were completely inadequate for the job. The waiting room had about thirty chairs, and there were sometimes another dozen people standing. At regular intervals, a row of automatic-spray air fresheners on the wall spritzed the lukewarm stench. It didn't help much. The bathroom was always a mess, so Derik took out the paper towel dispenser and installed an air dryer. The cleaning lady started coming in early to get a head start on the daily cleanup. She found hypodermic needles in the garbage cans, in the parking lot, rattling inside empty soda cans.

Derik and Chris didn't talk much about what was really going on at South Florida Pain. They talked business, sure, but they only rarely referred to the fact that they'd suddenly become a strange brand of drug dealer. It wasn't something they wanted to talk about much. Not with each other, and definitely not with the doctors or anyone else. It was partly a precaution, in case anybody was listening, and partly because they were afraid of jinxing their business luck. Derik believed Chris was feeling the same as he was: like a pitcher throwing a perfect game. It was the seventh inning, and they couldn't talk up what was happening, so they kept their excitement to themselves, maybe shaking their heads or raising an eyebrow at each other when they saw an especially long line of zombies lined up in the morning. Derik wanted to laugh when he remembered how they'd talked about the pain clinic when it was first starting, Chris saying that Jeff might be able to hire Derik for $12 an hour.

No more long hot days at a worksite, covered in sweat and sawdust. Derik was paying every bill and had money left over. This was what all the years of hard work had been for. He couldn't walk away now. He'd finally made it.

They'd always figured they'd get shut down sooner or later. Now they were beginning to believe they were in the clear. Either way, for now, they'd grab as much as they could.

But, four months after South Florida Pain opened: a wake-up call.

On June 10, a guy came to the clinic, introduced himself as a Florida Department of Health investigator. A smug little sawed-off shit, Derik thought. He spoke street English and generally came off to Derik as more of a Fort Lauderdale city meter reader than a guy with an important state job. Nevertheless, he and Chris were on edge.

The investigator said it was a routine inspection, something they did for all doctors who dispensed controlled substances on-site. He didn't ask many questions, but Chris and Derik took the opportunity to ask *him* a few things they'd been wondering about. After all, he was a state health investigator. If he didn't know how a pain clinic was supposed to run, nobody did. They asked him if there was a limit on the quantity of prescriptions they should be issuing for a twenty-eight-day period. For instance, what number of 30-milligram oxycodone pills was considered to be OK? The investigator didn't seem like he wanted to give a number, but eventually conceded that 240 pills could be considered an upper limit, which matched what Dr. Overstreet had told Chris. They asked what they should do when patients came back to the clinic early and said their prescription had been lost or stolen and they needed an early refill. The investigator said the clinic could replace a portion of the prescription if the patient produced a police report that confirmed the theft. For instance, if there were fourteen days left in a twenty-eight-day prescription, they could write a scrip for half the pills. The inspector wasn't referring to any documents or using any official-sounding words. In fact, his answers just rambled, like he was making up things as he went, pulling rules out of his ass, whatever he thought made sense. He also kept telling them to refer to the DEA website.

The whole thing felt wrong to Derik, the way the guy seemed reluctant to give solid and specific information. He felt like he was getting set up.

He thought to himself: *You should just walk away. Now. Go back to building houses.*

The inspector looked around the building. He wasn't pleased when he saw Moe, Dianna's floppy-eared wiener dog. He said it was considered unsanitary to have a dog around medication, even though Moe wasn't in the dispensary room. He told Chris he wanted to see receipts for the medication the clinic had ordered. Then he started looking through random patient files, making photocopies as he went. He was particularly interested in prescriptions that had been filled in-house, kept pulling them out of the files and piling up the photocopies. Chris and Derik had a bad feeling about this because the doctors usually didn't completely fill out scrips that were filled in-house. They weren't trying to hide anything. It was just a time-saving measure. Why bother writing out the patient's name and address if the scrip was never even going to leave the building? If the patient wanted to fill the prescription elsewhere, the doctors filled it out completely, and Derik or Dianna photocopied it and put the copy in the file.

Derik thought the inspector looked pleased with himself as he put the copies in an envelope and sealed it. It was kind of funny. Chris and Derik were a couple of house builders who had only the slightest idea what they were doing in the pain clinic business, and they had found a way to crank tens of thousands of pills a day onto the street. And the state investigator was fine with that fact. Instead, he knocked them for not including the patients' names or addresses on some prescriptions. And he didn't like Moe being there.

The inspector left with his envelope of photocopied prescriptions, and Derik and Chris did what they usually did when they were together: laughed it off. They made fun of the little guy, his street accent and bad grammar. *That* guy was going to bring them down? No way.

Chris took the health department inspection more seriously than he let on to Derik. For one thing, he decided he would no longer rely on the doctors to know the rules and regulations around pain management. Other than her brief stint at One Stop Medical, Dr. Gittens was a family practitioner. Dr. Joseph was a gynecologist. They weren't pain management specialists, and they probably weren't even very good doctors, or else why would they be working here? Chris needed to figure things out on his own.

After a local pharmacy began refusing to fill South Florida Pain prescriptions and said it was heeding the advice of the DEA, Chris called the DEA for clarification. He wanted to know, once and for all, what the rules were. He expected to get some kind of runaround, but he got lucky, connected with a woman who was some kind of higher-up in Florida. And then he introduced himself, and the DEA official knew who he was right away. Even knew his address.

She said: Oh, yes, South Florida Pain Clinic. That's 500 West Oakland Park Boulevard, right?

The recognition freaked Chris out. A DEA official had his clinic's address on the tip of her tongue. He asked her some questions, and she did what the state health investigator had done, told him to consult the DEA website. She couldn't tell him anything more than what was there.

Chris consulted the DEA website. It contained a policy, published in 2006, for dispensing pain meds. In the introduction, the policy quoted some statistics, including a national survey from 2004 that found that thirty-one million Americans had used painkillers to get high. But the eye-opening number was the 2.4 million people in the previous year who had tried painkillers non-medically for the first time. That number was higher than the number of new users of cocaine or even marijuana. Among illicit drug users, pharmaceuticals were the biggest growth market.

Yet doctors hadn't reached a consensus on painkillers. When the DEA had drafted the policy, many health professionals had provided input, and they split into two groups with different primary concerns: those who felt that pain was undertreated, and those who believed that painkillers were overprescribed. The document quoted one authority who said: "It takes only a few untrained or unscrupulous physicians to create large pockets of addicts." But the document also said "undertreatment of pain is recognized as a serious public health problem," and Chris liked the sound of that line, filed it away to use later.

The document said painkillers like oxycodone could only be prescribed or dispensed for a "legitimate medical purpose." And there's where things got really fuzzy. The policy said there were no specific guidelines that determined what was a legitimate medical purpose and what was not. Instead, courts must analyze the evidence surrounding each case individually, and to be found guilty of unlawful prescribing of controlled substances, a physician's illegal activity must be "glaring."

In 1978, a federal appeals court had created a list of actions commonly taken by doctors who were writing illegal prescriptions, and the DEA policy said that list was still relevant. Bad docs, according to the policy, tended to write lots of scrips for large numbers of pills. They gave no physical exams. They warned patients to fill their scrips at multiple drugstores. They wrote scrips too often. They called drugs by their street names and generally acted like drug dealers.

The policy gave a few examples of bad doctors—Chris paid close attention to this part—but their practices were way more blatant and crooked than anything South Florida Pain was doing. One doctor in the policy had given a patient seven to ten prescriptions in different people's names every *week*. Another physician had gone to the pharmacy to help his sixteen-year-old patient fill a prescription. Another had driven off the road after injecting himself with Demerol.

Chris reasoned that South Florida Pain's doctors could easily sidestep some of these problems by following a few simple rules. They would fill out diagnostic paperwork for every patient. They would schedule patient appointments no closer than twenty-eight days apart. And hopefully, his doctors would generally not let on to anybody if they knew what the patients were doing with the pills.

However, if Chris was going to make big money, Dr. Gittens and Dr. Joseph had to keep writing big and servicing big numbers. And one thing the policy made very clear was that the DEA reserved the right to investigate any doctor or clinic it wanted to investigate. So Chris wanted to know if there was a trigger number that would cause the DEA to red-flag South Florida Pain as a possible pill mill. Dr. Overstreet had said 240 pills per prescription was the magic number, and the health department investigator had seemed to confirm it. The DEA policy was vague, saying "what constitutes 'an inordinately large quantity of controlled substances'... can vary greatly from patient to patient," and that cases against doctors "typically involve facts that demonstrate blatant criminal conduct."

The policy gave only the following specific example: "(I)f a physician were to prescribe 1,600 (sixteen hundred) tablets per day of a schedule II opioid to a single patient, this would certainly warrant investigation as there is no conceivable medical basis for anyone to ingest that quantity of such a powerful narcotic in a single day."

Sixteen hundred pills a day to a single patient! That example was so over-the-top that it was useless as a guideline. Chris wondered if the DEA purposely left certain information ambiguous, so clinics wouldn't know how to avoid getting busted.

A few weeks after the health department inspection, a man stuck his head in the patient window and said he was Juan Ortega, a reporter from the *Sun-Sentinel*. Ortega had heard about South Florida Pain from a man who drove past the clinic on the way to work each morning. The commuter had noticed the growing lines of patients and called the newspaper about it. Ortega had spoken to the owner of the bridal headpiece shop next door and a law firm up the block. The neighbors were complaining about the long lines and disruptive patients in the parking lots. The reporter had also tried to speak to patients in line, but they wouldn't talk.

Chris agreed to the interview, didn't think much about it. He brought Ortega back to his office, where he had multiple security camera monitors showing various angles of the clinic property. He agreed to let the reporter record the interview on a handheld video camera. Ortega pointed the little camera at Chris's face and started asking questions.

Chris said the clinic was treating patients with medication and exercise. He said his doctors thoroughly examined patients and checked medical records before prescribing. He said they were committed to catching patients who were obtaining prescriptions from multiple doctors. He showed the reporter a filing cabinet in his office. It was filled, he said, with files of patients they'd banned for suspicious activities. At first, Chris refused to identify the names of the doctors, but Ortega had looked up the clinic on the health department website. Dr. Gittens, Dr. Joseph, and a part-time doctor listed the clinic address as their worksite. When the reporter told him the doctors were in good standing with the health department, Chris confirmed that they all worked there.* Ortega asked why there were so many out-of-state vehicles in the parking lot, and Chris sidestepped the question, acted like he didn't know. Chris also wouldn't say whether he was advertising the clinic on billboards.

Chris paraphrased a line from the DEA policy on prescribing painkillers.

"Pain is a big problem right now, and we're just doing our part," Chris said, his mug completely deadpan.

Chris also told the reporter that he was trying to expand the parking lot in the rear of the building by demolishing the landlady's back yard. "That'll solve all of our parking problems here," he said.

Ortega's story came out a day or two later—Neighbors Calling Clinic A Pain—underneath a big color photo of the front of the clinic, shot with a long lens from across Oakland Park Boulevard. The photo

* The health department had not yet issued a report about its June 2008 inspection of South Florida Pain.

showed a couple dozen people loitering beneath the big red-lettered sign on the clinic's low roof, a mix of men and women who looked to be in their thirties and forties, mostly. One young guy leaned on a walking cane.

The story wasn't too bad, Derik thought. It focused mostly on the neighboring businesses' complaints, one saying, "It's been horrendous. The people hang out all day." Ortega had checked police records and reported that local cops had been called to the clinic six times, including one time in May because someone had stolen a patient's pills. The story dropped a few hints about what was going on—the out-of-state patients, the pill thief, the fact that city leaders were looking into whether the clinic was complying with all municipal requirements. But it never mentioned painkillers or narcotics. An uninformed reader or someone giving the story a quick scan might come away thinking it was a minor dispute between a couple of local businesses over parking.

Chris and Derik enjoyed the video that accompanied the story on the newspaper website, especially the part where Chris said, with a straight face: "Pain is a big problem right now, and we're just doing our part." Derik loved that statement, especially since there was a random balloon bobbing in the background of the shot, like Chris was at some kid's birthday party. Derik couldn't remember where the balloon had come from, but somehow it made the whole thing even sillier. They played the video over and over, laughing. Chris had played the part well, Derik thought. He was solemn and earnest, just a well-meaning health care professional trying to solve the difficult problem of pain.

A week after the *Sun-Sentinel* article came out, Derik was having a bad thirty-first birthday. He came to work hung over from the night before. Then, two neighborhood thugs attacked two elderly patients in the parking lot, grabbed their meds, and took off. Derik chased them down some back streets, past the quiet ranch houses. They splashed across a canal and got away, and Derik slogged back to the clinic, soaking wet and in a foul mood.

It was Friday, a payday. After Dr. Gittens got her check, she told Derik that this would be her last day at the clinic. Derik was shocked. Dr. Gittens had always showed more interest than the other doctors in how the pain clinic was run. She was the one who said every patient needed to have an MRI. She was always asking questions about how they kept the books, how much the various medications cost, which MRI services were best. She was a nice woman, and she'd seemed invested in the clinic's future.

On the other hand, she'd been acting a little different lately. Before, she'd been friendly, meeting Derik and his roommate out for drinks. Her brother, who'd helped her move to Florida three months earlier, had showed up again, asking questions about licensing and how they ran the office. Derik had thought it was odd when he saw her studying the price lists they'd made for medications. Still, Derik couldn't understand why she was leaving so suddenly. He asked her to stay on for a week or two, give a reasonable notice so he could find another full-time doctor. Otherwise, they'd have to go back to servicing clients until midnight. But Gittens said no, she had made up her mind. She tried to give him a hug as she left, but Derik just walked away.

A few days later, Derik was riding in to work with his roommate, as usual. When they pulled off I-95 and headed east on Oakland Park Boulevard, a new sign caught Derik's eye, off to the right. A place called Oakland Plaza Medical Center. The sign said it offered pain management. Same side of the busy boulevard as South Florida Pain, just off the interstate, a half-mile closer to the exit than South Florida Pain.

He got into work and talked it over with Chris, who'd also seen the sign on his way in with Dianna. They were worried. What if patients coming off the interstate saw the other clinic's sign and started pulling in there? They believed whoever had put up this clinic was trying to steal their business.

So Derik paid a visit to the new clinic. It was in a building that looked like a warehouse, tucked between a window-tinting shop and a decorative concrete showroom. But the interior had been renovated, with nice stone countertops.

And that's when Derik saw Dr. Gittens's brother, working at the new clinic. No sign of Dr. Gittens herself, but her strange recent behavior suddenly made sense, the sudden interest in the inner workings of the clinic, her quitting without notice. She'd obviously decided to go into the business by herself, siphoning off the patient traffic from I-95.

Chris and Derik knew that if Gittens could piggyback on the success of South Florida Pain, nothing was stopping anybody from doing the same thing. The word was out, that there was money to be made in pain management. To stay on top, South Florida Pain needed to grow. It needed a bigger space, more doctors. More pain clinics were popping up every day, and Chris wanted to be the biggest and the best.

That was how Chris was. He'd wrestled back in high school, and he'd win lopsided matches, taking down a weaker opponent over and over. Afterward, his dad would ask why he didn't just pin the guy, take the quicker victory? But Chris didn't just want to win. He wanted to dominate the other guy, control him, mash his face into the mat. The more patients the clinic got, the more Chris wanted. He wanted every hillbilly streaming into Florida to know about South Florida Pain.

He began scouting new locations.

The local cops turned up the heat. The clinic sat just within the border of Wilton Manors, but the boulevard was patrolled by Oakland Park cops. They'd park their cruisers just to the east and west of the clinic and roll up on patients as they left the clinic. Patients said the cops would search the cars, question them, arrest them, take their pills. Other times, they'd cruise by the parking lot and scope out the patients' tags, run them, and then come into the clinic to get them if their insurance or registration wasn't up to date. Sometimes they'd tow cars right out of the lot.

Chris and Derik figured the *Sun-Sentinel* story had motivated the police to lean on them. Finally, Chris called the station to complain, and two officers came out to the clinic to talk to him and Derik, a regular patrol cop who had pulled over a lot of patients and a lieutenant. Chris and Derik told them they were trying to abide by the laws.

Chris said: Listen, just because they come here doesn't mean they get pills. They don't even necessarily get to see the doctor.

The lieutenant seemed to get it, and Chris thought maybe he'd order the junior officer to lay off. But the very next day the guy was still at it, pulling patients over as they left the clinic. Time for a confrontation, Chris thought. So he told a patient what was going on, and hopped in the patient's car when he was leaving. Sure enough, the cop pulled them over, and Chris dialed his lawyer's cell phone to report what was happening.

The patrol officer told him to get off the phone, and Chris refused. The cop got annoyed, popped Chris for resisting arrest, and took him to the gigantic concrete Broward County Jail in Fort Lauderdale. It took forever for him to get processed, so Dianna and Derik shared a bottle of tequila at a downtown bar. Derik got hammered and started a fight. They were kicked out of the bar and went to the jail to post bond. Derik caused a scene in the bond unit and almost got arrested right there in the jail. So Dianna drove him home to West Palm at midnight and then went back for Chris, who had to wait for an hour after he got out. Chris yelled at her for making him wait, and Derik felt bad when he heard about it since it was his fault for getting drunk. Chris pleaded no contest to resisting arrest without violence and was sentenced to one day of probation and a fine.

~

The arrest made up Chris's mind. It was time to leave Oakland Park Boulevard. He'd been thinking about it for weeks, after everything that had happened that summer. The health department investigator, and the DEA woman who knew his name. The angry neighbors, and the newspaper story. Gittens splitting to open her own clinic, other competitors popping up all over the place. Now, local cops were turning up the heat.

The clinic needed a new home. South Florida Pain had the potential to be a juggernaut, but a juggernaut couldn't operate out of a shithole bungalow with eight parking spaces.

It was also time to grow and mature. Time to hire more doctors and staff, create some rules, get serious. The clinic was inhaling $40,000 to $50,000 a day. And Chris believed that $250,000 a week was just scratching the surface. Like the railroad-and-oil tycoons of the nineteenth century, or the tech billionaires of the 1990s, Chris and Derik, of all the random people, had enjoyed perfect, exquisite, history-making timing. They'd stumbled into a Bizarro-world, a window of opportunity in which hard drugs were, for the moment, legal. Because if they weren't legal, how were Chris and Derik able to conduct their business in broad daylight? They had a big sign with red letters saying Pain Clinic. They'd been in the *Sun-Sentinel*, a big color picture of the zombies standing in line. The DEA was receiving their 222 forms every week, tracking their incoming drug shipments. The Florida Department of Health had sent in its inspector to rifle through their patient files. And nobody had shut them down.

But Chris and Derik knew that someone would find a way to end their ride, if they didn't grow up now. That meant doing something that did not come naturally to them: following the rules. It was time to hire a dog walker, stop bringing Moe in to the clinic. No more fun-and-games, no more letting patients take the neighborhood hostage. No more sloppy record-keeping, letting favored patients slide on their drug tests and MRIs.

And here was the beautiful part: By now, they could *afford* to be tough on the patients. They could kick anybody out, for the most minor infractions. Because for every one they kicked out, there were five waiting to jump in line.

They were going to make millions, many times over, and they had to protect the operation at any cost, even if that meant going straight.

Part II

4

Once he'd made up his mind to move, Chris George didn't waste any time. A few days after his arrest, he leased an office suite for the clinic a couple miles west of I-95 on Cypress Creek Road. The new space was huge, about six times the size of the little bungalow on Oakland Park Boulevard. It was in an office complex called the Cypress Creek Executive Court, which backed up to a row of airplane hangars next to the two-strip Fort Lauderdale Executive Airport. The quiet office park was nothing like the haphazard strip of businesses on busy Oakland Park Boulevard. It included travel agencies, insurance offices, and small law firms, and featured pleasant concrete walks, well-tended palms, wooden benches, and most importantly, lots of parking: about two hundred spaces.

After work on Friday, Chris and Derik Nolan went to Home Depot and ordered materials for a quick build-out. The supplies were delivered to the new office on Saturday, and that day they roughed out a ten-foot interior wall with a doorway and a window, to separate the waiting room from the examination rooms and filing areas. It was a makeshift job, with stapled-on particleboard walls propped up by two-by-fours. It didn't even reach the ceiling because a real wall would have required them to pull building permits. It looked like a temporary triage clinic in a war zone or something. But it would do. They were only planning to be there for a few months. Some other tenants were scheduled to move out soon, freeing up a nicer space.

Sunday, they rented a U-Haul truck and moved everything from one building to the other—the waiting-room chairs, the examination tables that no patient ever lay on, the gun safes where they kept the drugs. Derik had done an inventory of the drugs a couple weeks earlier. He hadn't wanted to hand-count each of the thousands of pills, so he'd come up with what he thought was a common-sense solution. He counted out and weighed some pills and then weighed them all and did the math. He wasn't sure what kind of regulations existed regarding the transport and inventory of controlled substances, but he just wanted to make sure no one was boosting pills. The count came out fairly accurate, give or take.

Monday morning, South Florida Pain Clinic opened in its new location. Chris stationed Dianna at the Oakland Park Boulevard building, where she answered the phone and told callers how to find the new location. When patients showed up in person, she gave them flyers with directions to the new clinic.

At the Cypress Creek location, things were slow for about an hour, and then the patients with Dianna's directions started pulling into the lot.

New location, new rules. From now on, Chris said, every patient had to have a valid MRI report that was less than two years old, and every patient had to take a drug test before seeing a doctor. No exceptions.

The MRI rule created a small problem. MRIs required a prescription, and having the doctors see patients twice would slow things down. So the doctors gave Derik a pad of blank prescriptions they'd already signed, and Derik would just fill it in, charging $50 per MRI prescription. He'd ask each patient where it hurt. If they said lower back, he'd write, "MRI of lumbar." If they said it was the neck, he'd write that. They'd go get the MRI done and come back for their doctor's appointment. Derik wasn't sure how an MRI machine worked or even what the letters "MRI" stood for. But writing prescriptions was simple, he found, not like something you needed to go to med school for anyway.

Under Chris's new rules, patients had to take a drug test every three months. Derik gave those patients a small clear plastic cup with a blue lid and a panel on the side. The patient took the cup to the restroom and came out with a full cup. Most of the time, no one actually watched the patients pee. Derik collected the cups, and when there was a trayful, he'd snap on rubber gloves and peel back the stickers on the panel to see which drugs were present in the patient's system. New patients were supposed to have clean urine, unless they said they had been prescribed something already. Return patients were supposed to be positive for oxycodone, but not illegal drugs like ecstasy or cocaine or marijuana.

Patients also were required to fill out numerous pages of paperwork before seeing a doctor, forms and policies Chris and Derik had collected, starting with the documents they'd taken from the other clinic before South Florida Pain opened. There was a pain management agreement, in which patients vowed not to abuse the medication. The one-page agreement instructed the patients to tell their physicians the truth about the intensity of their pain. To not share, sell, or trade pills. To safeguard it from thieves. To not use illegal drugs. To not go to other pain management doctors and South Florida Pain at the same time. Patients who broke the rules would be discharged and no longer welcome at the clinic. One key passage read:

> *I understand payment of the office visit DOES NOT GUARANTEE MEDICATION. Prescriptions are only written if the Doctor deems it necessary. We reserve the right to deny medication to those we feel are drug seekers or abusers. NO REFUNDS WILL BE GIVEN.*

Patients also signed a Diversion Policy, which covered the same territory, more or less. Another form asked whether the patients were Florida residents and, if not, why they hadn't sought treatment closer to home. A typical response: "They will not give enough to help with pain and when you ask for stronger they look down on you." Chris created that out-of-stater form himself. If the health department showed up again and asked why they had so many non-Florida patients, he figured he could use the patients' statements to shield himself.

Chris had found most of the forms and policies online, including the Patient Comfort Assessment Guide, a survey created by Purdue Pharma that asked patients to describe and rate their pain in great detail. (Among other questions, it asked if the pain fit the following descriptions: stabbing, gnawing, exhausting, shooting, burning, nagging, penetrating, miserable, or unbearable, plus a few more. Some patients circled every word.) Chris barely skimmed the documents and never discussed them with the doctors. He just wanted to make sure that each patient's file was stuffed with paperwork, drug screens, MRI reports, and signed policies. Thick patient files, he believed, would make it more difficult for authorities to claim that South Florida Pain was just a drug-dealing operation.

They needed more doctors. Dr. Gittens was gone, and the new office had much more space. Also, the more doctors Chris had, the more drugs the wholesalers would allow him to order. He wanted a mix of full-timers and part-timers so he could open early and stay open late, be as accommodating as possible. Chris placed another round of job ads on Craigslist, and doctors kept calling.

When interviewing doctors, Chris didn't want to come off as unprofessional or criminal. He tried to speak well, look successful. But he did want the doctors to understand what they were signing up for. So he didn't exactly turn on the charm. He wore his typical outfit—torn jeans and a T-shirt. He barely looked at resumes, asked few questions about medical expertise or credentials. The interviews were brief. Chris was a mumbler, had a monotone, monosyllabic way of speaking to outsiders. He'd tell the physicians they would be working to provide services for chronic pain. He'd ask if they had a DEA registration and a medical license and whether they were comfortable prescribing narcotics. If doctors said they lacked experience in pain management, Chris said that didn't matter, they could learn on the job. He would show the doctor some patient charts to give a sense of the dosages the other doctors were prescribing. And then he'd talk about the pay. At $75 per appointment, South Florida Pain was seeing enough patients to pay doctors between $2,000 to $4,000 a day. Plus $1,000 cash a week for the use of their DEA registration number to order drugs.

The true test came when Chris had an applicant shadow another doctor, to see if he or she could stomach the ceaseless flow of patients receiving prescription after prescription of the same controlled substances. Two interviewees walked out after these observation sessions, saying they couldn't do it.

But all the other doctors who came in for interviews took the job, no matter what they saw at the clinic. It became a joke between Chris and Derik. The long lines, the desperate patients, none of it seemed to make a difference. The doctors saw what was going on at South Florida Pain, and they were OK with it once they heard they'd be making $75 a patient.

The physicians were a mixed bag: male, female, young, old, black, white, Hispanic, Jewish, US-born, international, gay, straight. Mixed specialties too: gynecologists, plastic surgeons, family practitioners.

The doctors tended to be a little odd. One physician wanted to see only female patients, and it turned out that he was digging into patient files and stalking the good-looking ones. Another had such bad body odor that Derik was forced to talk to him about it, which was awkward. Another left after a few months and started his own pain clinic, as Dr. Gittens had done. Others had gambling problems, or drug problems, or student-debt problems. One belonged to a swingers group and tried to recruit Derik.

It was a great part-time gig, Derik thought, to come in for a couple hours in the evening after your real job, see a dozen patients and walk out with a grand in your pocket. The part-timers clamored for as many hours as they could get, and some wanted to come aboard full-time. Derik had mixed feelings about the medical staffing. The doctors were key to the entire business, of course. But fewer doctors had meant longer lines, which meant more patients handing Derik money to jump the line.

If the doctors struggled with their consciences, they kept it to themselves. Except one, a part-timer, Dr. Patrick Graham, a plastic surgeon in Boca Raton who worked at the clinic in the evenings, maybe once a week. Graham was in his early sixties. He'd interviewed at the Oakland Park Boulevard location, where Gittens had shown him the ropes before she quit. He'd spent half a day shadowing her as she treated about fifteen patients. During the first few appointments Graham observed, Dr. Gittens listened to the patients' heart and lungs, had them bend over, checked ears, noses, and throats, had them do some range-of-motion exercises. But as the morning wore on, Gittens had spent less time with the patients, her exams growing more cursory. Everybody got similarly large doses of narcotics. By the time Graham was done shadowing Gittens, he believed he understood how things were done at South Florida Pain.

Around Derik, Graham would drop hints that he knew the clinic was a pill mill, that he knew the score. Around the other doctors, he played dumb. Sometimes he'd complain to Derik that Chris had hired a new doctor, worried it would cut down his patient load. Other times, he'd come to Derik and say that there was nothing wrong with a patient and he couldn't write a scrip for him, like he'd had a sudden attack of conscience. Derik would point out that he'd already written twenty scrips that day for similar patients. Dr. Graham would continue to argue.

Finally Derik would say: Whatever, dude. I guess I need a new doctor.

That's when Dr. Graham would give up.

Graham would say: Fine, then.

And he'd go write the scrip.

Graham was interesting, Derik thought. It was like he wanted a little push from Derik. To make himself feel better, like he had no choice. So Derik would give it.

Derik didn't push the other doctors. If a doc wanted him to bounce a patient who had inadequate documentation or infected track marks, he bounced the patient. There was no upside to arguing with the doctors, nothing to be gained by pulling back the curtain and too openly revealing or discussing what they were doing.

Chris and Derik reasoned that the number one problem at the Oakland Park Boulevard location had been the tiny waiting room, which meant the patients roamed the neighborhood, shooting up, nodding off, shoplifting, squabbling, selling pills, and generally acting like junkies. Chris and Derik hadn't minded this behavior in the early months, even encouraged it sometimes, but after a while it was like they were begging the cops to show up. Which was why they'd been forced to move. Chris didn't want the same thing to happen again, so the rule at the new location became: no loitering in the parking lot.

They put the homeless man who'd hung around the Oakland Park Boulevard location in charge of monitoring the new building's exterior. The vagrant had been arrested for crack possession and was living in a halfway house now, which was a step up from the laundry where he'd previously slept. Chris and Derik had felt bad about leaving their homeless security guard behind when they moved to the Cypress Creek location, so they'd told him they'd give him a promotion if he came with them. The homeless man had happily agreed. They'd see him riding his bike the six miles from Oakland Park Boulevard each day, a scrawny figure in cowboy hat and boots, pedaling his bike in heavy traffic. Derik bought him a walkie-talkie and a shirt that read Security. He instructed the security guard to call him on the walkie-talkie when patients were parking in the other businesses' spots or pissing in the hedges. But the security guard never remembered to wear the security shirt and couldn't seem to get the hang of actually communicating through the walkie-talkie. When Derik heard a burst of static on his walkie-talkie, he knew his security guard was trying to reach him, and he'd head out to the parking lot. The guard couldn't take care of issues himself because the patients didn't take him seriously. When it became obvious that the homeless man wasn't getting the job done, Chris and Derik advertised for a new security guard and hired a three-hundred-pound Puerto Rican guy who came for his interview wearing a security guard uniform he'd bought somewhere. The scrawny vagrant and the giant tag-teamed the parking lot with varying levels of success.

The inside staff was growing too. Chris and Derik needed people to handle the increased paperwork. Derik hired several friends, either guys he'd grown up with or had met building houses. Derik's roommate, who'd come aboard earlier in the summer. Pedro, who'd worked for Derik on and off ever since his plumbing days. The brothers of Derik's high school girlfriend, as well as her father, a biker who'd been an addict himself but had been clean for a couple of years. When Derik told friends about the money they could make, they quit good jobs—union plumbers, electricians—to be security guards or work the patient window at South Florida Pain. Even one guy who was a mortgage broker talked to Derik about coming to work at the clinic. It felt good to create jobs for friends who needed work, something that made Derik look both bighearted and powerful. And having his own crew strengthened Derik's grasp on the operation, made him even more essential to Chris.

Most of the guys they hired were good-looking, clean-cut men, jacked up on steroids, wearing tight T-shirts and jeans. So Chris and Derik figured they should hire some good-looking girls too. They put an ad on Craigslist: *Receptionist needed for busy pain clinic. No resume or experience needed. Just send picture.* And they got lots of pictures, some professional headshots and some full-body pictures in swimsuits or lingerie, plus a couple of nasty messages, asking if they were running a doctor's office or a modeling service. They had a good time deciding which women had what it took to land an interview. One former bikini model and high-end escort immediately caught Chris's eye. Dianna didn't like all the women hanging around Chris. They fought more and more, and she stopped coming to the clinic.

Staff-wise, the clinic was less doctor's office than South Beach club—all tanned biceps and fake boobs. Derik loved it. He wanted the clinic to be a place where people enjoyed themselves—a junkie paradise. He bought black-market copies of movies that were still in the theaters and played them on the waiting room's massive flat-screen TVs. They installed vending machines, and the staffers flirted with the patients, sweetie-this and honey-that.

Chris didn't interact with the patients or staff much, so Derik was the center of the frenzy, directing traffic, deciding who got in and who didn't, like a nightclub doorman. Sometimes he felt like a celebrity. The patients drove him crazy, but he *loved* the power, how they'd do whatever he wanted because he controlled the thing they wanted most. He could tell a patient to put on a blindfold and run across Cypress Creek Boulevard, and the guy would do it, no questions asked.

Under Derik's watch, sponsors who were funding groups of patients got VIP treatment. They entered through the employee entrance, got to see the doctors right away. After coming for a couple months, patients often began to think they should be part of the clinic's inner circle. Some patients became downright obsessed with the clinic and its staff. Suddenly, guys from Kentucky started dressing like Derik and the rest of the crew, asking them where they'd bought their shirts. Some brought in moonshine as gifts for Derik or the doctors, showing him pictures of their kids, or posted about the clinic on underground junkie websites and on druggie threads on general interest forums like Topix.com. *Derik's a good guy, but it's hard to get face-time with him . . . Don't go outside for any reason today or else you'll get banned . . . Traffic's backed up on Cypress Creek going west toward SF Pain today, take this route instead. . . .*

Patients told Derik the street price of oxy 30s back home had dropped to $10, mainly because South Florida Pain was flooding the market. They said people who would have never visited Florida in the past were coming just to experience South Florida Pain. And people who used to come down just to get a prescription for themselves were sponsoring their own carloads. They got an e-mail from a sheriff in Kentucky. The guy sounded angry: *I arrested another one of your patients last night. I can't pull over a single car without finding an appointment card for your clinic. Thanks for destroying my community.*

South Florida Pain wasn't alone. Pain clinics were opening up all over Broward County, and patients told Derik the others were trying to copy his style, but no one had really succeeded. Derik told them nobody could match his showmanship, his panache. And it seemed to be true, judging by the lines in the waiting room. Everyone said South Florida Pain was the biggest pain clinic around.

On the other hand, being honest with himself, Derik had to admit the patients weren't coming for the ambiance. The clinic was popular because it usually had pills in stock. After six months, Derik understood these people, knew they'd drive to a shithole in Anchorage if that was the closest place to get pills. No matter what they looked like or how they spoke, they were junkies, which meant they had no humility or pride. They were all about getting the fix.

Take the women Derik and his roommate were dating, for example.

The first time the girls had come into the clinic, just before the move from Oakland Park Boulevard, Derik and his roommate were all over them. One was a Marine, but cute and sweet, big blue eyes, blonde hair. She had military disability paperwork for an injury, some kind of lower spine thing. Her friend was Brazilian, great body, olive skin. She told the doctors she'd been mugged, beaten up.

Early on, Derik had hooked up with female patients from time to time. Nothing serious, just a quick good time in a back room. He knew those patients were just hoping to score some extra pills, but he enjoyed himself anyway. Derik thought these women were different. They seemed out of place among the clinic patients, uncomfortable, which made Derik like them. No way these young, fresh-faced girls were junkies.

The girls flirted with Derik and his roommate at the clinic and ended up going back to the guys' apartment after work. Derik ended up with the Brazilian woman, his roommate with the Marine. Derik's girl was amazing in bed, no inhibitions. Derik, always quick to jump into things, started hanging out with her every night, even met her mother. He liked her jet-black hair, her Brazilian lilt.

Not a week had gone by, however, before Derik realized that something was wrong with his new girl. He'd find her staring in the mirror for hours, glazed over, mesmerized by her face, picking at it. He'd take her to a restaurant with friends, and she'd cause a scene, start crying. He'd be alone with her and she'd start going into withdrawal, begging him for pills, acting like a straight-up addict.

Derik began to wonder if she was with him just because he was the man with access to the pills, if the whole relationship was just another junkie stunt. On the other hand, he couldn't believe she was as bad as the pillheads he spent all day around, people who would do anything for a fix.

Almost a month into the relationship, she slept over one night, and Derik awoke to hear her phone buzzing. It was 2:00 a.m., and she was asleep, so Derik took a look at the phone. It was her friend, texting from his roommate's bedroom in the same apartment. The girls had been texting back and forth for hours. His roommate's girlfriend needed a pill to get her through the night, and she was trying to cut a deal with Derik's girl, offering to give her dirt on other women Derik was seeing. It was the same kind of wretched bargaining Derik was used to seeing from the low-down zombies at South Florida Pain. It made him sick. He turned off the phone and tried to go to sleep.

The next morning, he told her to hit the bricks. He wasn't surprised when the girls denied what was going on, but he couldn't believe it when his roommate took their side, defended them. His roommate was head-over-heels into his new girlfriend, had bought her a car and paid her bills, couldn't see that she was using him.

Derik, on the other hand, was no longer naive. The relationship had taught him one thing: No matter what they looked or acted like, all the patients were junkies—and junkies cared about one thing only.

As the staff grew, so did the variety of bribes and payoffs from customers. Everyone had a hustle going. Some employees took payoffs to let patients cut in line. Others charged extra at the counter. The staffers in charge of drug tests could make sure a test came back clean, for a price. Some employees became patients at the clinic, seeing the doctors and getting their own scrips and then selling their pills to patients.

Chris didn't want people selling their own pills on the side, and Derik agreed, at least in principle.* They basically had a license to deal legal drugs. It was foolhardy to sell them illegally. But try telling that to the rest of the staff, who, after all, weren't making nearly as much money as Chris and Derik.

On the other hand, Chris and Derik disagreed about the graft system. Chris thought it looked unprofessional for patients to be tipping the staff, like people trying to jump the line at a club. He worried that patients might run out of money or not come as often, or they might decide that South Florida Pain was too expensive for them.

Derik not only supported the payoffs, he was in charge of the system. When new staffers came on board, Derik told them that he'd be taking a 50-percent cut of any extra money they'd made, in exchange for shielding them from Chris.

Derik's salary had jumped to $3,000 a week at that point, and before long, he was taking in maybe another $5,000 to $10,000 a week in payoffs. At the current rate of income, he'd clear half a million this year, and there was no reason to think that number wouldn't keep on growing—as long as they didn't get shut down.

Chris himself was set to make multiple millions in 2008. Seven months in, the clinic was servicing more than one hundred patients a day, and the number was forever rising. One hundred patients paying hundreds of dollars apiece for the doctor visit and the meds meant the clinic was taking in tens of thousands of dollars a day. They bought more garbage cans for the cashier windows and ran the full loads of cash back to Chris's office over and over throughout the day, where it got dumped in one enormous garbage bag.

Mounds of bills became a common sight around the clinic, as ordinary as a pile of raked leaves on a fall day. On occasion, Chris had more

* Others who worked at the clinic later said that Derik did, on occasion, sell pills directly.

than a million dollars of cash in his office, just lying around in a bag or a box on the floor. Derik saw the money and felt no thrill. The drugs were locked up in a safe, but they didn't take major security measures to protect the money. Most of the people working at the clinic were Derik's friends, and he trusted them. Besides, everyone was making so much money from their various hustles, and in a way, Derik believed the graft system protected the larger cash flow. As long as everyone was making lots of money, no one was going to upset the apple cart by robbing the clinic itself.

Derik also didn't spend much time worrying about an outside crew robbing the clinic. He had installed lots of cameras and had his odd-couple security guards roving the parking lot. He didn't like guns, never carried one. He had a bad history with them, starting, of course, with his father murdering his second wife. And Derik knew himself. He didn't exactly avoid trouble. As long as there was cocaine and booze around, he was going to get in fights. If he carried a gun, he'd eventually use it, like his father had, and he'd wind up dead or in prison. Besides, he was 210 pounds of muscle and steroids, which made him feel invincible, with or without a gun.

Still, the cash was a problem. Chris had seen a movie called *Blow*, based on a true story about one of the biggest cocaine dealers of the 1980s, and he couldn't forget the part where the guy was arrested and his millions seized.

So, not long after the move to Cypress Creek, Chris had a sit-down with a private investigator who supposedly knew how to deal with large amounts of cash. The investigator was a skinny old guy, close to seventy years old. Talked a lot about his days as a DEA agent in the 70s and 80s, before he'd gone bad and spent thirty-eight months in the joint. Lots of stories straight out of *Miami Vice*—cocaine, cash, and Colombians.

Chris asked the guy about "cleaning" money, how to do it. Chris didn't know if he was using the right terminology—laundering versus cleaning versus just basic investing with cash. The investigator said he was looking to start an adult video store but was short on cash and maybe they could help each other out. Chris agreed to meet, morc interested in picking the guy's brain than really working with him.

Chris met the investigator at the Moonlite Diner, a chrome 50s-style restaurant two miles east of the new clinic location. At the restaurant, the fast-talking investigator drank coffee and explained how it was done. He'd help Chris establish an account at an offshore bank, maybe in the Cayman Islands, and take the cash there. He'd done it before, he said. Once he'd walked into a bank on Grand Cayman with $7 million in Colombian drug cash, and no one blinked an eye. The going rate was six points, the PI said, but the price was negotiable. Chris was less worried about the rate than the idea of just handing over hundreds of thousands to someone.

"I wouldn't ever trust anyone to launder that kind of money," Chris said.

"Then, well, you guys go fucking put the money in," the investigator said. "I'll just set it up for you. You do the accounts. I won't even have access. You have the numbers. You have the password. It's your thing, you put it in, OK?"

The key was, he said, Chris also needed to set up an offshore business that he could borrow money from to invest in legitimate projects in the United States. And then he'd pay his offshore business back, and the money would be clean. Chris asked some questions, but held the guy off.

"I'm still going to wait a while," Chris said.

"It's up to you. I mean, you know your situation," the investigator said. "The only reason I brought it up is 'cause you brought it up to me. I would've never even fucking mentioned it. You could start small. You could start with fifty or a hundred K."

Chris realized that what he wanted was not to launder his money. The pain clinic money was legitimate, and he was going to pay taxes on it. He just wanted a place to put the cash. But Derik was right, this guy couldn't be trusted. Before he cut ties with him, though, Chris wanted the ex-DEA agent's take on something.

"DEA doesn't like me," Chris said.

"No shit," the investigator said. "They don't like me much either. So what?"

Chris told him how he'd called the DEA offices and the woman had known the address of the Oakland Park Boulevard clinic as soon as he'd said his name.

"She knew it just like that?" the investigator said.

"Yeah," Chris said.

"Jesus," the investigator said.

But then the guy backtracked, tried to brush it off. There were lots of pain clinics and the DEA had to monitor all of them. It wasn't a big deal that the woman knew who he was.

"That doesn't mean you're doing anything wrong," the investigator said.

"It's not good, though," Chris said.

"No, it ain't good," the investigator said. "It'd be better if she never heard of you. But it's OK."

If South Florida Pain was a target, he said, Chris would have known about it already.

"It takes them a while," Chris said.

"Well, how long you been open?" the investigator said.

"Eight months."

"If there was a problem, you would have heard a long time ago," he said. "Just my guess. It's a legit business. There's no law against making money, you know what I'm saying?"

Chris was always searching for a bank willing to take the cash. He'd be with one bank for a month, but no banker wanted to take in this amount of cash day after day, even though Chris met with the management and insisted his cash flow was legitimate and he was going to pay taxes on everything. There were just too many federal reports to fill out for large amounts of cash.* Banks didn't want to deal with the Currency Transaction Reports and Suspicious Activity Reports and scrutiny from the IRS or the OOC or the FFIEC or the other alphabet-soup agencies that keep an eye on financial crime, especially South Florida banks that had lived through the cocaine cowboy days of the 1980s. Every major bank ditched the clinic, one by one, and wouldn't say why. It was a constant problem because Chris had to have money in the bank to cover the doctors' payroll, though he paid employees cash whenever he could.

In late September 2008, it happened again. Chris tried to deposit more than $250,000 in one of his banks, and the bank not only refused to take the money but dropped him as a customer. They wrote him a cashier's check for the balance in his account. So Chris went to the house he and Dianna were renting in the Talavera development in Palm Beach County and piled the quarter million in a kitchen cabinet. One day, in early October, Chris came home and found broken glass in the bathroom. Someone had punched through the window to get inside. He checked the kitchen cabinet. That stash was gone.

Chris and Derik reasoned that the burglar was probably someone they knew, someone who knew where to find the money. They narrowed their list of suspects down to four people, including Jeff, who believed that some portion of the pain clinic's profits rightfully belonged to him.

The next few days included a series of bizarre incidents, as Chris and Derik hunted for the money.† Chris persuaded a locksmith to help him break into the car that belonged to a friend of Jeff. He and Jeff had a screaming match at their mother's home, and guns were drawn. Chris also hired a polygraph expert to give lie-detector tests to the guys he suspected of the theft. The tests purportedly ruled out Jeff. And then suspicions focused on a friend of Jeff who had worked at South Beach Rejuvenation.

---

* The Bank Secrecy Act of 1970 requires US financial institutions to help the government fight money laundering by reporting suspicious activity and filing reports of cash transactions exceeding $10,000. Banks may refuse to handle clients in high-volume cash businesses if they believe the business might be illegitimate or illegal.

† The kidnapping is described briefly in court documents and testimony. The version of events told here is how Derik Nolan recalls it. Other sources declined to talk about it.

The twins had grown up with the man, who had a long list of arrests for carrying a concealed weapon, DUI, marijuana possession, and trespassing.

Jeff was furious that his friend might have stolen the money, so he agreed to help lure him to his house one day in early October. Chris and Derik waited at Jeff's, which was located in the Versailles development where Vanilla Ice, the rapper, lived and was soon to begin filming a new reality show about a home he was remodeling in the development. Jeff destroyed the homes he lived in, parked broken-down Lamborghinis in the yard, urinated in the pool. Derik checked out the new house, shaking his head. It was in better condition than Jeff's previous homes, but it reminded him of a kid's clubhouse. Dirty dishes in the sink, no food in the fridge, and toys everywhere: fireworks, martial arts throwing stars, air rifles. In one bedroom, a huge pile of cash lay under a blanket.

When Jeff and his friend arrived, Derik did his thing, punching the friend and then flipping him. The man landed on his head on the hard floor. He was knocked out for a moment, his body rigid as a plank. When he came to, his eyes were screwy. Jeff pulled out a gun and a pair of handcuffs—he was always coming up with random items like that. Their captive started going berserk, thrashing around, so Derik snapped the cuffs onto his wrists. Jeff yelled questions and waved the gun around. He fired the gun at point-blank range, the bullet creasing the cuffed man's scalp and burying itself in the floor.

Now their captive was terrified and brain-scrambled from hitting the floor with his skull. He didn't seem to fully comprehend what they were saying, but he knew enough not to admit that he'd stolen the money. So it was a standoff.

Derik and the George brothers huddled. Chris and Jeff wanted to let their friend go, to pay him to not tell police about what they'd done to him. Derik believed things had gone too far to just let the man walk out of the house. It wasn't a situation that money could solve, something Chris and Jeff never seemed to understand. Derik lost the debate. They decided to let him go, although Jeff couldn't find the handcuff key for a while.

Later, Chris told Derik he'd given the man $10,000 and persuaded him to sign some sort of legal document, swearing that the incident had never happened. To Derik, it seemed like the dumbest thing he'd ever heard of. You couldn't walk both sides of the line, couldn't be a gangster *and* a straight citizen. You had to pick a side, and they'd already chosen theirs.

On the other hand, the outlaw life was stressful, and Derik understood the need for a little normalcy. That's why he'd begun seeing the pharmacy tech at South Florida Pain.

Derik wasn't as attracted to his new girlfriend as he had been to his Brazilian ex-girlfriend, but he liked her and he loved her young daughter. He rented an apartment in Tamarac for the three of them. The relationship wasn't particularly physical, but he needed something normal to come home to after a day of running South Florida Pain. Without that, Derik knew every night would be as crazy as the days, just an endless cycle of blow and alcohol and hookers and women like the Brazilian addict. He also didn't mind the veneer of respectability his new relationship gave him. Taking care of his girlfriend and her daughter made Derik feel like a good guy.

The days were chaos. Always interesting, but always exhausting too. Patients going into withdrawal, their bodies turning on them, skin as gray and wet as an oyster. Every so often, a patient would just slide off a chair in the waiting room and fish out, flopping around on the floor like a hooked tarpon on a boat deck. The first time Derik saw a seizure, the patient fell and split his head wide open, blood everywhere, Derik and one of the doctors frantically trying to wake the guy up. As the patient numbers rose, the seizures grew more frequent. It became almost routine: Derik would yell for a doctor, run and dial 911. No one ever died right there in the office, but it was a concern, another reason to try to shield themselves legally. Derik knew junkies could die from too much dope—everyone knew that—but the idea of patients dying of overdose was abstract. He knew it could happen, but it was easy to not think about.

Some of the junkie stunts amused Derik, and some pissed him off, like when patients tried to bring their kids into the waiting room with them. The clinic was no place for children. But he was always curious to see how far people would go to get their fix or how dumb the pills made them. One pet peeve: how some of the zombies could never get the hang of tightening the drug test cup lids. They'd fumble the handoff and drop the cups, which turned them into what Derik called "exploding urine bombs." At least once a day, Derik would dodge one or get soaked, one of his least-favorite parts of the job.

Most of the time, nobody watched the patients actually urinate into the cups. Derik knew patients were using other people's urine. He knew this because the toilets where they did the drug tests were constantly clogged with containers and condoms that patients had used to smuggle in the substitute urine. Sometimes a pee-filled condom tucked into someone's shirt would burst, soaking the patient. And at the end of the day, the parking lot outside often had broken condoms on it, ruptured and melting onto the hot asphalt.

Derik played dumb with the patients, like he couldn't see the bulges in their jacket pockets when he took them to the bathroom for the urine test. But he couldn't afford to be *too* accommodating with them. He could never be sure whether someone was working with the police, hoping Derik would screw up and say something incriminating. So if a patient was too dumb to figure out how to cheat the test or stupid enough to get caught with a container of urine, Derik would kick that patient out. A couple of times, patients were caught using a Whizzinator, basically a fake penis attached to a plastic bladder of synthetic urine that was belted to the patient's hips.

A few times a day, each doctor called Derik back to discharge a patient. Most often it was for track marks, which he'd become good at identifying. The patients always had an excuse. The marks, they said, were from a recent hospital IV. Or from cutting briar bushes. Or the cat had scratched them.

Many patients didn't realize how easy it was to get a prescription, so they overdid the fakery, coming in wearing a neck brace or even a cast. Sometimes the staff would find crutches discarded in the waiting room by a patient who had received medication. One day, Derik told a patient in a wheelchair that he was being kicked out for going to another pain clinic. The guy just popped out of the wheelchair and came after Derik.

What some patients never grasped was that the staff at South Florida Pain was on their side, that Derik and Chris *wanted* them to get their drugs. All the patients had to do was follow the official rules. Don't doctor shop. Don't sell pills in the parking lot. Don't let track marks fester. Don't come in high. Don't be too obvious about smuggling in urine, and make sure it's not suspiciously clean or suspiciously dirty. And don't behave like a drug addict—acting desperate or begging to have your dosages "upped"—because that might make the doctors feel like drug dealers.

These rules protected everybody, and if the patients followed them, they'd get their meds. At first, Derik had believed that the patients would do anything to preserve their access to their pills, so of course they would follow his rules. Over time, he found that the junkies' desire for drugs was constantly at odds with their tendency to screw up.

So the parking lot at the new location remained a constant headache, a lawless zone where some patients felt like it was OK to bang a pill into their arm in full view of everybody. Despite all the amenities Derik provided in the waiting room, nothing seemed to keep the patients from loitering outside. The problem was the wait. It was always too long, and patients needed to grab a smoke or crush a pill before they got too sick. There were fights out there, including one where a guy had a canine tooth knocked out by a blow from a can of Mountain Dew. And always people pissing in the hedges, which was understandable if you were at a concert or something, but you couldn't just whip out your dick in an office park on a major thoroughfare.

Derik tried to be a good communicator. Several times a day, he would stand in the waiting room and address everybody in his raspy, New York shout: *OK, everybody, if you want to see the doctor today, here are the rules.*

You come here, I need you to stay inside. No hanging out in the parking lot, no shooting up outside. And then when you're done, you take off.

Early one morning before the clinic opened, Derik was catching a smoke on the north side of the building, which faced Cypress Creek Road. A big RV passed on the other side of the boulevard, coming from the direction of I-95, then swung in a big U-turn and turned into the office parking lot. Derik had a feeling they were clinic patients. Sure enough, the big camper came to a halt, parking sideways across several spots. The door on the side of the RV popped open, and a large family came streaming out, what looked like three generations, young and old. The family proceeded to settle in for a long day, propping up a canopy on the side of the RV, unrolling an outdoor carpet on the asphalt, setting up a grill and some chairs.

Derik thought: You gotta be shitting me.

He gaped at the scene for a while, then finally walked over.

Derik said: Hey, does this look like a Miami Dolphins game?

The people didn't seem to understand. Derik explained that they were drawing attention to the clinic, making the operation look unprofessional.

Derik said: This isn't a concert or a game. This is a trip to the doctor's office. It's not supposed to be a fun family outing.

A big woman who seemed to be the head of the family just scowled. Derik made them pack up the vehicle. Then he put them at the front of the line for the doctor, got them out of there as soon as possible.

Everyone, always, had a scam. The patients would try to "tip" the doctors, hoping they'd be given extra drugs. Or they'd cause a problem outside just so the staff would have to call Derik out, and they'd have a chance to talk to him alone. The conversation was always the same. The patient would call him by his first name, like they were pals.

The patient would say: Look, Derik, I've been coming here for five months now. I bring three people with me every time. I drive twenty hours one way. I follow all your rules. I don't go to any other doctors.

Then the patient would bring up whatever deal he was trying to cut. Could Derik give his girlfriend a break, let her see the doctor even though she had oozing track marks? Could Derik cut the red tape, let him skip the doctor visit and just sell him, say, a couple thousand pills, straight out of the pharmacy?

They could never see the big picture, that Derik wasn't going to risk a million-dollar-a-month enterprise by doing a straight-up drug deal with someone he barely knew. The red tape, the bureaucracy, the rules and regulations protected everyone. He and Chris had learned this the hard way when they'd been chased off from Oakland Park Boulevard. It was a new era at the South Florida Pain Clinic, and Derik was getting used to telling people no. It went against his friendly nature and his outlaw instincts, but Derik was learning that the best way to deal drugs was to keep it impersonal and keep it legal.

One October morning, Derik and Chris stood underneath the covered walkway outside the clinic door, the early-morning sun casting palm-tree shadows against the concrete walls. From a distance, if you didn't count Derik's half-grown-out Mohawk, the friends looked like mirror images—two six-footers wearing designer jeans and black T-shirts, hair clippered short and tapered.

Derik was heading to the airport, where he and Jeff were going to catch a plane to Los Angeles for a party at the Playboy Mansion. Derik and Jeff hadn't been speaking to each other much, aside from the incident, two weeks earlier, when they'd grabbed Jeff's friend after Chris's money went missing. The dispute between the George twins over South Florida Pain had spilled over into Derik's relationship with Jeff. But Jeff was trying to make things right with Derik, and he'd offered to take Derik to a party at the Mansion on October 17. Jeff knew a girl who'd been a Playboy bunny. It was an early Halloween party, and they were going to dress like gangsters.

Derik's driver's license was still suspended, so he relied on others to drive him around, though sometimes he didn't bother and just drove himself anyway. Chris was going to give Derik a ride. On the way to the car, Derik and Chris had stopped to talk for a moment.

And that's when Derik saw his friend's eyes widen just a little, and they both turned to look at a middle-aged woman with short-cropped red hair and a black suit approaching them. Holding a microphone. Followed by a cameraman.

"Morning," she said. "Mr. George?"

Chris didn't panic. He turned slowly and sidled toward the clinic door, trying to look casual. Derik followed. The woman followed Chris, speaking to his broad back. Her voice was authoritative, sharp.

"We have pictures of people snorting, shooting up in this parking lot after coming out of your clinic," she said. "I mean, what do you have to say about what's going on here?"

Chris opened the clinic door, and the woman stuck the microphone inside. It had a 7 News logo on it. Chris spoke over his shoulder.

"I . . . I don't believe you're right," he said.

The glass door's pneumatic closer was easing it shut too slowly, so Chris reached back to yank it closed.

"That's *all* you have to say?" the woman said.

Derik had made it inside too, and he and Chris started chuckling, slightly in shock. Then they realized that Dr. Joseph had not arrived yet. They peered outside and saw the little Haitian physician pulling into the lot.

Chris told Derik to get him. Block him from the camera.

Derik went back out, but the cameraman beat him to the doctor's car. Dr. Joseph got out, staring warily as the redheaded woman approached. He actually looked very doctor-like, a stethoscope around his neck and a manila file full of papers under his arm.

"Are you certified in pain management?" the reporter asked Dr. Joseph.

Derik swept in, wrapping his arm around the diminutive doctor and guiding him toward the clinic door. The reporter jogged ahead, asking more questions. "Why do you think so many people are coming from out of state to see you here?"

Chris had answered the reporter's previous question, so Derik figured it couldn't hurt if he said something too.

"'Cause they're from the Bible Belt states, and they can't get pain medications," Derik said, and hustled the doctor inside.

Derik stayed inside—worrying he was going to miss his flight—until he thought the reporter had left. He walked out and lit a cigarette, and then she popped up again, from behind one of the columns, scaring the shit out of him.

She asked what his name was. He didn't tell her. She asked if he was one of the clinic owners. Derik, wanting to keep her guessing, said he might be. He told her that she was on private property, that they'd leased the parking area and she needed to get her camera off it. But she was tough and seemed to know what she was talking about when she called his bluff, saying he didn't lease the whole area and couldn't tell her to leave a public access area. She wouldn't back down. She chased him back inside. Derik finally sneaked out of the office and barely made his flight to Los Angeles.

A week after Derik got back from LA, the story about South Florida Pain Clinic aired on WSVN-TV. Chris and Derik didn't get Channel 7 at their homes up in Palm Beach County, which is why they hadn't recognized the redheaded woman, Carmel Cafiero, who was some kind of investigative reporter. But Derik found out about the South Florida Pain story as soon as it aired, when basically everyone he knew in Broward and Miami-Dade, including his grandma in Deerfield Beach, started calling him, saying he was on TV and what kind of trouble was he getting himself into now?

Chris and Derik watched the video on the Internet. Cafiero's story pretty much laid the whole operation wide open. It showed the Oakland Park Boulevard location with its big South Florida Pain Clinic sign. It showed Kentucky, Ohio, and West Virginia license plates on cars in the clinic lot, the numbers blurred out. Grainy, headless shots of patients leaving clinics, zooming in on the plastic bags in their hands. Patients arguing in parking lots. And the money shot: a close-up, through a car window, of a man in his car, crushing and dissolving a pill, then slow-motion footage of him pulling out a hypodermic needle.

Cafiero's report said that Broward County was the nation's number-one dispensing site for oxycodone, that doctors in the county had dispensed more than 3.3 million pills in the first six months of 2008. A Broward County Sheriff's Office spokeswoman said: "The appearance is that they are pill mills, simply handing drugs out, hand over fist. We're talking hundreds of thousands of individuals trafficking into the state of Florida specifically to obtain pharmaceutical drugs." The report showed photos of a white body bag on a grassy strip next to a highway, and Cafiero said in her voiceover: "And when they leave the clinics high, police say some of them die in accidents or overdose on the side of the road."

The last third of the report was devoted to Cafiero's ambush of South Florida Pain. Chris was named in the story, but he was only on-screen for a few seconds, as Cafiero chased him inside. Derik wasn't named but was the star of the piece. Looking thuggish in a black skull-and-crossbones T-shirt, they slo-mo'd a grainy shot of him staring intently at the ground and exhaling a lungful of cigarette smoke. Later, he "rescued" Dr. Joseph and ushered him inside, wrapping a tribal-tattooed arm around the little doctor's shoulder. The incongruity between the compact physician and the mysterious hulking guy with the wraparound shades propped on his forehead was striking.

Still, one line in Cafiero's voiceover made everyone feel better.

"But the problem for law enforcement is that what these clinics are doing is perfectly legal," she said.

There you go, the guys said. Perfectly legal.

After the kidnapping incident, Chris and Jeff went back to not speaking to each other, and the lawsuits between the brothers proceeded. Jeff finally had opened his own clinic in West Palm Beach, calling it East Coast Pain and modeling it after South Florida Pain. But he was juggling South Beach Rejuvenation and other enterprises, including trying to start a strip club and running a timeshare resale business. So Jeff hadn't focused on building East Coast Pain, and his doctors saw only a fraction of the patients South Florida Pain was handling.

As he and Jeff had originally planned, Chris wanted a string of clinics in multiple locations. He wanted a presence in West Palm Beach to compete with Jeff's clinic. He also wanted to get Dianna out of South Florida Pain and into her own place. As they'd hired more staff, Dianna sat around and did nothing, mostly. She had been bored for months. She didn't like all the girls around the office, especially the former bikini model who liked to sit on Chris's lap in his office.

So Chris talked about opening a new clinic in West Palm Beach. Dianna would run it. He told her to set up a corporation in her name on Sunbiz, the Florida Department of State's website. She did it, but it went no further. Dianna was increasingly unhappy. She didn't like the cash lying around the house. She didn't like how Chris was so focused on the money all the time, and not her. Fixated on it, like the more he had the more he wanted. She didn't like the way the cops had targeted the Oakland Park Boulevard clinic, and the customers at the new location scared her and grossed her out. They were even more zombie-like than before, really strung out and smelly and unkempt.

She complained to Chris. It wasn't normal to make this much money, to have cops showing up all the time, to have acquaintances stealing hundreds of thousands of dollars out of your house. She'd worked in strip clubs for years and managed to avoid trouble, which wasn't easy. Now she was afraid they'd both land in prison.

Chris told her to not worry so much. The pain clinic was operating in a gray area. It was frowned upon, but there was nothing the authorities could do, because it was legal.

That October, almost exactly one year after they'd hooked up in West Port, Dianna left Chris and went back to the life. She lived out of her car, crashing at friends' houses, and got a job dancing at Rachel's, the strip club steak house in West Palm Beach. Chris put plans for his new West Palm Beach clinic on hold.

One morning, about a week after the Carmel Cafiero report, one of the security guards told Derik that one of the girls was there for her interview. They needed a receptionist, so Derik had run another "just send picture" ad on Craigslist, got a bunch of modeling headshots and cheesecake photos, and set up interviews. It was early in the morning when the guard approached Derik—they hadn't even opened yet—and Derik figured the girl must be eager.

Derik went to the back room and a tall black woman greeted him. Too old for this job, Derik thought. He was aggravated, thinking the woman must have sent in a picture that wasn't hers, and he gave her some attitude.

Derik said: Sorry, you're not the look we're going for.

The woman looked annoyed.

She said: What is this, a doctor's office or a modeling agency? And what's up with your parking lot? It looks like a Mercedes dealership out there.

That was weird, Derik thought. What did she care what kind of cars they drove? But he shrugged it off, let her leave, forgot about it.

Until the next day, when the guard again approached him before opening hours.

The guard said: Yo, D. That woman's here to see you again.

And Derik turned around to see the tall woman standing in the employees-only area of the pain clinic. With about seven other people. Holding a Drug Enforcement Administration badge.

She made some smart-ass comment, but Derik was in shock and the words didn't even register.

The visitors were a mix of Florida Department of Health, Broward County Sheriff's Office, and DEA. They said they were there to inspect the clinic.

A detective from the sheriff's office said: Shut it down, and get all of your employees together.

He asked everyone to produce identification, and Derik said he didn't have a driver's license, which was true.

A DEA agent said: You don't have a driver's license? That's odd, considering we just saw you drive up in a Mercedes that costs, what would you say, $100,000?

Derik said: I guess you got me.

He asked if they had a warrant, and they said they didn't need one because it was just an inspection. Derik had no idea whether this was correct, but he got the employees together and gave the agents an ID card that he had obtained after losing his license. The officers and agents split into teams. The female DEA agent took Chris into an office, where they holed up for a long time. They wanted the clinic's dispensing logs. They told him they were inspecting South Florida Pain because of the quantities of oxycodone that had been ordered in the doctors' names.

Another pair wanted to audit the pharmacy, examine purchasing records and inventories to make sure the pills the clinic bought were going to actual patients. Derik definitely didn't want them doing this; God knew what the pill counts would be. So he pretended to not have keys to the pharmacy, said they'd have to wait for the pharmacy tech. He hoped to head her off, but she showed up.

Another pair of officers interviewed staffers. Two others interviewed Dr. Joseph, the first doctor to arrive that day. That interview was short. They emerged with the little doctor, and one agent said that Dr. Joseph had volunteered to surrender his DEA registration, which allowed him to prescribe and dispense controlled substances, in exchange for not being prosecuted, and they were going to seize his medications.

Derik protested. The pills were worth a lot of money. They were just going to take them? Derik said he wanted to transfer the meds to another doctor's name, and the agents said it didn't work like that. They were confiscating Dr. Joseph's drugs.

Dr. Joseph, the doctor who'd been at the clinic the longest, just walked out the door, probably bewildered because his English wasn't great. The agents spent an hour questioning another physician, Dr. Beau Boshers.

They asked the new doctor how many patients a day he saw, what kind of exams he gave, whether patients came from out of state. Dr. Boshers had worked at the clinic only for a couple of weeks, and he already suspected the place was an unusually well-insulated pill mill, though he certainly wasn't going to admit it to federal agents. He barely examined his patients, but he believed he was protected by the MRI reports and the diagnostic paperwork he filled out for each patient. He'd earned his medical degree in his mid-thirties and worked for several years as a hospital-based internal medicine doctor. The money had been good, but the hours were long and the work grueling. By comparison, the pain clinic was easy money.

Derik sneaked away from the agents for a moment and started calling the other doctors, telling them to not come to work. He headed off a couple doctors that way, though one later surrendered his registration just like Dr. Joseph had. The cops kept asking Derik when the other doctors would be arriving, and Derik played dumb, said they were supposed to be here, they must not be coming in.

He enjoyed the cat-and-mouse game, but he was worried that the clinic's run was over. While he waited to see what would happen, Derik sat with Dr. Boshers in the waiting room and watched TV. *Rambo* was playing on one of the big flat-screens. Groups of patients loitered outside in the parking lot, hoping the clinic would reopen. Every once in a while, the bold or desperate ones came up to the door and pressed their faces to the glass.

Around midday, one of the cops told Derik they'd run his identification and he was in big trouble. Not for the clinic or the drugs, but for driving with a suspended license. Not to mention the fact that he was on probation and wasn't supposed to leave Palm Beach County. He could be looking at years in prison. Multiple years.

Derik felt the same way he'd felt when the health department investigator had made copies of the incomplete MRI prescriptions in June. All the shit he was pulling, and these guys were going to violate him on a *traffic* charge? But he knew the prospect of prison time was real. The memory of his stretch in St. Lucie County Jail, ten months ago, was still fresh.

But they didn't arrest him. Around 2:00 p.m., the inspectors and cops just packed up and left. They took Dr. Joseph's stock of pills with them, and they were mouthy on the way out the door.

One said: Just remember, Derik, we let you go. But I have a feeling we're gonna have further business.

When they were gone, Derik walked outside and addressed the patients.

He said: Thanks for waiting, everybody. Come on in!

The patients flowed inside, and Dr. Boshers got to work writing scrips. One doctor down, but back in business.

Even before the inspection, Chris had decided it was time to make some moves—for the good of everyone. One of the pharmaceutical wholesalers had called Chris after the Carmel Cafiero report aired and said the company couldn't sell drugs to South Florida Pain Clinic any longer. The wholesaler specifically mentioned Derik's presence in Cafiero's story.

The wholesaler said: That guy just *looks* like a drug dealer. We can't be doing business with you guys anymore.

The wholesaler also suggested that Chris change the clinic's name, make a fresh start.

Chris thought about it and decided the wholesaler was right. First off, the clinic's reputation was both a blessing and a curse. Their word of mouth had been great. People knew the doctors at South Florida Pain wrote big and the guys made it as easy as possible. Prospective patients still came every day to the old location on Oakland Park Boulevard, months after it had shut down. Derik had hired a guy for $500 a week to just sit there in his car and hand out flyers with directions to the new clinic.

But after the *Sun-Sentinel* story and picture and now the Cafiero report, the big red-lettered South Florida Pain Clinic sign on Oakland Park Boulevard had become a symbol of pill mills. They'd changed locations, but the name itself was still a target. They needed a new one.

And they needed a new face. Despite the improvements they'd made to the business, Chris and Derik themselves had become liabilities. Chris would continue to own the clinic, but he needed a straw owner. It couldn't be Derik, especially after the Cafiero report. His relationship with Dianna was on the rocks, so she wouldn't work either. It needed to be someone without a police record. Someone respectable, who could be the face of the clinic. Someone who could start fresh with the wholesalers and the banks.

Back in North Port, Chris had worked with a guy named Ethan Baumhoff, an ex-cop. Originally from Missouri, Ethan had spent five years in the Army and then a decade as a police officer in various small departments before moving to Florida and going into construction. Ethan was a grown-up, thirty-seven years old and married with kids. He had a clean record, as far as Chris knew, and his background in law enforcement would look good to anyone investigating the clinic. Chris talked to Ethan, who agreed to be the manager of the pain clinic.

Chris told Derik what the wholesaler had said about him looking like a drug dealer, and Derik was offended.

Derik said: What the fuck do you want me to do? Get a face-lift? Tattoos removed? Lose the New York accent?

But he was really outraged when Chris said he was hiring Ethan as manager. He'd never liked Ethan, even back in North Port. Ethan was completely different than Derik and Chris—a rules-oriented guy, a stickler with a Napoleon complex. Worst of all, he'd been a cop, which meant that he had cop instincts and cop leanings. He would ruin the freewheeling chemistry of the place that Derik had created by hiring a mixture of friends and hot girls.

Chris said: That's the point. He's a strong representative for the clinic. He'll really have no say, but we'll put him out there to make it look like he does.

Derik didn't like it, but Chris's mind was made up.

During his first few weeks, Ethan Baumhoff spent most of his time in Chris's office, learning about the clinic's circulatory system of drugs and money. Chris wanted him to reestablish ties with the wholesalers who had dropped them after the Cafiero story and get the drug shipments flowing again. Chris also wanted to find some more wholesalers who would sell to him. Conveniently, the DEA website had a list of wholesalers, and Chris had Ethan call every one of them.

Ethan would also handle the money, establishing accounts with the banks and hauling the money back and forth. He carried the cash in a blue duffel bag, and because it contained so much money, he also carried a gun.

Derik continued to run the rest of the office, herding the patients, keeping an eye on employees, making fun of Ethan. His dislike of the new guy deepened as Ethan spent hours holed up in Chris's office.

One of the first things Chris had Ethan do was create a new limited liability company under Ethan's name and address so no one would be able to connect it to South Florida Pain. He had a lawyer write up a letter that made it clear that Chris was the real owner, but the state records would show that Ethan was the registered agent.

As soon as one problem was solved, another would emerge. They'd been in the Cypress Creek Executive Court only a couple of months when the office park people said they wanted the pain clinic out in December. Despite Derik's efforts to keep order in the parking lots, there were too many complaints from the other tenants, and now the once-sleepy office court was a target for journalists and law enforcement.

The new office complex was just a mile east on Cypress Creek Road, closer to I-95. The tenants of the new location were more industrial, less customer-based, and Chris hoped that meant they'd be less concerned about the activities at the pain clinic. This time, they spent more time and money on the renovation—stone counters, carpeting, artwork. Chris hired a contractor, but they needed the job done quickly, so after the clinic was closed for the night, Derik would go to the new location and work until midnight.

Chris came up with a new name for the clinic, nothing that he pondered over too deeply. Ethan registered it on the secretary of state website, and when they moved in December to another new location, they started using the new name. They didn't want or need eye-catching signs at the new location. Their customers would find them. So their new name was listed only in small print in a column, along with all the other tenants, on the red directory sign at the office park entrance:

American Pain.

In November 2008, the Florida Department of Health finally issued administrative complaints from its inspection of the Oakland Park Boulevard clinic the previous summer. Derik and Chris remembered the little health inspector with his bad grammar, pleased with himself as he stuffed the photocopied prescriptions into an envelope.

In writing, some of the violations seemed laughably minor:

The investigator reported the following deficiencies:

a. No generic drug sign was displayed.

b. Several prescriptions were dispensed to patients but contained no patient names or addresses.

c. Several prescriptions were dispensed to patients but were not initialed and dated.

d. Several prescriptions were signed by Respondent even though they were not for specific patients.

Other charges seemed more serious, including claims that doctors had not documented any evaluations of patients before prescribing large amounts of narcotics.

But the thing was, the complaints were directed at Dr. Rachael Gittens and Dr. Enock Joseph, neither of whom even worked at the pain clinic anymore. Dr. Gittens had left to open her own clinic. And they hadn't seen Dr. Joseph since the DEA inspection, when the Haitian gynecologist had given up his DEA registration, rendering him useless to the clinic. So it was no great concern to Chris or Derik when they read that the physicians might be facing "restriction of practice, imposition of an administrative fine, issuance of a reprimand, placement of the Respondent on probation, corrective action, refund of fees billed or collected, remedial education and/or any other relief that the Board deems appropriate."

And that was it. Neither the DEA nor the health department made a move to shut down the clinic, and this fact bolstered Chris's confidence. The DEA and the state health department were targeting the *doctors*, not the people who owned or ran the clinic. Chris and Derik were off the hook. They could always get more doctors.

And over the next few weeks, Chris did hire two more full-time doctors—Dr. Jacobo Dreszer and Dr. Cynthia Cadet—to replace the doctors lost after the DEA inspection. Dr. Dreszer was a hot-tempered Jewish guy originally from Colombia. He'd been an anesthesiologist for thirty years, which made Chris happy because it looked good to have a guy who actually had some expertise in pain management. Dr. Dreszer had a son who was also a doctor, and the younger Dreszer was also set to start work at the clinic in a couple of months. Roni Dreszer had received his MD from Drexel University four years earlier, but he'd been booted from his surgical residency at a hospital in Philadelphia. His problems had a lot to do with his love of gambling and Percocets. He owed $300,000 in student loans and approximately $30,000 to credit card companies. His first job as a full-fledged doctor would be working for Chris George's pain clinic. Derik found this humorous, along with the fact that Roni Dreszer's mother had driven him to and from his job interview.

Derik liked all the new docs, but Dr. Cynthia Cadet was the one he connected with the most. She was a small and slender black woman with fine features. She'd attended Cornell University on an ROTC scholarship and had been a major in the Air Force. She was kind and compassionate with the patients, listening to their fears and concerns, as opposed to some of the doctors who barely spoke to them. She never seemed to be in a hurry. Even if it was late at night and everyone else wanted to go home, she'd get absorbed in conversations with patients. Derik had to knock on her door a couple of times to ask her to hurry up. But everyone—patients and Chris alike—loved the fact that she generally wrote big scrips. Even on the first visit.

Derik didn't get to know Cadet very well until one evening when he was in the little break room in the rear of the clinic. He'd found some tortillas left over from lunch, and he was conducting a little experiment, covering them with sour cream and tossing them to the ceiling to see how long they would stick up there. Cadet came through the room on her way home, then stopped and stared at Derik like he was crazy.

She said: What are you doing?

Derik said: I'm sticking tortillas to the ceiling.

She said: Oh!

He said: You want to try?

She gave it a shot, and after that, Derik and Cadet were friends. He bought Christmas gifts for her two kids. He walked her to her car at night. She seemed like one of the happiest people Derik had ever met, out of her element among the junkies and schemers of American Pain. But she seemed unaware that she didn't fit in with the other doctors, who appeared to be more clued in to what they were doing, bickering with each other about patient loads. Floating into the office each morning, tottering slightly on her high heels like a girl, singing out, "Hi, Derik!" as she passed his office, a big smile on her face.

They didn't bring their homeless security guard along to the new location. The guard was nearly useless at preventing problems in the parking lot. He still couldn't even operate the walkie-talkie. But Derik didn't want to fire him outright, so he instead posted the vagrant employee at the old location and told him to hand out flyers directing patients to the new place up the road. The homeless man liked being in on the real action of the clinic, and he looked crushed when Derik gave him his new duties.

Before long, patients began approaching Derik, irritated, asking why his guy was charging for directions from the old location to the new location. Five bucks a pop.

Derik went down to the old location and spied on his employee from an adjacent parking lot. The vagrant man stood near the entrance of the old clinic, waving down patients as they pulled in looking for American Pain. He did his crazed little dance steps, gesticulating with his skinny arms, exchanging flyers for bills through the car window, like a corner boy with a bag of drugs.

And then, the final straw. He sidled over to some trash cans, extracted a pipe from its hiding place, lit it, and took a pull. He was back on crack.

Derik fired the homeless man. He slipped him a few hundred bucks and never saw him again. Later, the cleaning lady said the ex-staffer had asked her to tell Derik he was sorry and he wanted his old job back. Derik just laughed and forgot about it.

The clinic wasn't the same laid-back place it had been when it was operating out of the bungalow on Oakland Park Boulevard. Chris and Derik knew the DEA was watching them now, along with the TV reporter, Carmel Cafiero. Something fundamental about the operation had changed when Chris hired Ethan and changed the name. The clinic had become a place where there was too much at stake to keep a crack-addicted stray dog around for laughs.

South Florida Pain was gone. The future belonged to American Pain.

Derik took the clinic gang out for an office Christmas party at the Solid Gold strip club. Most of the others came, including Chris and Dianna, who were back together, some staffers, and three of the new full-time doctors: Beau Boshers and both Dreszers, father and son. Derik didn't invite Ethan Baumhoff. After the move, Ethan had tried to assert more control over the operations, which was Derik's territory.

He'd say to Derik: We gotta get this thing more legal. This could really be big.

Derik told Ethan to stay out of his business, go back to counting the money.

So Ethan had started in on Chris. He wanted the staff to start dressing more professionally, dress shirts and slacks Monday through Thursday, and casual Fridays. Derik had responded to this directive by showing up for work in a nice pair of $300 jeans with a T-shirt that read "Fuck You." He didn't need Ethan at the Christmas party.

Solid Gold had a high-end steak house inside with glittering chandeliers and tablecloths as soft and white as a fresh snowfall, so they had dinner first. Derik had the beef Wellington and picked up the $1,500 tab. Then they headed into the club for drinks. Dr. Boshers was off-the-chain, buying lap dances for everybody. The younger Dreszer was a party animal too. He liked cocaine and prostitutes and once dropped $300,000 on a private poker game. It was a fun time, one of those blurred nights when the events of the previous year seemed like a colossal and astonishing practical joke. Twelve months earlier, Derik had been losing his mind in St. Lucie County Jail, his life in pieces—no driver's license, no job, no friends, no prospects. Now he was running the biggest pain clinic in Florida, surrounded by friends, awash in money.

He'd even hired a personal driver. The DEA agent's warning about Derik's illegal driving had scared him—the thought of getting a long prison sentence for such a minor thing, especially when he was so close to being set for life. So he'd called his cousin up in New York, and told him to move down to Florida. Derik's cousin liked guns, carried a couple of registered .45s in his belt everywhere he went. The cousin moved in with Derik and became his driver/bodyguard. You couldn't be too careful.

Derik's plans were vague but glorious. He and Chris talked about it sometimes, the future. They planned to keep going for five, six years, until Derik was in his mid-thirties and he'd personally banked some millions, and then they'd sell the clinics. Derik would find a woman like Dianna, and the four of them would hit the road or the open seas, travel the world together.

But that was the future. Right now, South Florida was everything a man could want. It was the pink heart of a grain-fed steak filet wrapped in a flaky perfect pastry shell. It was pure, wonderful, fresh-off-the-boat Miami cocaine. It was beautiful women who would take off their clothes and do what you wanted, because you had a thick roll of bills to spend on them. It was the anticipation of holding primo tickets to the Dolphins game or the UFC fight. It was the supple leather passenger seat of your own purring Mercedes, driven by a strapped bodyguard who was also your cousin. It was that invincible inner hum from monster doses of steroids flowing through your bloodstream.

South Florida during Christmas 2008 was all of those things to Derik, everything that was the opposite of Binghamton, New York, and its icy winters and dark memories. South Florida was paradise, and Derik and his best friend were its kings.

5

On New Year's Day 2009 in Rockcastle County, Kentucky, Alice Mason got a call from her son's girlfriend, Lisa. Alice was, as usual, on her farm at the end of Hummingbird Lane.

On the phone, Lisa said that Alice's son had up and run off. No one knew where Stacy was.

The news surprised Alice. Stacy and Lisa had been together for five years, living together almost as long. They had their ups and downs, like couples do, but those two loved each other, and Alice hoped and expected they'd get married someday. Alice talked to them if they brought up problems, but otherwise she didn't meddle. She knew enough after fifty-three years of life to let them work things out on their own.

But Alice had been fretting about Stacy ever since his accident in August, four months earlier. Stacy made good money pouring and finishing concrete, $700 or $800 a week when work was steady. But that meant long days during the warm months, out the door before sunrise. Stacy was behind the wheel of his Tacoma pickup at 5:30 a.m. one day, heading to a job site, when he dozed off on Interstate 75. A trucker saw the Tacoma drifting and blasted the horn. Stacy jerked awake, overcorrected the wheel, and flipped his pickup. The impact crushed the Tacoma's roof into the passenger seat. On the other side of the cab, Stacy was flung about but not really hurt. He called Alice and said the truck was totaled, but he was fine, in fact he was catching a ride to work. Later that day, on the job, someone bumped into Stacy from behind, just a little nudge, but the pain shot down his back, and Stacy realized he *wasn't* fine. He was hurt bad.

The pain grew as the days went on. Stacy went to see a local doctor, and she prescribed him some painkillers.

Throughout the fall, Stacy tried to go back to work, but he couldn't lift a wheelbarrow. His gait was a little off, and he had a hard time lifting his legs, especially going up stairs.

But when Stacy and Lisa had driven out to the farm for Christmas dinner, everything seemed fine. Stacy was loaded down with gifts. A Mossy Oak camouflage hunting jacket for his little brother, Kevin. A toaster oven for Alice. A guitar-and-drums setup for the video game player.

Now Lisa was calling, saying Stacy was gone, wasn't returning her calls. Had Alice seen him?

Alice said she sure hadn't seen Stacy. Not since Christmas dinner.

Lisa said: Well, we got into it. He left, and he said he was going out to the farm to stay in the trailer.

Lisa didn't say what they'd argued about, and Alice didn't ask.

Alice said: Well, good Lord, Lisa, if he's down there, he probably about froze to death. It was *cold* last night.

Alice got off the phone and left the main house, tromping past the barn and the ever-sniffing beagles and the game roosters leashed to their blue plastic barrels and Stacy's bulldog Red. Over the frozen ridge and down to the white single-wide where Lisa and Stacy had lived through one winter and one summer, on the Mason farm but just out of sight from the main house. Stacy wasn't there.

Kevin, Alice's youngest, was home for the holiday, so Alice told Kevin to call his brother's cell phone. Kevin dialed the number, and Stacy picked up. Stacy said he'd be home later that day. He didn't say where he'd been.

Alice was only partially relieved. She was a worrier. She worried about all three of her boys. Even though Stacy had just turned thirty, she still called him her "young'un." Stacy smiled like a boy, open and friendly. If there were kids around, they were climbing on Stacy like he was a tree. Or he was rolling around on the floor with them. Until he hurt his back.

At one time, Stacy used to drink a little bit, but what he loved was pot. Alice had heard that more than once, and she didn't like it. But he hadn't done those things around her or his daddy, never talked about it.

And now he was with Lisa, a clean-living girl who didn't tolerate drugs or alcohol. Lisa wouldn't even take an aspirin if she had a headache. Stacy had straightened out once they got together.

But now, something was going on—Alice could sense it. She knew that when there were problems, mothers were generally the last to hear.

At the time Stacy took off, he and Lisa were living in town, which was Mount Vernon, about ten miles from the Mason farm. Their little white house in the steeply pitched yard belonged to Lisa's mother, and Lisa had grown up there. The night before, New Year's Eve, Lisa had called her mother over and over, frantic with worry about Stacy's whereabouts.

Lisa said she knew Stacy was lying about something. It was out of character for Stacy to be hiding something. He was usually so open, even when he'd done something wrong.

Lisa's mom, Shelby, had known Stacy since he was a teenager. She didn't know his mother and father—they kept to themselves out on the farm, went to a little backwoods church. Stacy was a good-looking boy with broad cheekbones and wide pale-blue eyes. A polite country boy, all "yes, ma'am" and "no ma'am." But he had a rebel streak, to Shelby's mind. He favored T-shirts with cutoff sleeves that showed off his strong arms, pulled back his long blonde hair into a ponytail that Shelby didn't like. He created his own heavy-metal band named Feel and wrote song lyrics that sounded to Shelby like devil music. He was the lead singer. The band never really took off, but Stacy kept writing songs. After he and Lisa got together, Stacy sat down with Shelby and talked to her about the lyrics, and she came to believe that the words were darkly spiritual.

Shelby grew to love Stacy like he was her own son. He and Lisa were so different. Stacy had grown up with nothing but the beautiful slice of Kentucky hilltop that his family owned, and that's all he really wanted. Lisa wanted more and was willing to work hard for it. Lisa was a pretty girl with reddish-blonde ringlets, a hard worker ever since she was a teenager. She'd worked her way into a good job at a nearby tourist attraction. Somehow, she and Stacy fit each other.

Like Alice, Shelby didn't want to get in the middle of the argument. She figured Lisa and Stacy would work things out, because that's what couples did. They had arguments, and then they worked them out. But it worried her that Lisa said she'd been calling Stacy over and over.

The next morning, New Year's Day, Shelby noticed a message on her phone from Stacy. It had come early that morning. He sounded upset, even scared. Stacy said he needed a ride. He didn't understand why nobody cared enough to come pick him up. Something happens to me, Stacy said, you'll be sorry.

He wasn't making much sense, didn't sound like himself, and Shelby was worried. She started calling around, looking for him.

Later that morning, a friend of Stacy pulled up near the house where Shelby was staying, and Stacy got out of the car. He looked pale and weak. He moved funny as he climbed the steps to the house. Shelby asked if he was all right.

His reply was breathless: Yeah, yeah. Where's Lisa?

Shelby said Lisa was up the highway in Berea, returning a new TV to the Walmart where Shelby worked. Lisa and Stacy had bought it for Christmas, but money was tight since Stacy hadn't been able to pour concrete for months, and Lisa had decided they couldn't afford it.

Shelby said: Stacy, come in and sit down, you need to sit down.

Stacy said: No, no, I'm fine.

Shelby said: Stacy, you need to get some sleep. You don't look good.

Stacy said he didn't need sleep, he was fine. He got back in the car, and his friend drove away.

Kevin was alone at the farm about 3:00 p.m. that afternoon, sprawled on the couch watching the Georgia Bulldogs bowl game, when Stacy came in carrying a garbage bag. The brothers didn't say much to each other. Maybe they nodded. Maybe they exchanged a word or two. Kevin certainly didn't start questioning Stacy about where he'd been all this time, while everyone worried. Mom would do that later.

Stacy dropped his bag in the back bedroom and headed back outside.

At halftime, Kevin got up and looked outside but didn't see Stacy or the friend who'd brought him home. A few minutes later, his parents came home. Kevin told them Stacy had returned, but he might have taken off again. Alice and Eugene left the house to check the trailer. Kevin kept watching the game.

A few minutes later, Kevin heard his mother hollering, and he looked outside and saw her running down the hill toward the house, screaming for him to call the ambulance, and suddenly everything clicked in his mind and he knew exactly what had happened even as he refused to believe it.

Alice returned to where they'd found Stacy hunkered over a barrel behind the barn, on his knees like he was praying. She held his body on the cold ground. Eugene lay beside her. Kevin came up to the barn after calling 911, and he just sank to the ground too, leaning his back against the barn, bewildered.

Rocking and crying and holding Stacy as tight as she could, Alice felt something hard against her ribs, something inside Stacy's jacket. She slipped her hand into Stacy's jacket pocket and pulled out two pill bottles. She gave them to Eugene and went on grieving.

The ambulance took forever to find the farm at the end of Hummingbird Lane, maybe thirty-five or forty minutes. When the paramedics finally got there, they called the coroner's office.

In town, Shelby got a call from Stacy's cousin. They'd spoken earlier in the day during her hunt for Stacy.

He said: Something's wrong. I called some neighbors down there and they said there's a bunch of ambulances and stuff on Hummingbird Lane. Police cars and stuff.

Shelby hung up and starting looking for a ride from someone who knew where the Mason farm was. Before she could find a driver, Stacy's cousin called back.

He said: Stacy's dead.

Shelby went to Lisa's house and told her. Lisa lost it. Screaming, waving her hands, running in circles. She said it was her fault. She said she shouldn't have argued with Stacy.

Shelby took her to the emergency room at Rockcastle Regional. Shelby's son-in-law had to carry Lisa inside.

Billy Dowell knew the Mason family the way he knew most Rockcastle County families: He'd embalmed and buried their ancestors. Dowell was a funeral home director and also the elected coroner of Rockcastle County since 1966. Now in his seventies and well over six feet tall, he towered over everyone else at death scenes. Local cops called him "The High Coroner."

He loaded Stacy's body into the dark blue van that bore the letters Rockcastle County Coroner on the side and carried it to Dowell & Martin Funeral Home. The body spent the night in the funeral home cooler, and the next day, Billy Dowell loaded it again and drove eighty miles to the state medical examiner's office in Frankfort. He rode with the body up to the third floor, weighed it, and then, as was his custom during the postmortem, went to the break room to have a cup of coffee and yak with whoever was around. He'd watched autopsies before and believed if you'd seen one, you'd seen them all.

The autopsy technicians disrobed Stacy and recorded his height, weight, hair color, skin color, tattoos, and scars. No obvious needle puncture marks, no track marks or drug residue on nostrils. No evidence of natural disease. They removed blood from the femoral vein near the groin, urine from the bladder, and vitreous humor from the eyeball. Those fluids were packaged, labeled, and sent to a toxicology laboratory in Indiana to be screened for drugs.

The techs made a Y-shaped incision from the upper chest to just above the groin, and the organs were removed, weighed, examined. The most significant finding was that his right lung weighed 920 grams, and his left weighed 720 grams. A normal pair of lungs typically weigh approximately 1,000 grams together. There was no infection or lesions in Stacy's lungs—they were just sodden with fluid buildup.

And even without the tox screen, that finding pretty much nailed down the cause of death. Heavy, congested lungs are the hallmark of respiratory depression caused by opioid overdose. High doses of opioids mute pain, and they also mute the psychological discomfort caused by carbon dioxide buildup, the useful rush of panic you feel after too long underwater. Carbon dioxide is produced by the body's metabolic processes, and it's flushed out of the blood with each pump of the lungs. When the lungs slow, receptors in the brainstem detect higher levels of the chemical and trigger a breathing reflex. That's why you can't kill yourself by holding your breath. Even if you managed to hold it long enough to pass out, the breathing reflex would kick in.

So Stacy had felt fine even as the carbon dioxide thickened in his bloodstream. His breathing reflex drowsed, and so did he, kneeling over the barrel behind the barn. His inhalations and exhalations slowed to four a minute . . . then two . . . then one. His heart continued to push blood throughout the body, but his lungs didn't do their part. Millions of air sacs in the lungs began to flood, drowning him in his own blood serum. The few slack breaths he did take forced bloody foam up into his mouth and nose. His brain swelled with fluid. His heart, starved for oxygen, pittered into wild arrhythmia.

The postmortem over, Billy Dowell zipped the corpse into a body bag, loaded it into the coroner's van, and headed back toward Rockcastle County.

Alice, Lisa, and Shelby. The three women who loved Stacy. They had questions. Of course, what had killed him? But also, where had he been the last couple of days? Why was he so weak and exhausted? Why hadn't he gotten Lisa's voicemail messages?

Shelby talked to Stacy's friend, the one who'd dropped him off at the farm. Stacy's friend said he'd picked up Stacy at Peg's, the little grocery off the interstate. Then Stacy's friend said something crazy. He said when he picked him up, Stacy said he'd just got back from Florida.

Florida? This made no sense to Shelby. Stacy had never been on an airplane. Never seen the ocean. He'd barely been out of Kentucky. No way he'd been to Florida.

Stacy's friend said Stacy had started the argument with Lisa so he could leave and go to a pain clinic in Florida. To get pills. Stacy had gone with a group of people he didn't know well, the friend said. They'd driven all night and just gotten back on New Year's morning.

It was outlandish, but Lisa now believed the story. After she calmed down some, Lisa told her mother how the argument had started. Stacy had said he might go to a pain clinic to try to get some pills. His doctor in Mount Vernon had cut him off, he told Lisa. Cold turkey. He needed the painkillers if he was ever going to get back to work. They argued, and he said he was leaving, going to the farm.

Alice was all torn up and people spoke carefully around her, but Lisa told her about the Florida rumor.

Alice couldn't imagine it, Stacy going all the way to Florida, where he didn't know a soul. But then, a couple days after Stacy died, Alice remembered the pill bottles she'd taken out of his jacket pocket.

Alice told her husband to get the bottles so she could look at them. And sure enough, the name of Stacy's doctor in Mount Vernon wasn't the name printed on the labels. Instead, there was a name she'd never seen before, a name she didn't know how to pronounce: Dr. Cynthia Cadet.

There were three bottles. One contained alprazolam, and two contained oxycodone, two different dosages, 15 milligrams and 30 milligrams.

Oxycodone. Alice had heard of oxycodone. She believed it was some kind of cancer drug.

The alprazolam and the 15-milligram oxycodone had been filled at a place called America's Pharmacy. The 30-milligram oxycodone was from a place called Speedy Scripts II. The addresses were Fort Lauderdale. Florida.

They went through the garbage bag Stacy had brought home. Mostly clothes, but also some papers. A photocopied sheet with drawings of people doing stretching exercises. A pharmacy receipt with the Speedy Scripts II logo at the top, the words tilted slightly to call attention to the speediness, like they were about to zip off the page. Stacy's name and the farm's address. The doctor again: Dr. Cynthia Cadet. Oxycodone HCL 30-milligram tablet. Quantity: 240. Stacy had paid $247.30, cash.

The receipt contained a long set of printed-out instructions.

". . . used to treat moderate to severe pain . . ."

". . . acts on certain centers of the brain . . ."

". . . Follow your doctor's instructions exactly as prescribed . . ."

". . . take this medication only 'as needed' for acute pain (e.g., pain after surgery) or on a regular schedule for chronic pain (e.g., cancer pain) . . ."

". . . withdrawal symptoms . . . anxiety, irritability, sweating, trouble sleeping, diarrhea . . ."

". . . SIDE EFFECTS: Nausea, vomiting, constipation, mild itching, drowsiness, dry mouth, lightheadedness, loss of appetite . . ."

Then two more sets of receipts from America's Pharmacy. The logo: a druggist's mortar and pestle on top of an American flag. And some advertising in bold letters: "GENERICS STARTING AT $2.99. BUY 1, GET 1, FREE." Stacy had paid $20 for the alprazolam and $100 for the oxycodone.

Alice also found a card, the kind the doctor's office gives patients to remind them of their next appointment. Stacy already had another appointment with Dr. Cynthia Cadet set for January 28 at 1:00 p.m., three and a half weeks away, at a place called American Pain.

They also found Stacy's MRI reports, the ones Stacy's doctor had ordered back in August after the accident. There were two of them, one for the cervical spine and one for the thoracic spine. Lots of words like "reactive osteophytes at C5-C6" and "diffuse bulging disc" and "small left paracentral disc protrusion at T8-T9."

One other thing they found with Stacy's things: a green plastic bottle, probably Mountain Dew, the label ripped away, heavy with coarse-grained sand.

They reckoned Stacy had seen the ocean after all.

Alice knew about the Internet, of course, but she didn't mess with computers. She didn't even know how to turn one on. But young Kevin was a wonder with electronic things, excited that something he called DSL was finally making its way out to Hummingbird Lane.

Kevin was glad to have a way to help. He'd known more than Alice about Stacy and the pills. He knew Stacy had begun crushing and snorting the Lortabs the doctor had prescribed him. He knew that Stacy had started going to the pharmacy a couple days before he was supposed to, trying to get refills early. He'd seen his brother high on the pills. But Stacy high wasn't too different than Stacy sober. He was the same mellow, friendly guy, maybe a little more so.

So Kevin hadn't worried much about the pills. A doctor had prescribed them. How bad could they be? And anyway, Kevin was busy with college and work. Kevin was going to have his own computer shop someday, be his own boss. College and computers were things Stacy and the rest of the family didn't know much about. Stacy would have been happy to work masonry and live on the farm the rest of his life. But Stacy encouraged Kevin's ambitions. He wanted the best for Kevin.

Kevin began searching for information about pain clinics in Florida. He wanted to know what his brother had seen and done on his trip.

Kevin looked up American Pain. On Topix and other websites, folks from Kentucky were talking about the clinic like it was somewhere in Somerset or Lexington instead of seventeen hours away. Apparently,

Kevin told his mother, lots of people from Kentucky were going down to Florida to get pills. You just took them an MRI or a CAT scan and that's pretty much all you needed.

Kevin looked up oxycodone. He read that a usual starting dose for an adult was maybe two 10-milligram pills a day. Dr. Cadet had prescribed Stacy a twenty-eight-day supply of 240 30-milligram pills. More than *eight* 30-milligram pills every day.

And that didn't include the 15-milligram oxycodone pills. Or the alprazolam.

Kevin was no doctor, but this didn't sound right. Not for a patient's first visit.

Alice got the prescription bottles and flushed the pills down the toilet.

Eugene always wanted to be buried on his land, so he and Alice decided to start a family plot on the pretty sloping meadow where the horses grazed, not far from the main house. Stacy's tombstone would be the first.

But they decided it just seemed too lonely to put Stacy out there by himself, so they ordered their own stones at the same time, leaving the final dates to be engraved later.

Lisa, always organized, helped Alice plan Stacy's funeral and burial. Lisa helped design the tombstone, adding a guitar and music notes. The mother and the girlfriend made arrangements, Lisa paying for things whenever Alice let her. And they talked and talked about Stacy, the trip to Florida, the pain pills. And as the initial shock dulled, what took its place was anger.

Why in the world, Alice wondered, had that Dr. Cynthia Cadet prescribed Stacy so much medication? She couldn't get her head around it. That lady doctor giving him not one, but *two* bottles of the exact same kind of medication. The question was never far from her mind: Why in the world would a doctor do that?

Lisa came out to the farm, bringing news stories she'd found on the Internet about people dying of overdoses after receiving drugs from

Florida pain clinics. She showed the articles to Alice and Kevin. People were dying in Florida too. Even if the police in Kentucky couldn't do anything, maybe someone down there in Florida could.

The funeral home brought Stacy's body to Sand Hill Baptist Church the evening before the funeral. The small white frame church stood at the crossroads of two wooded lanes cut into the mountainside. Alice spent the night there with him.

The next day, the sanctuary was overflowing with hundreds of people.

Rev. Tommy Miller, an auto mechanic during the week, preached a sermon of peace and forgiveness, but inside he was angry. If you asked him to speak his mind, he'd tell you he was hearing more and more about the pills, to the point where it seemed every family had a tragic story to tell. And the government was doing little that he could see. Oh, they had money to bust hardworking coal truck drivers for speeding, an easy form of local revenue, but they didn't bust drug dealers unless they had $200,000 in the bank, an amount of money worth the trouble of seizing.

Shelby, Lisa's mother, came to the funeral. While Lisa and Stacy had been living together all these years, more or less common-law married, Shelby had been out to the farm on Hummingbird Lane only once before. The property contained a scattering of dwellings: the clean-swept and simple main house, two trailer homes for various Mason kin, a row of rooster hutches fashioned from barrels, the rust-streaked tin barn. A milk cow, three skinny mares, and a gelding. The Masons were hill-country people, meaning they took their time getting to know you. You were lucky to hear two words out of Eugene. On that single visit, Shelby had seen but not really met Alice. Stacy's mother was maybe not quite five feet tall, shaped like a beanbag, face reddened by sun and wind, some teeth gone, the rest stained brown by the chaw of tobacco usually lodged in her gums. During warm months, she preferred to get around her farm on grubby bare feet, an oversized stars-and-stripes baseball cap perched backward over her chopped-off white hair.

At the funeral, Shelby met a different Alice. Grief had demolished her barriers. The little woman grabbed Shelby and hugged her close, wanting Lisa's mother to feel at home even on this day. Alice had Stacy's pale eyes, eyes like a girl's, showing exactly what she was feeling. One minute, they were all mischief. The next, a hard look of wrath. Then, over and over on this day, crumpling into deep wells of sorrow.

Shelby saw Lisa and Alice fueling each other's fire, and she worried about it. Lisa was so stubborn once she set her mind on something.

And Lisa was the one who said it first.

Lisa told Alice: We have to find out what happened. We have to go to Florida.

Sheriff Mike Peters had been called out to Hummingbird Lane on the day Stacy died. He didn't know the Mason family, who kept to themselves out in the woods and presumably obeyed the law. Alice Mason was completely torn up, as was to be expected. She seemed like a nice lady to Sheriff Peters, about as simple and country as you could find these days, pinning up her laundry on the clotheslines behind her house.

Sheriff Peters had talked to Alice and Eugene Mason, taken some notes, and written up a report. Stacy's toxicology report came back a few weeks after his death. The medical examiner found that Stacy had died from "acute oxycodone and alprazolam intoxication." Trace amounts of hydrocodone and marijuana were also detected in his system.

Sheriff Peters didn't take it any further than that. What was he going to do? He'd been elected to his first term as sheriff two years earlier. He had a simple redbrick office and a tan Ford Explorer and three deputies to cover 17,056 residents spread out over 314 square miles of terrain. Their job already included transporting prisoners, collecting taxes, providing court security, and serving court papers. What could he do about doctors in Florida?

When Sheriff Peters was a boy, which wasn't yesterday, the biggest drug problem in Rockcastle County was the town drunk. A sheriff could do something about that problem, throw the drunk in the tank now and again. And then came marijuana. Don't get him wrong, weed was illegal, but if people smoking pot was the worst problem in the Rock, things would be pretty good. Sheriff Peters knew plenty of folks he would call alcoholics or potheads. Friends, neighbors, family. Most could hold down a steady job, and he didn't know any who stole to support their habits.

Pills were different. At their worst, pillheads needed two or three hundred bucks a day to get by and would steal from family members to get a fix. And painkillers weren't like crystal meth, which was something that tended to be restricted to a certain lowlife element. Pills truly changed the county, turning normally law-abiding folks into junkies and thieves and bad parents.

The organized gangs and cartels that supply the United States with illegal drugs had always avoided eastern Kentucky, for pretty much the same reasons major businesses stay away: too many hills, too few people. So folks who wanted to get high made do with what they had, which for a long time meant cooking moonshine. Certain families made a good living from making and running shine. Other folks in the community may have disapproved of liquor, but they also tended to distrust the government and outsiders. Local resources like timber and coal seemed mainly to enrich folks from other places. At least moonshine revenue stayed in the mountains.

As vets came back from Vietnam with a taste for new highs, moonshine gave way to marijuana. Turned out the rugged mountains and humid climate of eastern Kentucky were excellent for growing weed. By the 1980s marijuana was believed to be the state's number one cash crop. Most pot farmers grew high-grade plants in clusters no bigger than the John Deere Model Ds they once used to bring in forty acres of burley tobacco. A sixty-square-foot plot could yield about $60,000. Pot was harvested three times a year, and buyers came in to evaluate and bid on it just as tobacco buyers had for generations. In some areas, 40 percent of the community was involved in the trade, which meant basically everybody was dependent on its cash, from the feed-and-seed to the filling station.

Most Appalachian marijuana rings were organized within families. Life in eastern Kentucky revolves around extended families. People figured out who they were by looking at their clan—more than the church, the job, the club, the school. Certain families controlled the majority of the marijuana trade. They also ran the other black-market establishments and trades, the illegal roadhouses and prostitution rings. Through interstate marijuana contacts, they eventually branched into transshipment of harder drugs. A light plane full of cocaine would fly in from Louisiana or Florida and land on an abandoned airstrip in the mountains, where it would be off-loaded and transported via pickup truck along an old bootlegger route to Pittsburgh or Chicago.

Twenty years ago, there was no widespread black-market trade in painkillers. But pills were always part of life in the coalfields. Mining camp doctors prescribed painkillers liberally. They were overwhelmed by torn bodies and black lung and backs damaged by hunching over for hours in narrow shafts. Miners took to trading pills, deciding themselves when they needed medication. The other primary jobs—timber and farming and construction—also involved manual labor, which meant injuries . . . and pills. It didn't help that the state had one of the highest cancer rates in the country and that doctors were scarce. Painkillers got folks back on their feet and back to work faster than physical therapy or other intensive treatments.

OxyContin appeared in 1996, and its purity and strength was like nothing eastern Kentucky had ever witnessed. Stocking pharmacy shelves with pure oxycodone pills in the mountains was like throwing dry timber on a smoldering ground fire—the whole forest blew up. OxyContin didn't spread like weed or cocaine, because there was no pipeline needed. Pills were already everywhere, systematically and legally funneled through a national distribution system. OxyContin abuse didn't spread like a product. It spread like an idea: in conversations, over the Internet and the phone, and face-to-face.

Between 1998 and 2001, a cluster of nine counties on both sides of the Kentucky/West Virginia border received more prescription narcotics per capita than anywhere else in the country. The pills were everywhere, and it was a casual thing. In the early days, say 1999 or 2000, the dealer tended to be the old lady down the street who was prescribed twice as many pills as she used. Often as not, a drug deal went like this—you dropped by the old lady's house, maybe had a cup of coffee at the kitchen table, asked after the family, traded a few stories, then cash for an old bottle of pills.

Casual . . . until the user tried to stop using. Young people trying the pills were familiar with smoking weed and drinking beer. They'd had no exposure to hardcore opiates. They weren't ready for the withdrawal, the fever and sweats and throbbing pain as every cell in the body ached for a fix. They went back for more.

Supply and demand kicked in, and the street price bumped up to about $1 per milligram. Theft and petty crime reports rose. Pharmacies were robbed. Emergency room doctors saw more and more people complaining of pain. In a matter of months, police departments went from receiving an OxyContin-related call every couple of months to three or four phone calls a day. Perry County Park, a wooded roadside recreation area with a walking track and a mini-golf course, turned into an open-air pill market. They nicknamed it "Pillville."

In 2003, the *Lexington Herald-Leader* released a trove of stories about how painkillers were crippling eastern Kentucky. The series included dozens of stories about how the drug had turned eastern Kentucky into the Wild West, sketches of backwoods judges and their connections to drug defendants, nuggets about how the Kentucky State Police didn't trust local law or prosecutors. The package detailed how no less than four former sheriffs who'd been removed from office due to criminal charges—mostly drug-related—had run for office again in eastern Kentucky in 2002. How two sheriff's candidates in different counties had been murdered that election season—again, drug-related. One piece reported on the state's biggest pill mill, a clinic located in a tiny Greenup County town forty miles down the Ohio River from Huntington, West Virginia.

Five doctors there eventually pleaded guilty to churning out prescription after prescription.

Hal Rogers, the US representative from eastern Kentucky since 1980, read the *Herald-Leader* series and reacted like the twelve-term congressman he was. Two months later, he unveiled a regional drug task force called Operation UNITE. The organization, funded by federal grants, would combine law enforcement, treatment, and education under one umbrella. Over the next three years, UNITE's officers confiscated more than fifty thousand pills and arrested some eighteen hundred people. The state also passed tighter controls on doctors and painkillers.

Purdue Pharma was also changing how it did business in Kentucky. In 2001, Purdue retooled its sales pitch for drug reps in fifteen Kentucky counties. Those reps were told to discuss only abuse prevention with their doctors. Purdue also told its reps that the company would no longer pay them bonuses on OxyContin sold to doctors who were arrested for improper prescribing.

And the measures worked. Sort of. After 2003, the number of painkillers prescribed and sold in Kentucky plateaued. Reporters turned to other matters.

But officials soon noticed contradictory trends. Despite the leveling off of sales figures in Kentucky, and outright decreases in eastern Kentucky, the number of fatal drug overdoses in the state continued to rise. Steeply. In 2001, there were 339. The next year, 435. Year after that, 551. In 2006, 711.

Same went for babies born addicted to drugs. In 2001, sixty-two Kentucky newborns were hospitalized for neonatal abstinence syndrome. The next year, ninety-three. Two years after that, 166. By 2007, 275.

Most overdose deaths in Kentucky involved a mixture of drugs. The most common drugs, by far, were alprazolam and oxycodone. There might be thirty or forty cocaine-related deaths in a typical year. Maybe one heroin death, often none.

So where were the drugs coming from?

What gradually became clear in 2005 and 2006 and 2007 was that Kentucky users were leaving the state for their drugs. Seven states border Kentucky, with seven different sets of drug laws and regulations and seven different levels of prescription drug scrutiny. Few states kept track of prescriptions as closely as Kentucky. Eastern Kentuckians were arrested with pills from doctors in Detroit; Philadelphia; Cincinnati; Slidell, Louisiana. But increasingly, the destination for painkillers was Florida, which didn't track prescriptions of controlled substances at all.

One early Florida pill runner was a sixty-four-year-old Kentucky grandmother named Jewell Padgett. Two-dozen people were traveling from Kentucky to Florida to buy pills, and Padgett paid for expenses and kept a portion of the pills. After Padgett was arrested in 2006, her son blamed the whole thing on Kentucky doctors who were afraid to prescribe painkillers since the crackdown. His ailing mother was forced to travel to Florida. He said: "They wouldn't give her medication she needed. They're scared up here."

Around that time, another go-to candyman for several Kentucky oxycodone rings was Dr. Roger Browne, who had a practice in Coral Springs, Florida. Dr. Browne made the mistake of getting too close to his patients. First, a girlfriend got arrested for selling pills back home in Carter County. She told the feds in Lexington about Dr. Browne. Another patient started working with the feds and wore a wire one night when he met the doctor for drinks. The informant told the doctor that he'd bring some buddies on his next trip to Florida.

"That'll work," Dr. Browne said.

The buddies were federal drug agents. In April 2008, they raided Dr. Browne's clinic and found the medical records of almost five hundred Kentucky residents. Dr. Browne pleaded guilty to conspiring to distribute oxycodone and was sentenced to two and a half years in prison.

Didn't matter. By mid-2008, the word was out all over eastern Kentucky: New pain clinics were opening every week in Broward County. Kentuckians began traveling to Florida by the van-load.

In Rockcastle County, Sheriff Peters was just beginning to learn about the pill pipeline in early 2009. That's around the time his friend

Shelby told him about the trip she and her daughter and Alice Mason had made to Florida to confront some pill mill doctor. The sheriff knew Lisa's mother pretty well. They'd worked together years ago at Renfro Valley, the country music concert venue. He wasn't happy that she'd put herself in harm's way like that. But he wasn't surprised. That was Shelby. No, what surprised him was that Alice Mason had traveled that far from Hummingbird Lane. He couldn't believe Shelby was talking about the same gap-toothed farmwoman he'd met. Folks like Alice Mason didn't travel to Lexington, let alone Fort Lauderdale.

Sheriff Peters was right. Only once had Alice spent more than a day outside of Kentucky. The big trip had happened around 1969. Alice had been thirteen or fourteen. Her mom's sister had moved down to Winter Haven, Florida, and one day she came back to Kentucky and picked up the whole family, except Alice's father, and took them to Florida for two weeks. Alice told her sons about the experience sometimes, how flat it was in Florida, the strange weather, how one time she saw the sky pouring rain on one side of her aunt's house and nary a drop on the other side. It was exciting. But Alice was glad to get back home to Rockcastle County after that trip, and she never left again, other than a couple of daytrips to state parks in Tennessee when the boys were little. She went to Mount Vernon a couple of times a week to pick up groceries, and that was about it. Young Kevin seemed to go everywhere in the world, but not Alice. She stayed home. Florida had so many people, and not people she knew.

But she had to understand what happened to Stacy, why the doctor had prescribed him so many oxycodones. She thought about this question all the time, what she would say to Dr. Cadet, wondering what Dr. Cadet would say. There had to be a reason.

So when Lisa said they should go to Florida, Alice surprised herself by saying, yes, she wanted to go.

Almost four weeks after Stacy died, a massive storm moved south through Kentucky. Driving rain fell through an upper layer of warm air, then froze in the colder layer below. Shelby woke to find all of Mount Vernon coated in a half-inch sheath of ice. Every surface was glazed over and glittering—twigs, power lines, fences, mailboxes.

Shelby got in her car to head to her shift at Walmart, and just made it off her hill before sliding backward into someone's yard. She called the store to let them know she wouldn't be in. No answer. She called another number, and someone picked up and said the ice storm had pulled off an impossible feat. It had shut down Walmart.

Shelby called Lisa.

Shelby told her daughter: I'm off work, so I can go, if we go now. If you and Alice are bound and determined to go, I got the money and the time off. Let's go to Florida.

Somehow the three women made it out of ice-covered Kentucky, heading south in Lisa's little white Suzuki sedan, Lisa driving, Shelby in the passenger seat, Alice alone with her thoughts in the back seat. Alice reckoned Stacy also had taken 1-75 to Florida a month earlier. Tracing his last trip made the journey even harder. The women didn't talk much. Alice cried more than once.

Shelby was skeptical about the trip, what it would accomplish. But she wasn't about to let Lisa and Alice go by themselves. Shelby had talked to some people about American Pain. The clinic had security guards. People thought there were police officers involved in the operation too. Alice and Lisa were deep in grief and anger. Shelby was worried they'd just bust into the place and get in trouble or get hurt. Shelby believed she was good at listening to people, at finding out things, paying attention to the clues of their posture and gestures and expressions. She had experience with security, both at Renfro Valley and Walmart. She figured she could help.

They left in the early afternoon and drove straight through the night, stopping only for fuel and McDonalds. In Georgia, a tire went flat and they put on the feeble-looking spare doughnut tire. They pulled into a roadside service station to get the tire changed, but the service station didn't have the right kind of tire.

A Georgia State Police trooper was there, a woman. She saw the Kentucky tags on Lisa's Suzuki and started aggressively asking all three women questions. Where were they going? Why?

Even after all those miles, Lisa was loaded with energy, oddly excited. She'd insisted on driving the whole way down. She wasn't intimidated by the state trooper's tone. The opposite, in fact. She got out of the car, pulled out Stacy's American Pain appointment card, the one with the American flag on the front, said she was going down to Fort Lauderdale to confront the doctor who'd given Stacy the oxycodone that killed him.

The trooper didn't seem to understand.

She said: I just want to know why all you Kentuckians are coming through my state all the time.

By this time, both women were red-faced, in each others' faces. Shelby was in the car. She didn't want the lady cop to arrest Lisa. But she also didn't want to get out and make things worse. Then Lisa let the trooper have it.

Lisa said: I'll tell you why all us Kentuckians are coming through your state. It's because your fucking doctors down here are killing our men!

Shelby cringed, convinced this was going to end with Lisa in handcuffs.

But something in Lisa's words seemed to satisfy the woman. She got in her patrol car and took off, burning rubber.

They never got the tire fixed, so Lisa drove the rest of the night on the doughnut tire, refusing to give up the wheel. They reached Fort Lauderdale around 10:00 a.m., and the temperature was in the mid-70s, a completely different world than the frozen mountains they'd left the previous afternoon, the air earthy and wet, the streaming multitude of cars shiny like they'd just exited a car wash, not covered in a gray film of salt and road grit. Even in her distracted state, Alice's eye was caught by the exotic flowerbeds around the fast-food restaurants, especially the amazing purple-leaved plants she didn't know the name of.

The American Pain Clinic looked like everything else in this part of Fort Lauderdale not near the beach: low to the ground, nondescript, well planned. It was just another business in a complex of tan and featureless office buildings, surrounded by geometric plots of green Bermuda grass and perfect rows of identical palms, like telephone poles on a highway. A red sign at the entrance of the complex displayed dozens of agencies by their office suite number: real estate, insurance, home nursing care. And the pain clinic in office suite 204.

Shelby knew from the folks she'd questioned back home that they were supposed to park in a separate fenced-in lot behind the complex reserved for out-of-state vehicles. Only Florida drivers could park near the entrance of the clinic. But Lisa was so agitated to finally be there that she just pulled right up to the door marked 204. A big man in a black shirt approached, and Shelby thought she could tell that he knew the women didn't belong there. His shirt read Security. He asked who they were, annoyed. He said they were violating the parking rules. Out-of-staters had to go to the cage in back.

Lisa and Alice weren't concerned with the guard. They got out and beelined for the door, leaving the car where it was. Apologetic, Shelby took Lisa's place behind the wheel.

Shelby said: I'm sorry, she's in a lot of pain. She's in a hurry to get inside. Where do you want me to park?

Alice went inside the clinic.

Lord, the waiting room was full of people. Loud, too, everyone talking and sitting in chairs and standing in lines and people who worked there hollering names. Alice stood in line for a window. When her turn came, she told the person behind it that she wanted to talk to Dr. Cadet. Alice wasn't sure she was saying the doctor's name right, but the employee told her to take a seat and they'd have someone talk to her.

Alice sat and watched the people coming and going. The room filled up and emptied three times while she waited. People shuffled in and joined a line, and sat down, and went back to the doctor, came back out. And the staff herded the people here and there, in and out. One patient dawdled in the waiting room after getting his medication, but a security guard moved him on his way.

The security guard said: You got what you came for. Now it's time to go.

It put Alice in mind of a crowded stockpen, a line of hogs waiting for the slaughter. It made her mad.

When Shelby entered the waiting room, she recognized someone: a dark-haired man who'd pulled a knife on her at Walmart back home. He had a black-ink tattoo creeping up his neck. Shelby often caught people in the store tucking items in their bags or under their shirts. Once, she'd watched a family eat their way through the entire grocery section, but she let them go because they looked like they needed the nourishment. The man with the knife had been stealing car batteries or Sudafed or rock salt, she couldn't remember. What she did remember was the knife in her face when she confronted him. She'd let him run out of Walmart, and the cops picked him up later.

Now he was sitting here in Fort Lauderdale. He glanced at Shelby, looking like he might have recognized her, and she felt afraid. She was wearing a gray T-shirt and jeans and looked haggard and unkempt after a day and night in the Suzuki. She wasn't sure the knife man could place her or that he could or would do anything if he did. But it made her realize even more that this was a bad scene, nowhere for Lisa and Alice to be. Shelby messed up her hair even more, hoping no one else would recognize her.

A man came out and introduced himself to the three women. Around fifty, thin with a long dark ponytail. He looked like a biker. He and a security guard asked the women to come outside with him.

Outside, the women explained who they were, said they'd come to speak to Dr. Cadet about Stacy Mason's death. The man with the ponytail said he remembered Stacy, the musician. He'd spoken to him. Stacy was a nice guy, he said. He was sorry to hear that Stacy had passed away. Stacy was in a lot of pain, the man said, and if the doctors in Kentucky had helped him, he wouldn't have had to come all the way to Florida.

But he said he couldn't let all three women talk to Dr. Cadet. Only Stacy's mother. Shelby wasn't happy about this. She didn't think Alice would get much information. But it didn't seem right to tell Stacy's mother that she thought she or Lisa should be the one to confront Dr. Cadet.

So Shelby and Lisa began asking questions then and there. The women asked why the doctor had given Stacy so much oxycodone. That amount of oxycodone was dangerous.

The man with the ponytail said: People build up a tolerance to these medications.

Shelby said: But he'd never been down here before! If you read his file, you'd know that.

She asked the man if he was a doctor, and he said no.

Shelby said: That would explain why you don't know what you're talking about. You're used to giving prescriptions to drug dealers who are selling it and know what it'll do. We want to talk to the doctor.

The ponytailed man said: Well, I'm sorry. I'm sorry. But not all of you can go back there.

A police cruiser drifted up to the clinic door, and an officer stuck his head out the window.

He said: Y'all got a problem here?

The ponytailed man said no and explained what was going on. Shelby thought the officer would take her side, but he didn't.

The officer told the women: You need to go on back to Kentucky.

Even the police are against us, Shelby thought.

Shelby and Lisa went back inside to wait with Alice. A couple other faces in the waiting room looked familiar to Shelby, but she wasn't certain that she knew them. Shelby noticed the towering stack of filing cabinets behind the clerks. Drawers and drawers, full of patient files. And each of those files was a person, Shelby thought, someone who maybe had a mother and a girlfriend who was worried about them. All those people, all that misery, filed away in those cabinets.

Finally they called Alice's name, and they took her back to Dr. Cadet's office.

Dr. Cadet came in and introduced herself, and Alice was surprised that she was a black woman. And so young and small and quiet. Alice finally asked the question she'd been wondering every moment for the past month.

She said: I want to know, why in the world you gave my son *two* bottles of oxycodone? The same kind of medicine?

Dr. Cadet just stared at the floor. Two men entered the room. They said they were doctors at the clinic. They did the talking for Dr. Cadet, like the little doctor needed to be protected from Alice.

Alice repeated her question, and the men doctors answered, not Cadet. They seemed to know about Stacy, like they'd read his paperwork. They said he was in bad shape with his back and needed medication. But they didn't say why he needed so much.

Alice asked if they could make a copy of Stacy's file for her.

The doctors said no.

Alice said: That's all right. I got all the proof I need at home anyway.

And she left.

Shelby knew the trip was a failure when she saw Alice coming out only a few minutes after she'd gone back to talk to the doctor.

The women got back in Lisa's Suzuki and headed toward the highway, looking for a place to get the tire fixed. Alice cried and told the other women what had happened. How Dr. Cadet just sat there and stared at the floor, no expression. They'd come all this way and hadn't learned a thing.

Alice said: It'd be different if the doctor had cried. Or if she'd been upset about what happened to Stacy. But she didn't care.

Nobody in Kentucky could do anything about Dr. Cynthia Cadet, and nobody in Florida seemed to care.

~

But just a twenty-minute drive away, a woman named Jennifer Turner was zeroing in on American Pain.

Turner, a special agent of the FBI, was stationed in an unmarked three-story building somewhere in Broward County. The building contained a couple hundred police officers and federal agents of every stripe. The covert multi-agency facility was supposed to provide a physical location where the missions and data and expertise of varied law enforcement organizations could collide and spark. It was a place where a special agent from the Bureau of Alcohol, Tobacco, Firearms and Explosives could easily share coffee with a police detective from Pompano Beach. Where a Broward deputy sheriff could just walk over to the next office suite to pick the brain of an analyst from the Department of Homeland Security.

Until a few months earlier, Turner had investigated health care fraud. Because of its retiree population, South Florida was the center of the universe for this type of crime. Turner had spent years chasing medical equipment manufacturers who offered free products to seniors in exchange for their Medicare numbers, or surveilling corrupt doctors who billed health insurers for services never rendered.

Turner was thirty-eight, tall and athletic, with blonde, shoulder-length hair. She loved being an FBI agent, which had been her goal since she was a young girl. She was talkative and ardent, perhaps even idealistic in her devotion to the bureau. She knew the rules and believed in them, but to both her partners and her targets, she came off as someone who could understand opposing points of view, someone who maybe could be counted on to be in their corner, if they did the right thing. She could be harsh in the interrogation room but then follow it up with a compliment or nice gesture, straightening the tie of a government witness about to testify. She was *nice*. But her eyes—weary and shrewd—kept you guessing.

Turner had recently transferred from health care fraud to organized crime—Russian organized crime specifically—and she hadn't quite found her footing in the new assignment. She was helping with a few investigations, but she wanted to find something she could really put her arms around, something that would take advantage of her skills and experience. A case of her own.

One day in late 2008, Turner was in the break room of the multiagency building, half-listening to a conversation between police officers from Davie and Hollywood and the Broward Sheriff's Office. They were standing near a watercooler, talking about pain clinics. New clinics were popping up all over the place, they said, causing lots of problems.

A police captain said: You know, some of these clinics have Russian doctors in them.

Russian doctors. Turner turned to the group.

She said: Excuse me?

The captain said: I thought that might get your attention.

Turner pumped him for more information. He said the patients were selling pills, urinating on public property, shoplifting from nearby stores. Many of the patients were from other states. Often, when they got pulled over, the patients had not only pills, but marijuana and cocaine in the car. Local police were trying to crack down on these activities, focusing on the patients, but they weren't equipped to look into the clinics themselves.

Local police had talked also to the DEA about the pain clinics, but the drug agency considered legal opioids to be the purview of the DEA's regulatory branch, the Office of Diversion Control. DEA special agents were primarily focused on cocaine and heroin, not pills manufactured by pharmaceutical companies and prescribed by doctors.

Turner was intrigued but skeptical. This could be an investigation that would take advantage of her health care experience but still fit into her current assignment. But where was the crime? Oxycodone was legal, and doctors were allowed to prescribe it. At first blush, the whole thing sounded to her like an exaggeration, a problem that had been blown out of proportion. How big could this possibly be? Yes, it was interstate drug trafficking, but was it truly organized crime or just a few individuals? And how many people would really travel from Kentucky or West Virginia just to go to a doctor?

She decided to look into it. She talked to some local police departments for background and began doing surveillance of the biggest problem clinics. She saw long lines outside the buildings, zombie-like patients wandering around the neighborhoods. She watched Carmel Cafiero's reports on a place called South Florida Pain and was surprised by the guys who seemed to be running the place. They were so young. She saw billboards advertising pain clinics, notices in the free weekly newspapers.

Turner took her information to an assistant US attorney. Like Turner, the prosecutor wasn't sure whether a federal case could be built around pill mills, but he encouraged her anyway.

He said: Someone's making a ton of money here. Let's keep digging.

6

By early 2009, Chris George was worried. His secret was out. American Pain was still the top dog, but the pack was now a herd.

That was the problem with legitimate business, Chris realized—it was transparent. Everyone could see what you were doing and just copy it. There'd always been individual candymen in Florida, the doctors who'd built a reputation for being loose with the prescription pad. But American Pain had helped turn a handful of clinics into a major growth industry, inspiring shady entrepreneurs and basically handing them a template for the pain-pill business. Some of the new pain-clinic owners had started out as sponsors at American Pain. They'd bring dozens of people to the clinic every month, funding their visits and then collecting half the pills. Making a nice profit, but it was never enough. Pretty soon, they'd start thinking about opening their own places.

The new clinics borrowed Chris's aggressive marketing techniques: search engine optimization, out-of-state Yellow Pages promotions, advertisements in the *New Times* and *City Link*. Before long, every other billboard seemed to be plugging pain management, as if an epidemic of agony had swept across the state.

The pain clinics kept an eye on each other. One would start promoting half-off specials on certain days of the week, and then a slew of them would do the same in the following week's *New Times*. Some clinics paid patients $25 for bringing in a new patient; others rewarded new patients directly with $25 gasoline cards. For a while, Chris offered free initial visits to attract new patients, but when others started doing it, patients began simply moving around from clinic to clinic, taking advantage of the special offers on initial visits. So Chris started offering a free *second* visit.

A new clinic was opening every three days, on average, and Chris spent a lot of time driving around, checking out the new guys, trying to figure out who was behind each clinic and whether it was a real threat. Most of the offices were tiny, with a single doctor. Others were strictly small-time, the doctor fearful to hand out narcotics in quantities that would keep patients coming back. Many didn't have strong wholesaler connections, and couldn't dispense pills themselves.

Chris wanted American Pain to appear more legitimate than the horde of upstarts. He gave Baumhoff a new title—"compliance officer"—and sent him to Florida Board of Medicine meetings, so they could monitor the latest policies and laws about pain management.

By 2009, the American Pain doctors were regularly receiving letters of inquiry from the health department about overprescribing, usually triggered by complaints from patients' relatives. Chris didn't want the doctors worrying about legal problems. He kept an attorney on retainer, and when the doctors received letters, they'd turn them over to Ethan, who would forward them to the lawyer. The doctors would pull the file of the patient in question and write a report about the patient's treatment.

They joined the American Academy of Pain Management, which involved paying a small fee and getting a membership certificate. Chris displayed the certificate in the clinic. They also paid a law firm $10,000 to write a standard operating procedure manual. Ethan gave copies of the manual to every employee and doctor and told them to read it and sign it and return it to him, so he'd have something to show the DEA if they came back. Everyone ignored his instructions. No one returned the manuals.

Ethan also told the doctors that the DEA targeted clinics that ordered nothing but controlled substances. He asked the physicians to send him lists of medications that he could order so the clinic wouldn't look like a pill mill. Again, no one followed through.

Chris backed Ethan's new dress policy, and despite Derik's opposition, the staff began to follow it: no jeans Monday through Thursday, and collared shirts and medical scrubs were acceptable, as long as they were clean and had no holes.

When patients e-mailed American Pain to inquire about treatment, Ethan responded cautiously: "I cannot and will not guarantee you will be prescribed medication. What I can tell you is that you will have a quality examination done by a qualified physician. If you are interested we take walk-ins from 9–5 Monday through Friday."

Chris believed American Pain was the biggest pain clinic in Florida, which almost by default meant it was the biggest in the United States and maybe the world. Chris wanted to be even bigger. He wanted clinics across the country, in every state that would allow him to own one. That way, if Florida ever got its act together and successfully banned him from owning one, the money flow would barely be interrupted.

Meanwhile, he kept hiring until he had five full-time doctors, plus a number of part-timers and a staff of about twenty. Parking-lot security guards, who were paid in cash. Inside, more security, cashiers, pharmacy techs, and receptionists, all on the payroll. And the cleaning woman, an independent contractor.

Fort Lauderdale code enforcement officers began to pressure the clinic, and in March, Chris moved for the third time, this time to Boca Raton, where they stayed for the rest of 2009, the longest the clinic had ever remained in one place. They took over the lion's share of a strip mall, about ten thousand square feet, with a huge waiting room that could seat 150 patients. The Boca location looked great, not like the seedy little clinics popping up everywhere. Boca had artwork and big flat-screen TVs on the walls, potted palms, high ceilings with exposed trusses and beams, and nice off-white carpeting they had to switch out every few months after the zombies had ruined it with spilled Mountain Dew and smuggled urine.

More patients meant more problems. In Boca Raton, seizures became a weekly occurrence. If the patient looked really bad, Derik called one of the doctors to help. The rest of the time, he just called 911. The parking lot became a sex-for-drugs zone, patients trading pills for back-seat blow jobs. Derik heard about these encounters regularly from his security team, and he witnessed them himself a few times. He couldn't bear to interrupt another guy's moment; he just walked away. Next door to the clinic was an Italian restaurant called the Basil Garden. Shortly after the clinic moved in, the restaurant stopped offering lunch, and Derik believed it was because they preferred to wait until American Pain was closed to start serving patrons so they wouldn't have to deal with the pain clinic clientele. Some neighborhood residents took advantage of the situation and began charging $20 to park in their yards.

The same month that American Pain moved to Boca Raton, Chris opened a second, smaller clinic in Dianna's name. Their breakup had lasted only a couple of months. But Chris had begged her to come back, and eventually she had. She believed she had nowhere else to go, and she was ready to fully embrace Chris's pain clinic venture.* The clinic in her name was called Executive Pain. It was in an office plaza in West Palm Beach, sandwiched between another medical clinic and a dental office. Starting out, the staff was just two part-time doctors and two nonmedical employees, Dianna and Ethan Baumhoff's wife.

At first, Chris saw Executive Pain as a backup location, in case American Pain got chased out of Boca. He also wanted to keep Dianna busy and happy running her own place away from American Pain. He knew it was smart to stake a claim in West Palm Beach. Broward County was overrun with pain clinics, and the commerce was moving north into Palm Beach County.

As time passed, Chris gradually figured out how best to utilize the second clinic. As American Pain had become more stringent with its patients, maybe one in ten patients walked out the door without a prescription. Derik and his staff rejected patients for failing drug tests, and the doctors kicked them out for having track marks, for openly jonesing, for begging the doctor for drugs, whatever happened to make that doctor uncomfortable. But Chris hated to lose a patient. So Executive Pain

* This is based on Dianna's court testimony. She declined to be interviewed, and Chris did not discuss his relationship with her in detail.

became a second chance for the patients he called "dirtbags"—the 10 percent who didn't pass muster at American Pain.

Over time, they developed a cover story for these referrals. When they bounced an American Pain patient for track marks, the official rationale was that they were sending the patient to Executive for treatment. The clinic paid for a doctor to take an online class in drug detoxification. They bought some Suboxone, an opiate-detox drug, and put lettering on the door that said Detox Available. Only one patient ever asked for it. The rest of the patients referred from American to Executive simply asked for pain meds when they got to the new clinic.

By the end of 2009, Executive Pain had hired several more doctors and was servicing eighty patients or more a day, pulling in between $15,000 and $40,000 a day: much less than American Pain, but still one of the bigger clinics around.

The atmosphere at Executive Pain was loose. Some of the doctors called the patients "pillbillies" and joked about the ones with lots of track marks. They came up with a nickname for the flow of patients from American to Executive: "The Pain Train." Two employees snapped pictures of themselves rolling in piles of cash in Dianna's office.

A few months in, Chris offered his mother, Denice Haggerty, a clerical position at Executive Pain. Previously, she'd worked at a large property management firm for twelve years, working her way from bookkeeper to vice president of administrative services, and then she'd worked for the twins' father at Majestic Homes, but she left when her ex-husband's company was facing bankruptcy. Since then, she'd been bored at home, so she took the job at Executive. Friends later speculated that it was because she was trying to get closer to Chris.

Derik almost never went to Executive, but he had a hard time picturing Denice there, a pleasant middle-aged Wellington housewife type among all the dirtbags. Derik knew he didn't have the most normal family, but he thought of Denice as the classic mom figure. Nicest lady in the world, even if she drank a few too many glasses of wine at night. After her divorce from John George, she'd married a firefighter, but she and Chris's dad seemed to get along. Sometimes John came to the big family get-togethers Denice hosted regularly at her house, up to thirty-five people at a time. She also donated to animal shelters and hospices and crocheted afghans for a homeless shelter in Youngstown, Ohio. How on earth she'd ever brought Chris and Jeff into the world and ended up working at Executive, Derik would never understand.

Chris had his full-time doctors sign a power of attorney so Ethan could use their DEA registrations to order pills. Ethan bought pills as fast as he could, but it was never enough for Chris. American Pain had a year's head start on most of the new clinics, and he and Ethan had developed relationships with a dozen or so wholesalers. Chris had realized his access to pills was his key advantage over other pain clinics, and he told Ethan to protect his relationships with the wholesalers and keep them to himself.

In early 2009, the wholesalers were saying their supplies of oxycodone were running low due to the glut of new pain clinics in South Florida. Which meant that American Pain's dispensary was "dry" more often. When that happened, Chris took it out on Ethan, shouting: You're costing me $5,000 a day!

When they did have to send patients to outside pharmacies, they tried to direct them to ones that wouldn't cause problems. Pharmacists, especially those in other states, constantly called the clinic to make sure the prescriptions were from a legitimate doctor and not a stolen prescription pad. Derik believed he usually could tell by their tone of voice whether they were just calling to cover their asses—so they could say they did their due diligence—or if they were really trying to verify whether the scrip was legitimate. Over time, Chris and Derik learned which pharmacies to avoid. Large chain pharmacies tended not to carry large enough quantities of controlled substances to meet the demands of hundreds of patients a day. They would also eventually red-flag American Pain patients. Independent mom-and-pop pharmacies were hit and miss, so Derik was always keeping an ear out for the ones that stocked a lot of oxy and would fill painkiller scrips without asking questions. Derik put up signs in the clinic ordering patients not to fill scrips at Walgreens and CVS. He went down through the listings in the phone book, calling pharmacy after pharmacy and asking if they stocked oxycodone and accepted patients from other states. If those questions didn't seem to raise a red flag with the pharmacist, it was a safe bet that patients wouldn't run into problems there.

But it was a lot of work, and Chris began thinking about investing in a larger chunk of the pharmaceutical supply chain. Sending patients to outside pharmacies was not only a pain in the ass, it was lost revenue. Also, he assumed Florida would eventually outlaw the dispensing of drugs from pain clinics. All of these factors led him to a conclusion: He wanted his own pharmacy.

He found one for sale in Orlando, a place called QuickPharm. The pharmacy had a DEA license and a staff pharmacist who wanted to stay on. Best of all was the location. Patients driving back home to Kentucky, Tennessee, and West Virginia passed through Orlando on the Florida Turnpike, so it was a convenient place to send them to get their scrips filled. The pharmacy wasn't making much money, but Chris wasn't worried. American Pain would supply the patients.

Chris met with the owner of QuickPharm and agreed to pay $120,000 for the business, plus power of attorney to use the owner's DEA license so he could begin ordering and selling drugs immediately. Chris registered Ethan Baumhoff's brother-in-law, Daryl Stewart, as the president of the company.

Chris also began building out a second pharmacy in Boca Raton, a nine-hundred-square-foot space. It took six months to start the store from scratch because he lacked a license, a process that involved state and DEA inspections. He didn't want to be connected to the pharmacy, so he put that one in the name of an old friend, Andrew Harrington. Drew had been begging Chris for a job at American Pain, and he had no criminal record. Chris would put in the money, Drew would do the work, and they'd split the profits down the middle.

The next rung of the industry, the pharmaceutical wholesaler business, also interested Chris. From what he could tell, it was a tough racket to break into. He was told the two main generic oxycodone manufacturers were not selling to new wholesalers. So he looked into buying a preexisting wholesale company. He had his eye on one in St. Petersburg that had begun selling him oxy a few months earlier. It was called Medical Arts and was run by a pharmacist named Steven Goodman, who'd been in the profession since 1966. Chris made an offer, but Goodman was beginning to realize how much money he could make from selling to pain clinics and rejected it.

Chris didn't tell Derik about these plans ahead of time. He just walked into American Pain one day in March and announced that he'd bought a pharmacy and that they should start directing all out-of-state patients to QuickPharm in Orlando.

Derik was taken aback, but only for a moment. Nothing really surprised him anymore.

As the flow of patients and cash had continued to rise, Ethan was spending up to six hours each night counting the money. He'd sort it by denomination and wrap bank bands around the stacks. Chris didn't want to bother with counting one-dollar bills, so he instructed the cashiers to round up all fees to the nearest $10. Eventually Ethan began to check the proceeds from each window against the patient numbers, to make sure the cashiers weren't just pocketing bills. Ethan carried the cash home each night in a blue duffel bag and then deposited it in one of Chris's three banks the next morning. One bank was nervous about him holding such large amounts of cash in the waiting room, so they'd usher him to a private room in the back, where he'd count the money and make his deposit. One day, doing his daily deposit at Bank of America, Ethan noticed the bank's cutting-edge cash-counting machine. He noted the make and model and bought one for the clinic. The cash counter was the size of a toaster oven, lots of buttons and a little digital screen. Everyone enjoyed watching it work; it was a miracle of efficiency, riffling through hundreds of bills in seconds, sorting and counting and occasionally spitting out a note that was damaged or counterfeit.

The moment Derik realized that price had basically lost its meaning for him was Super Bowl Sunday in 2009. Three days before the big game, he and Chris decided to go, to just wing it, never mind the cost.

The game was in Tampa, only three and a half hours away, but even so, it wasn't cheap to go to the biggest sporting event in the country, especially at the last minute. Chris found tickets, five grand apiece. One of the American Pain clerks rented them a floor of a hotel in Tampa—$2,500 a night for three nights. They tried to charter a private jet but couldn't find one at the last minute, so they just drove. They hit Tampa's notorious strip clubs, saw comedians, and participated in the NFL Experience at Raymond James Stadium. During the game, Derik had ten grand in his pocket. By the time the weekend was over, they'd blown more than $20,000.

It just didn't matter. By now, Chris could afford to blow through $20,000 *every* weekend and have plenty left over. Each time Ethan deposited money, the banks filed a Currency Transaction Report in his name. During 2009, the three banks filed 147 reports for American Pain deposits in the amount of $14,094,979. And that's just what the banks took in. Chris had begun stashing cash in his mother's attic, where he had installed several safes. He had millions up there.

Chris bought Range Rovers, Mercedes, BMWs, and boats. In January 2009, he bought the three-year-old home he'd been renting for most of 2008. The property was in receivership—the bank suing the developer—so Chris got a great deal. He paid a flat half million for the 5,600-square-foot mansion with its pale yellow stucco exterior, gourmet kitchen, marble countertops, crown molding, and kidney-shaped pool. Later in the year, Chris bought two more unfinished homes in the same development that were also in receivership, one next door and one down the street, for a total of $420,000.

Over 2009, Derik made a lot of money too. Maybe a million bucks, though it was tough to pinpoint because so much was under-the-table cash—and he spent as quickly as he made it. He dropped a lot on clothes. Maybe twenty pairs of jeans from True Religion and Diesel. Basically every shirt from the Stone Rose collection—"luxury threads for the discerning gentleman"—$150 or so apiece. A Rolex. Nights, he basically lived in strip clubs and the Hard Rock Hollywood. In March, he and his girlfriend moved from their crappy apartment in Tamarac to a nice townhouse in Boynton Beach. Derik went to a furniture store and picked out an entire house's worth of furniture and had it delivered to the townhouse. Trips to Italy, Vegas, Bahamas, Puerto Rico. Sizable loans for friends and family, money he knew he'd never see again, five grand cash as a wedding gift for an old friend. Breast enhancements for his girlfriend—she, Dianna, and Ethan's wife all got boob jobs that summer, courtesy of Dr. Patrick Graham, a plastic surgeon who wrote pain-pill scrips part-time at American Pain. Lawyer fees for his one brother who was always in trouble, rehab for an old high school friend. There were times when he had $100,000 in a grocery bag in his car, just sitting there for weeks because he didn't know what to do with it.

And the cars! An SUV for his other brother, a Mazda RX8 for his girlfriend. And for himself, a $120,000 Mercedes CLS 63. It was sweet satisfaction when he took his sister—she was actually his cousin, but they'd grown up together after Derik's dad killed his mom, and they considered each other siblings—to the Mercedes dealership. He'd told her stories about American Pain, and she seemed to think he was exaggerating about the money. Derik wasn't above embellishing a story for effect or for personal gain, but he didn't need to stretch the truth about American Pain's cash flow. When he plunked down $25,000 as a down payment on a convertible, his sister started to believe.

His party expenses went up a notch too. Derik had always been a drinker, but he was doing more blow than usual. He also took oxycodone, as did most of the others at American Pain. Derik found that the pills took the edge off the cocaine. Oxy filled him with energy, the everyday aches and pains vanished. They made him feel like he could do backflips.

Derik's body generally had a number of pharmaceutical chemicals running through it. Oxycodone, for nights out. Anabolic steroids, of course, to keep the machine in prime condition. Adderall, to gun the engine—taking three at once was like snorting a bump of coke. Xanax, to bliss things out. Dr. Cadet wrote him scrips for Viagra and Cialis, which he told his girlfriend he'd gotten for one of the security guards who was too embarrassed to ask for them.

Most of the employees eventually became patients, and either used the drugs themselves or sold them. Saturday nights, Derik popped oxys with half of his American Pain crew. Monday mornings, the same guys lined up in Derik's office and he gave them their weekly testosterone injections.

Some people could handle having total access to any drug they wanted, and some couldn't. Derik himself did coke and oxy maybe once a week. The father of Derik's high school girlfriend was a biker and recovering alcoholic with three years of sober time. He wanted to be a drug counselor, but he started working at the clinic in 2008, and his addiction roared back to life. Within a month, he'd gotten a prescription from Dr. Joseph for Percocet 10 milligrams. Just a few weeks and he'd graduated to oxycodone 30 milligrams and was getting high at work. Dr. Boshers wrote for him even after the staffer told the doc he was an addict. The staffer was making thousands a week, more than he'd ever made, but he was upset when he saw pretty young female patients growing thinner with each monthly appointment, hair thinning, sores on their faces. He finally quit and went to a Veterans Administration rehab.

Derik's old friend wasn't the only one with oxycodone problems. One of the good-looking women they'd hired turned out to be a serious junkie, which was clear from the day she started. She could barely speak half the time. Eventually, she was so much trouble that they stationed her at the closed Oakland Park Boulevard location, giving directions to the new clinic. Eventually, another pain clinic called Derik, saying the employee had been doctor shopping. This was the ultimate taboo at American Pain, not because anybody gave a shit whether employees took drugs but because it was so easy to get caught, which could jeopardize the whole operation. Derik fired her.

Some days, the party spilled over into the workday, people boozing and doing who knows what else at the clinic. It infuriated Ethan, who didn't like trying to run herd over a bunch of Derik's pals. They didn't believe they answered to him, which suited Derik fine.

Almost all the doctors wrote Derik or other employees prescriptions at different points.* Jacobo Dreszer wrote Derik scrips for oxycodone 30s. Roni Dreszer wrote him for Adderall and amphetamines, sometimes just because the young doctor didn't want the drugs in his own name; Derik would fill the scrip in-house and hand the speed over to the young doctor. One employee also gave Dreszer cocaine; Dreszer was writing him scrips. Boshers and Cadet also wrote oxy scrips for other employees, and Boshers was on the stuff himself. The doctor, who was in his mid-forties, had pain from a bad disc in his back. He got oxycodone prescriptions from Dr. Joseph, then the Dreszers, and then Dr. Cadet. Each doctor upped him. When Boshers first came to American Pain, he'd started out taking 130 30-milligram oxycodone each month, and before long, he was taking the maximum Chris would allow the docs to prescribe: 240 of the pills each month, plus another sixty 15-milligram oxycodone for "breakthrough pain." The pills didn't help for long, but he did get hooked. Finally, he had an MRI done, and the radiologist told him that the disc in his lower back had ruptured, leaking fluid like a stepped-on jelly doughnut. He needed surgery, not higher and higher doses of narcotics.

Despite all the drugs and prescriptions exchanging hands, none of the new crop of doctors ever directly addressed what was really going on at American Pain, though little hints slipped out now and then.

Dr. Boshers was the physician who danced closest to the edge of the charade. A longtime patient would come into his office, someone the doctor felt comfortable with, and he'd joke: Here for your candy?

---

* This is according to interviews with Derik and court testimony. The only prescriptions actually found in Derik's patient file were from Dr. Jacobo Dreszer.

Roni Dreszer was an interesting one. When Dreszer first joined his father at the clinic, he wrote only very small amounts, a few dozen pills at a time. When a patient complained, Derik mentioned it to the young doctor, trying to be subtle about it. Dreszer didn't get it.

He said: I think some of these people don't really need as many pills as I'm giving them. It doesn't feel right.

Derik and Chris talked it over. They had never encountered this problem—every other doctor who made it through the interview process seemed to get the picture right away. Chris called the young doctor to his office.

Chris said: I can't tell you what to do, but people are leaving the clinic unhappy, and you really can't work here if you're not going to treat the patients as they want to be treated.

After that, Roni Dreszer wrote higher. He rarely prescribed more than 180 pills a month, but that was enough to satisfy most patients. Dreszer was kind of like Dr. Boshers, Derik thought—it didn't seem to bother him when patients asked for more meds or referred to the pills as "blues" or "mallies" or "roxies," though he did complain to the other doctors when patients offered him bribes. And Dreszer shared Derik's sense of humor about the whole phony medical scene at American Pain. One day, the young doctor emerged from his office and called out to Derik.

He said: Dr. Nolan? Dr. Nolan? I need a consult. Can you take a look at this patient?

Derik played along, followed Dreszer into his office. A male patient was there. Dreszer asked the man to drop his shorts, revealing a scrotum swollen to the size of a softball. Derik recoiled.

Dreszer said: What do you think of this, Dr. Nolan? What's your professional opinion?

Derik: Uh, I don't know. What's *your* professional opinion?

Dreszer: Well, I think he's retaining some fluids in his scrotum.

Derik: Yes, I think you are correct, Dr. Dreszer. He's retaining fluids.

Roni Dreszer's father took the job more seriously. The elder Dr. Dreszer would kick patients out if they asked to be upped or if they called the drugs by their street names. He didn't seem to like any direct acknowledgment of what American Pain was. He took pride in the fact that he'd had a long career as an anesthesiologist and was actually somewhat qualified to work in a pain clinic.

Chris was never satisfied, but he knew he couldn't push the doctors too much. He'd look at Dr. Cadet's patient intake box, stuffed with patient files, and say to the other doctors: If you wrote the amounts she does, your patient box would look like hers.

Or he'd tell the docs they needed to see more patients—fifty, seventy-five, eighty-five a day. The numbers kept growing, and the elder Dr. Dreszer, always excitable, pushed back.

He said: I am a human being, not a machine! If you don't stop this, I will have to leave!

Still, the elder Dreszer burned through patients as quickly as the other docs, and like the rest of them, he preferred return patients to new patients. Return patients took five minutes or less. New patients required a lot more introductory paperwork, so it took ten or fifteen minutes to process them, and the pay was the same. Some of the doctors asked Chris and the staff to give them only return patients.

To speed things up, Derik had a set of prescription stamps made for each doctor. That way, they wouldn't have to take the time to handwrite the same scrips over and over all day. He ordered stamps for Xanax, Percocet, Valium, and Soma, a muscle relaxant, as well as four stamps with different dosages of oxycodone 30 milligrams: 150 pills, 180 pills, 210 pills, and 240 pills. Derik had a catered lunch delivered to the clinic each day so the doctors could get back to work more quickly. He also hired a company to wash the physicians' cars, so they would focus on working instead of running errands. These conveniences also had the added benefit of limiting the doctors' exposure to the patients. Better they saw as little as possible of activities in the waiting room and parking lot. Chris wanted the docs in their offices, writing scrips.

The $75-per-patient pay system encouraged competitiveness. Once, Dr. Michael Aruta saw Dr. Jacobo Dreszer take a patient file out of Dr. Boshers's bin and call that patient back. Dr. Aruta considered this stealing, and he confronted Dr. Dreszer. The old man started yelling about how Dr. Aruta was a hack who couldn't make it in plastic surgery and didn't care about the patients. The younger Dr. Dreszer held back his father from attacking Aruta, but he told Aruta that he needed to start taking a bigger load of new patients instead of grabbing all the follow-ups. Derik stepped in and split up the doctors, and Aruta and Dreszer were enemies from that point on.

This atmosphere of greed at American Pain bothered Dr. Aruta, but the pay made up for it. Aruta needed money. Since 2003, he'd operated his own anti-aging, vein care, and appearance enhancement practice in Fort Lauderdale. He invested heavily in the business in 2007, which proved to be a mistake when the economy tanked. A year later, he closed the business more than $200,000 in debt. While searching for a job, he kept running across ads for pain clinics. They were popping up on every corner in South Florida. He knew some pain clinics had been shut down, and he wasn't sure they were legal, so he didn't pursue any of the positions at first. But after several months of looking for work, he took a job at a pain clinic called A-Pain in Hollywood. Seeing and prescribing for pain patients was easy. Too easy. He saw only eight to twelve patients a day at $50 a pop. Driving home one day, he saw a billboard advertising another pain clinic in Fort Lauderdale. He grabbed his phone right then and dialed the number and spoke to the clinic's owner, Chris George. They discussed Aruta's experience with pain medications, and Chris said he'd pay $75 per patient, plus $1,000 a week for the use of his DEA registration to order medication. Even better, Chris said he'd see at least forty patients a day, which meant $15,000 a week.

Aruta went to the clinic for an interview the next day and was heartened to see the busy waiting room, maybe seventy-five patients milling about. Aruta had worked at the 1,550-bed Jackson Memorial Hospital in Miami and the gigantic Cleveland Clinic. He was used to lots of patients. He *needed* lots of patients.

His interview with Chris George took about ten minutes. Chris glanced at Aruta's medical license and DEA registration but spent most of the time looking at the security-camera monitors in his office. Chris then handed him off to other staffers, who explained the medication ordering process and gave him a tour of the pharmacy. Aruta also shadowed one of the doctors and saw that the procedures were similar to A-Pain's.

But Aruta realized pretty quickly that it wasn't a typical medical practice. For one thing, the staff was juvenile, a bunch of kids in their twenties, constantly causing drama and pulling pranks. Their leader was Derik Nolan, who affected a loudmouth, tough-guy exterior, especially with the patients. But Aruta liked him anyway. Underneath, Derik was funny and affable and intelligent, and when he wanted to be, surprisingly articulate. He was also very skilled at getting rid of problem patients, which Aruta appreciated. Aruta had heard of patients attacking pain clinic doctors who wouldn't give them a prescription. He began carrying a gun to the clinic, as did Dr. Boshers. They wore their guns under their physician's coats as they attended to patients. Aruta was a careful man and kept an eye out for problems around the clinic. He called it situational awareness. So when Aruta wanted to get rid of somebody without writing a prescription, he simply excused himself and found Derik, who took care of it from there with minimal drama.

Derik was always making the rounds of the clinic, but Chris George was aloof and typically stayed in his office. When Chris did talk to the doctors, it was usually something critical. Early on, Aruta sometimes told overweight patients that they should improve their diets, stop drinking Mountain Dew, that losing weight helps with many pain problems. Chris told Aruta to knock it off, that patients were complaining and a couple of women had left his office in tears. Aruta knew Chris didn't want patients switching to another clinic, but it irked him that Chris would try to stop him from giving basic medical advice.

Three times, Aruta was called out to the waiting room to treat patients who were going into spasms. Once, before the doctors could act, a staffer unzipped a convulsing patient's pants and dumped ice cubes down his underpants, thinking the cold shock would jolt him out of the seizure. Ethan talked to the doctors about assembling a crash cart for these seizure episodes, but it never got done.

Sometimes, there was talk of patients who had died of overdoses, though Aruta hadn't heard of it happening to any of his patients. There was the man who died in Kentucky before Aruta started working at the clinic, the one whose mother and girlfriend had confronted Dr. Cadet. Any medical practice carried risks, Aruta told himself.

Over and over, Aruta thought about his procedures and convinced himself he was providing appropriate medical care. He and the other doctors talked about this a lot, whether they were breaking the law. They repeatedly assured each other that they were not. Sure, they saw lots of patients, and the visits were short, but that was because the doctors weren't doing complicated diagnoses. They were simply treating pain. Nobody could ever tell for sure whether someone else was in true pain, so it wasn't the doctors' fault if the patients lied. Furthermore, they regularly discharged patients who had track marks, sometimes several a day. The staff also discharged patients if they found they were going to other clinics. The doctors told each other that it was inevitable that some patients would abuse the medications. They were doing what they could to prevent it. If there were illegal activities occurring at the clinic, that was Chris George's problem. The doctors absolved themselves.

The worst thing Aruta foresaw happening was police shutting down the clinic, leaving him out of work again. Which would be bad, because the money was even better than George had promised. Aruta was making more than $20,000 a week. He'd never earned more than $140,000 in a year, and now he was making more than that every two months. He paid off his debts and started thinking about retirement. It was a great feeling.

Dr. Cadet was the one Derik couldn't figure out. On one hand, she generally wrote the highest, maybe because she hated to disappoint anybody. But she was a mixed bag, because she also took the longest with each patient, would get deep into conversation with them, perhaps less aware than the other docs of the $75 she was earning per patient. She seemed to care genuinely about their well-being, yet somehow she also justified giving them massive doses of addictive drugs.

One day, Dr. Cadet called Derik back to her office and introduced him to a female patient. Cadet said the woman was three months pregnant and scared to death she was damaging her fetus. This wasn't the first time American Pain had dealt with this issue. Relatives of pregnant patients had called Derik in the past, furious that the doctors were prescribing heavy narcotics to women about to give birth. A couple of times, cops had called him with the same complaint, saying they'd just arrested a pregnant woman with a scrip from the clinic, asking Derik, how he could live with himself? The answer, of course, was that he thought about it as little as possible. And when he did think about it, he knew what he was doing was wrong, but he told himself that he'd quit as soon as he'd saved up a million bucks or so. And anyway, it wasn't his fault. The patients were hooked because they weren't taking the medicine as prescribed.

But this patient was different. She *wanted* to detox from the oxy. Cadet asked Derik to research drug treatment centers and specialists and help the patient wean herself from the drugs. Derik did as Cadet asked, calling the woman's obstetrician, forwarding medical records, putting in a lot of time helping this one patient. And then he created a new policy that every female patient younger than forty-five years old had to take a pregnancy test.

It was a nice thing to do for the patient and her baby, and Derik did feel good about the new policy. But he didn't fool himself. It wasn't like helping this one woman made up for everything else they were doing.

This was Dr. Cadet's thing. She would write scrips for addicts all day long, but then she would call him back to her office, and show him a nice card that some coal miner had given her, thanking her for helping get him back on his feet. Or she'd introduce him to a patient and tell him a sad story about a problem the patient was dealing with, ask Derik for some kind of help. Derik would comply, and then he'd head back out into the sea of junkie desperation in the waiting room, shaking his head and wondering if Dr. Cadet was for real, actually oblivious to the shitstorm of misery they were unleashing on these people. Derik could laugh about it all, but he couldn't completely fool himself into thinking he was doing some sort of humanitarian service at American Pain.

Like Dr. Cadet, Chris George sometimes came to the aid of certain patients. Usually this happened when Derik had decided to kick someone out for doctor shopping or trying to sneak in to an appointment early or failing a drug test or something. If the patient somehow managed to get Chris's attention, Chris would often side with the patient. He'd say Derik was heartless and didn't understand what it was like to be in severe pain.

But Chris didn't spend much time dealing with patients. Derik did, and he'd heard too many sad stories, seen too many junkie stunts. He knew exactly what these people were. All of them, no exceptions. Derik was losing his patience with the zombies, not that he'd ever had a whole lot. He didn't think of them as human beings. The Brazilian girl he'd dated the previous year had taught him that a junkie was a junkie, no matter what she looked like. And the lesson had been reinforced in December, when an elderly couple from Kentucky had come to the clinic two weeks before their appointment. Patients were always trying to scam their way into an early appointment, because they couldn't make their pills last twenty-eight days. But this couple was different. They weren't desperate. They seemed like regular folks, nice. A grandfather and grandmother. They said they'd brought their grandkids to Disney, which was why they were early. Someone back home was sick, which was why they'd taken the grandkids on this last-minute trip. Their schedule wouldn't allow them to come back for their regular appointment, and they asked Derik to help them out.

The doctor agreed to write their scrips early, as long as they didn't fill them for two weeks. To ensure this, the doctor dated the scrips two weeks from the current date. The couple thanked him over and over, said he'd helped their family out during a tough time.

Less than an hour later, a pharmacy called. The old folks were trying to fill the prescriptions, and the pharmacist was suspicious because the dates were torn off. Derik called the couple, told them off, said he was turning them in to the cops. They seemed scared, but two weeks later, they had the nerve to try to come back on their regular appointment date. Derik told them to beat it.

From then on, he thought of all patients in the same way. No matter how they looked or spoke or dressed, they were all junkies to him. Which made the whole thing easier to stomach. Junkies were gonna get those pills—somehow, someway.

The bigger it got, the more money that poured into Chris's bank accounts, the harder he'd become to deal with. Over the year, he'd gone from monosyllabic and standoffish to downright mean sometimes, barking at the doctors for being too slow, chewing out Ethan for not keeping the place stocked with drugs, and yelling at Dianna for just about everything. He took to studying patient files each night to make sure the doctors were prescribing high enough. He seemed especially tough on the female doctors. One woman who worked part-time quit after he berated her. Chris also got on Dr. Cadet's case because she often took time off and left early—3:30 or 4:00 p.m.—to take care of her two young children. Usually, she was a model big writer, but once, in front of staffers, he blew up after looking at Cadet's file.

He said: I'm going to fix that bitch once and for all.

He stalked over to her office and told Cadet that she needed to get her numbers back up.

Derik smoothed things over with Cadet. Derik liked Cadet, and she liked him. She laughed at his antics, called him the Original Gangster. She was no longer the happiest person he knew, however. Her marriage was breaking up, and she seemed like a lost woman for a while. The divorce became final in October 2009. She needed help with practical matters. Derik helped her find a new car similar to his, a Mercedes CLS 550, arranging the test drive with the salesman at Mercedes-Benz of Delray and going with her. When she wanted to buy a beach house, Derik made some calls to some real estate people he knew from his construction years. He printed out some good deals, set up appointments for her to see them.

So Derik didn't like it when Chris yelled at Cadet. But at this point, Chris and Derik were clashing too. They almost had a fistfight one day because Chris asked Derik to give a deposition in Chris's lawsuit against Jeff. Derik wasn't going to put his name on any legal documents. At times, Derik considered quitting American Pain and opening his own clinic. He talked about it with Cadet, who said she would come with him. In fall 2009, he even put down a deposit on an office in Lake Park. But every time he was poised to jump, something stopped him. He and Chris would make amends, and Chris would boost his pay. Besides, Derik had been a key player in the creation of American Pain. He'd helped build a huge operation, and he didn't want to start over.

No matter what they called the clinic or where they moved, Carmel Cafiero from Channel 7 would eventually show up. Her cameraman had a knack for getting grainy, ominous B-roll footage of the clinic exterior. Customers counting hundred-dollar bills before heading inside. Or sitting in their cars wielding hypodermic needles. Security guards lumbering thuggishly through the parking lot in their black T-shirts, spitting slow-motion into the grass.

When cameras showed up, Chris and Derik snuck out the back door. They didn't need a repeat of the Cafiero report the previous fall, which had been a disaster. Wholesalers had dropped them, forcing Chris to change the clinic name and hire Ethan as his front man. Chris and Derik couldn't afford to be directly linked with American Pain.

Still, Derik believed it was his right to know who was in his parking lot, to ask questions about what they were doing, so he occasionally violated his policy of making himself scarce when a camera was around. Sometimes it was hard to tell who was a reporter and who was just nosy.

There were the amateurs, unaffiliated with any news organization, who would park outside the clinic and shoot video on their cell phones, including one woman who wore a wig and a hat so she wouldn't be recognized. Sometimes they'd even come inside and snap some pictures or shoot a short video of the crowded waiting room.

One day, Derik's crew chased off a woman who was cruising through the American Pain parking lot, shooting video on her cell phone. Turned out, she was posting the videos on her YouTube account, narrating her adventures as she went: "And now we got two security guys that are gonna come and tell me to get off their lot, maybe, I don't know." She shot video of Tennessee and Kentucky license plates, tsk-tsking until someone tapped on her window. "Get away from my car. Get *away* from my car!"

Later, Cafiero interviewed the woman for a segment on pain clinics, identifying her as a "citizen journalist." The citizen journalist looked delighted to be in the studio, a big smile on her face, and told a story about being waylaid by American Pain guards. "One has a knife and the other has a set of keys in between his knuckles. He goes . . ." scowling and deepening her voice, "'You don't want any of this! You better come with us.'"

One day at the clinic, some staffers who hadn't seen Carmel Cafiero's reports asked Derik about them. Derik found one of the Cafiero videos online and played it for the staff on his laptop. Aruta and Cadet were there too. Aruta was aghast when he saw a patient shooting up in the clinic parking lot.

Aruta discussed it with Cadet afterward. They both said they hoped the pharmaceutical companies would come up with a narcotic painkiller that couldn't be abused. But Aruta believed that drug diversion was a problem for the police. The patients were the ones who were violating the instructions printed right there on the pill bottle. How could *he* be held responsible? He and Cadet agreed: They had no control over what patients did with medication after they left the clinic.

And, in a way, the news coverage and the proliferation of pain clinics made everyone feel more secure. The clinics were everywhere, ads blanketing page after page of the *New Times*, billboards up and down I-95. They were operating out in the open, safely aboveboard.

Another time, Derik was walking to the convenience store across Federal Highway and saw a blonde woman and two men videoing the clinic. Derik approached, and all three strangers jumped into a maroon sedan and peeled out of the parking lot. Derik was suspicious, and curious.

Chris was leaving the office right at that moment, so Derik flagged him down and they followed the blonde woman's car in a black Range Rover. Chris called 911 and explained what was happening, and the dispatcher told him to stop following the people. Chris kept going. The car stopped at a gas station, and Derik got out, and the threesome took off again. Finally, headed south on I-95, the car pulled over to the side of the road. Cops showed up and told Chris and Derik that the people in the car were media and to leave them alone.

And that was that, until a few months later, when the whole scene played out on a forty-seven-minute documentary called *The OxyContin Express*, which Derik and Chris watched on hulu.com. The blonde woman was a documentary filmmaker named Mariana van Zeller. For the first fifteen minutes of her story, she shadowed a pill addict whose brother had died of an overdose. The guy, who looked familiar to Derik, let the camera follow him as he was rejected from a pain clinic and finally bought pills from a street dealer. He even let her shoot him crushing and smoking a pill off a scrap of tinfoil. Then the focus shifted to American Pain. The blonde woman shot video of the old South Florida Pain location on Oakland Park Boulevard. It had been closed down for almost a year, but the big red-lettered signs were still up and old customers still came by. Derik kept a guy parked out front to direct patients to the Boca location. "So we came here to check out this pain clinic because a lot of the law enforcement and doctors told us that a lot of the prescriptions are actually coming from this one pain clinic," van Zeller said to the camera. She got a map from Derik's guy, who sat in a tan Ford Ranger, a towel draped over his window to block the blazing South Florida sun. She followed the map to the clinic in Boca Raton, and that's when Derik spotted her. As Derik and Chris followed her, van Zeller drove and narrated at the same time, glancing nervously at the rear-view mirror: "So we were filming a pain clinic from across the street and essentially had the camera out for five minutes and this huge black SUV comes up with a guy all tattooed, a huge guy, and starts asking us, 'What the fuck are you doing? What are you filming?'"

Derik didn't remember being quite that aggressive. He thought he actually smiled, raised his hands in peace. And he considered himself neither "huge" nor covered in tattoos. But saying a 210-pound man with some ink had approached her wouldn't have made for good TV. Or won a Peabody Award, like *The OxyContin Express* did that year.

Still, it could have been worse. At least the blonde woman hadn't named him or Chris and had blurred out their faces on the video.

The Boca Raton police kept an eye on the clinic and regularly pulled over patients leaving the parking lot, but they were friendly enough to Chris and Derik and didn't give them a hard time. They came to the clinic asking for information on patients they suspected of doctor shopping. Derik helped the cops when he could, trying to stay on their good side.

Still, sometimes, Derik would look around at the hundreds of drug seekers in the waiting room and feel a stab of panic. There was no way they'd get away with this.

Derik would say: Chris, we gotta calm it down.

Chris would say: Nah, we're good, we'll be OK. Until they change the laws, we're legit.

Other times, it would be Derik telling Chris there was nothing to worry about. Sometimes they would agree they needed to be more cautious, but then over the course of the conversation, they'd talk themselves out of their own fears. Caution wasn't natural to either of them.

In October, Derik flew to Italy for a friend's wedding. While he was there, he got a phone call from his cousin. A former American Pain employee had been arrested on cocaine and gun charges, a guy named Pedro Martinez who had worked for Derik on and off for years, ever since Derik's plumbing days. Derik had fired him from American Pain after finding out he was selling pills.

When Derik got back home, he went to Pedro's house. Pedro was acting odd. He turned the TV volume up high and whispered as he told Derik what happened after his arrest. Pedro said he'd been held at a police station in Royal Palm Beach until another cop showed up, a deputy sheriff from Palm Beach County. Derik knew the deputy's name. He knew him well, actually. The cop had come to American Pain a number of times while investigating patients for doctor shopping. Derik had always been cooperative and handed over patients' medical records. The deputy was a friendly guy, always asking questions about the clinic.

Pedro said the deputy sheriff was some kind of DEA task force member, and he'd shown Pedro a big board with Chris and Derik's photos on it, along with half the American Pain staff. Like something out of a gangster movie, Pedro said, all these mugshots and arrows pointing from one guy to the next. Magnets with titles on them. Derik's title was "Enforcer."

Derik was surprised, and a little hurt, that the cop had been just posing as his buddy, even asking him to go out for a beer.

Pedro said: Well, these guys got you all marked up like you're going down like some big organized crime ring.

Derik said: Man, these guys are taking this shit a little too seriously.

Pedro's story didn't seem quite real, but it lingered in the back of Derik's mind, the Mafia-movie poster with his mugshot on it, and the title: Enforcer. Was the DEA really investigating American Pain? The lawyers had told them they were in the clear, that the doctors were ultimately responsible for what they prescribed. Pedro's story was bullshit. Had to be.

Derik Nolan, left, and Chris George pose for a picture at the American Pain 2009 Christmas party at the Breakers resort in Palm Beach.
PROVIDED BY DERIK NOLAN

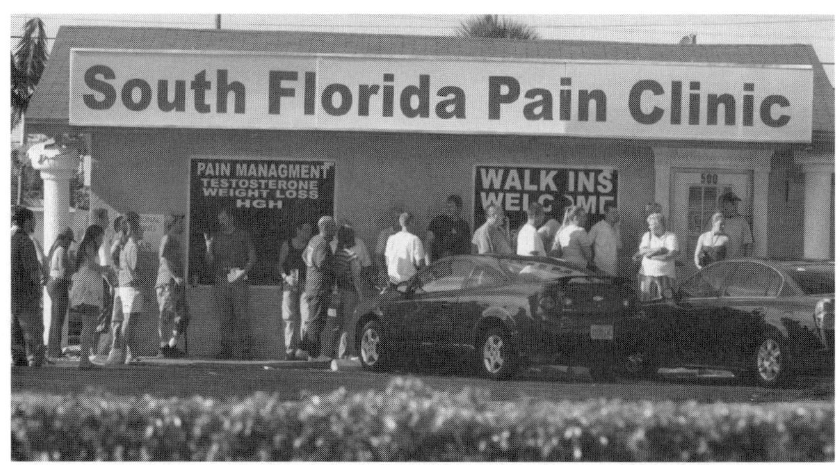

The South Florida Pain Clinic in its first location on Oakland Park Boulevard in July 2008. The Sun-Sentinel *ran this photo with Juan Ortega's story about the clinic.*
SUSAN STOCKER/SOUTH FLORIDA *SUN-SENTINEL*/ZUMAPRESS.COM

The American Pain waiting room on March 3, 2010, the day the FBI executed search warrants.
FBI

The final location of American Pain, a former bank building on Dixie Highway in Lake Worth, Florida.
JOHN TEMPLE

One of four safes found in the attic of Chris George's mother.
FBI

Derik Nolan, April 2015, in federal prison in Oakdale, Louisiana.
PROVIDED BY DERIK NOLAN

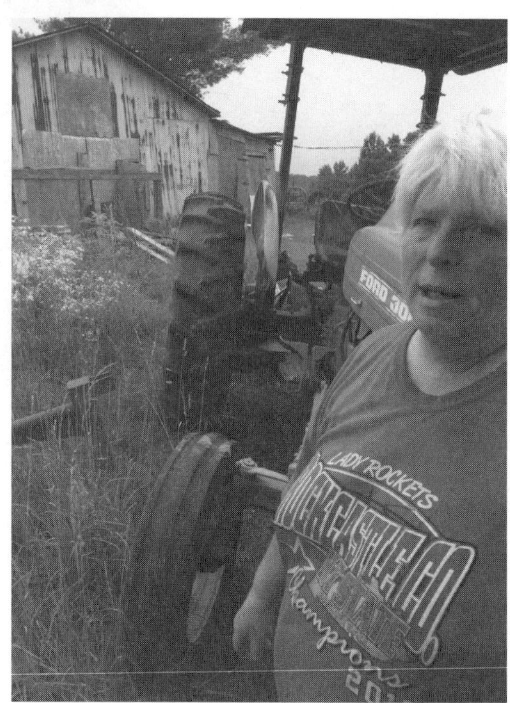

Alice Mason on her farm. Her son, Stacy Mason, died near the barn behind her.
JOHN TEMPLE

7

Early in 2009, Jennifer Turner flew to Kentucky to take a look at the flip side of the pill mill disaster—the Appalachian front.

The FBI special agent was no longer working alone. She was now heading up a rapidly growing task force that included the IRS, the US Attorney's Office, the Broward and Palm Beach sheriff's offices, local police departments, and the initially reluctant DEA. It had been only a few months since Turner had overheard the group of cops talking about pill mills at the watercooler, but there was a fresh urgency around her investigation. The state's prescription drug overdose death rate had risen to eleven a day, topping cocaine's. Florida doctors and pharmacists were distributing almost twice as many oxycodone pills as the next-highest state, Pennsylvania.* All the federal agencies now agreed; something had to be done.

Turner's partner on the Kentucky trip was a broad-shouldered DEA special agent named Mike Burt, a former cop with an expertise in wiretaps. In Lexington, Turner and Burt met with members of the Appalachia High Intensity Drug Trafficking Area (HIDTA) task force to trade information and discuss their shared problem. They decided that the HIDTA team would focus on sponsors and traffickers in their area, and the Florida task force would go after the biggest pill mills.

The special agents also interviewed anyone who could tell them more about the beach-to-mountains pill pipeline. They met with people like Barry Adams, a HIDTA member and a deputy sheriff of Rockcastle County. Adams was a farmer when he wasn't working, and he looked the

---

* In 2009, Florida doctors, pharmacists, and medical centers would distribute 523 million oxycodone pills. The next highest state was Pennsylvania with 267 million.

part in boots, jeans, and flannel. Like any Kentucky lawman, Adams was long familiar with 10-milligram Lortabs and 40-milligram or 80-milligram OxyContin. But the first time the sheriff's office had run across oxy 30s from Florida was the first day of 2009, when a young fellow named Stacy Mason had died on the Mason family farm.

Then, one cold afternoon ten days after Stacy Mason died, Adams was off-duty when he saw two men exchange something in the parking lot of Rose's One Stop gas station in Brodhead. One of the men drove away in a gray pickup truck, and Adams followed him. The truck wove across the centerline, other cars swerving to avoid it, before it slammed into a ditch. Adams tried to conduct a sobriety test, but the driver could barely stand. Adams searched him and found a magnetic key holder containing a bunch of pills, including some he'd never come across before: twenty-five round white tablets marked with 446 ETH. He looked them up and found they were 30-milligram oxycodone pills, manufactured by Ethex Corporation in St. Louis, same dosage as the ones Stacy Mason's mother had found on his body. Oxy 30s were new to Rockcastle County, and now the sheriff's office had come across them twice in less than two weeks.

That was the beginning. Adams and the other HIDTA members kept hearing more and more information about what they began calling "that Florida dope." Details about the new pill pipeline kept piling up, arrest by arrest, interrogation by interrogation.

The pill smuggling spread like a contagion, most often through family relationships, though police in West Virginia said Detroit gangs had moved into Huntington to take over the oxy trade. To Adams's mind, the rural trafficking networks grew like a spider's legs. One person—usually the head of a marijuana-growing or meth-dealing family—would begin sponsoring pill runs to Florida. The runners themselves were usually addicted to the pills. This gave the sponsors a hold over the runners, because addicts were always out of money and pills and would therefore make any deal. But junkies were terrible employees, always getting arrested or overdosing on the road or claiming the pills had been stolen.

A few of the most enterprising runners would eventually save a little money and begin sponsoring their own mules. Because the drugs were legal, the pill-running business didn't have the same barriers to entry as, say, the cocaine trade, where you had to know a supplier. Anyone with a car and a few hundred bucks could make a pill run. And profits from one run were enough to sponsor a carful of mules.

The pipeline inspired its own lingo. For self-evident reasons, the junkies called the oxycodone 30-milligram pills made by Mallinckrodt "blues," and the traffickers began calling I-75 "The Blue Highway." State police staked out the Tennessee-Kentucky border, pulling over multi-passenger cars in what they termed "pill stops." Allegiant Air offered a multitude of cheap round-trips between the mountains and South Florida, and the planes were so packed with drug runners that the flight was nicknamed "The Oxy Express." Observers found it interesting that the Allegiant planes were the same powder blue as the oxycodone pills.

Police in the states between Kentucky and Florida began to figure it out. If a multi-passenger car with Kentucky tags was heading north through Georgia, state troopers would find a reason to pull it over. They'd often find not just pills but brochures and business cards from clinics and pharmacies, and handwritten ledgers that detailed travel expenses for the sponsor. Sometimes the traffickers behind the wheel were high or they had illegal drugs along with the pills, which made it easy to make an arrest. If half the pills were gone from a twenty-eight-day prescription that had been issued the day before, that was probable cause to suspect drug dealing, and the cops would confiscate the pills. Some traffickers had visited multiple doctors and had more than one prescription for oxycodone, which was illegal. Those were relatively easy arrests to make.

But as the racket had matured, the traffickers were wising up, adapting to police pressure. Word got around that patients shouldn't sell their pills until they were safely home so their pill counts wouldn't be short if they got pulled over. Doctor shoppers who went to multiple pain clinics began to visit FedEx stores in between each doctor's visit, mailing home the pills so they wouldn't be caught with more than one oxycodone prescription at a time. Sometimes, patients would drive just over the Georgia line, then rent a car so they could slip past police who were on the alert for Tennessee or Kentucky or West Virginia plates. And police rarely found illegal drugs in pill runners' cars anymore.

As major Kentucky sponsors grew into kingpins, it became too complicated to make all the arrangements in Kentucky, handing out as much as $2,000 apiece to a carload of addicts in the hope that they would return intact with the pills. So a few of the biggest operators in Kentucky sent subordinates to live in South Florida, renting them a car and a long-term hotel room or even a bungalow. The sponsor in Kentucky would organize and send down the groups, and the coordinator in South Florida would take over from there, meeting the groups, giving them directions and cash, telling them which clinic employees to connect with, the peculiarities of specific doctors, explaining the unwritten and written rules of the pain clinics, guiding them through the process. The pill runners would meet the coordinator in the clinic waiting room. Sometimes they hadn't met the coordinator before, so one coordinator took to wearing a court jester hat or a Rastafarian hat with fake dreadlocks so he'd be easy to pick out in the waiting room. The runners were told: Look for the guy in the funny hat—he'll hook you up.

One day during their trip to Kentucky, Turner and Burt learned that a group of pill runners had wrecked while driving back from Florida. One of the traffickers was in the Lexington County Detention Center, and the special agents were invited to talk to him. Turner and Burt went to the jail and took seats in an interview room. Turner's back was to the door; Burt was sitting on the other side of the table. The door opened behind her, and Turner saw Burt's eyes widen in astonishment. She turned around to see a prisoner being led into the room. Bloody bandages concealed his massively swollen face and left ear. The accident had nearly severed the flesh from the front of his skull, and doctors had stitched his face back on.

Turner couldn't imagine the guy was able to speak, but she asked him if he was OK.

He mumbled through the bandages: Yes, ma'am.

So Turner went ahead with the interview, and the defendant willingly told her about his travels to Florida. Near the end of the interview, Turner was shocked when the man said he'd be heading back to Florida as soon as he got out of jail.

Turner said: Hold on. You're in jail, you just had this major accident, and you almost lost your life. Why on Earth would you go back to Florida to get pills?

The man explained, patiently: Well, ma'am, I'm addicted to them.

Turner wanted to understand. She had no addicts in her family, and she'd never met anyone like this. She could tell that he wanted her to understand too.

She said: OK, but why Florida? Why not just go somewhere closer?

The man turned to face her more directly.

He said: Because it's so easy to get pills there. Florida is the candy store.

When she left the jail, Turner was shaking. She thought: How are we ever going to stop this? It's so much more powerful than we are.

Whitney Summitt was seventeen the first time she made the run to American Pain. Her mother was an addict, her father in prison, and Whitney herself had started using drugs when she was fourteen. Her aunt, Pat Sandlin, had raised her, so when Aunt Pat told her to drive some folks from Louisville to Florida and back, Whitney did it. The doctors at American Pain wouldn't write for a minor, so during Whitney's first runs, she just drove and collected the pills afterward. Whitney had dropped out of school after the ninth grade, a young doughy girl with a moon face, but she was bold and businesslike. She made the seventeen-hour drive with as few stops as possible, and she told the three adults in the car exactly what their cut would be: their choice between fifty oxy 30s or $500. Most took the drugs.

Over the next few months, Whitney made the long drive about once a week with carloads of uncles, aunts, cousins, friends, even her father. She got to know the American Pain staff, knew she could slip the clerk at the window $50 and ask him to rush a patient, knew Dr. Graham and Dr. Cadet were considered to be the biggest writers. She showed her passengers how to tilt their hips in the MRI machine so their spines would look out of whack. If she didn't have a passenger who had clean urine that everyone could share, she brought a bottle of clean urine (clean-ish, actually—there was supposed to be some oxycodone in there, since you were supposedly a pain patient). It wasn't hard to get urine. Folks back home had taken to selling Mason jars of it at flea markets.

Whitney knew the fees by heart: $200 for a first-time visit, $250 for an MRI, $50 to bump a patient to the head of the line. Plus maybe $500 to fill the scrips. So sponsoring one runner's trip might set Aunt Pat back a thousand bucks, plus fifty of the oxy 30s, plus gas. The remaining 190 oxy 30s might net her $20 each back home, which was $3,800. And that didn't even include the ninety oxy 15s and ninety Xanaxes that the docs at American Pain usually tossed in.

A couple months after she turned eighteen, Whitney told Aunt Pat she reckoned she was old enough to do more than just drive. Aunt Pat agreed: It was time. In March 2009, Whitney took a full carload of people to American Pain and got her own paperwork. She paid the clerk $50 to sign off on her drug screen, since she knew she definitely had marijuana in her system, and possibly coke, in addition to oxycodone, which she was hooked on by now. She filled out the paperwork as quickly as possible. She knew it didn't really matter. One question asked where her pain was. She wrote: "Low back." On a scale of one to ten, how would she rate her pain? This was a no-brainer: Whitney circled ten. She circled a bunch of words that sounded painful. She said she'd taken prescription Lortabs for her back problems, which was true except that the pills hadn't been her prescription, and she hadn't been in pain.

Finally she was escorted to the office of a young male doctor she didn't recognize. He took one look at her, said: Exactly how old are you?

Whitney said: Eighteen.

The young doctor wasn't happy.

He said: I'm not comfortable writing you a prescription.

But he didn't outright say he wouldn't. So Whitney sat down next to the doctor's desk, and the doctor started checking items off on his paperwork, still looking unhappy. And maybe ten minutes later, she walked out with the scrip in her hand and went to wait for her passengers in the waiting room. When they came out, they went straight to the American Pain pharmacy to get them filled. Whitney waited until she got home to go to the pharmacy; the retail drugs were cheaper in Kentucky.

Whitney kept returning, but eventually a doctor at American Pain refused to write for her because she was under twenty-one. An employee sent her to Executive Pain, and she continued to get her pills. In between her own once-a-month appointments, she continued running other folks down every week or so.

By the time she turned nineteen, Whitney was no longer chubby. She'd lost weight and had stopped paying attention to her hair and clothing. Needle marks scarred her hands, the only place on her body she could still find a vessel. She was dissolving and injecting ten to twenty pills a day. The highs weren't really highs anymore, just a break from the bone-deep pain of withdrawal.

By this time, Florida's new pill-based economy was in full swing. Billboards plugged pain management. Dive motels catered to "oxy-tourists." Drugstores and MRI facilities flourished. And the pain clinics' parking lots were clogged with out-of-state vehicles.

Clinics opened and closed and changed locations and owners, and no one kept track of them, so it was hard to pin down an exact number, but officers in the Broward Sheriff's Office Pharmaceutical Drug Diversion Unit said the county had been home to four pain clinics in 2007.

Now, two years later, the unit tallied 115 pain clinics.

Odd connections had begun to emerge between flat, scorching, teeming South Florida and the green hills and slow brown rivers of the Appalachian Mountains. Broward County drug court judges saw defendants from places like Harlan County or Hazard at nearly every arraignment. Pain clinic staffers kept an eye on weather patterns in Kentucky and West Virginia; if a winter storm hit the mountains, business in Florida would be slow. Lots of Kentuckians and Tennesseeans began dying in South Florida motels that catered to the oxy-tourists. Likewise, coroners and ER doctors and airport security in Kentucky began recognizing the names of certain South Florida physicians after seeing them repeatedly on amber pill bottles they'd confiscated.

Sandwiched between Miami-Dade and Palm Beach Counties, Broward County was the epicenter of the new painkiller trade. The newspapers were catching on to the story. Board of Medicine members had been calling reporters at the major South Florida papers for some time, trying to get them to write about the proliferation of pain clinics, to little avail. The phrase "prescription drug abuse" sounded lackluster, especially to reporters who were used to covering huge, international, illegal cocaine busts. But suddenly the pill mills were everywhere, and business owners and residents in oxy hotspots seethed and politicians mulled legislation. A Broward County grand jury was appointed to study pill mills.

And reporters at the *Palm Beach Post* and the *Sun-Sentinel* began to pay attention. The *Sun-Sentinel* ran a story in April 2009 that said every single one of the fifty largest-selling oxycodone clinics in the United States was located in Florida. Thirty-three of them were in Broward County. A single small municipality, Oakland Park, was home to eighteen clinics within a two-mile radius.

Many people were upset about the pill mills, but parents of pill seekers had the deepest reservoir of rage—people like Karen Perry, a Palm Beach County woman who founded the Narcotics Overdose Prevention & Education (NOPE) Task Force after her son died in 2003. NOPE ran support groups and conducted educational presentations in schools. Pete Jackson, a biologist in Illinois, whose eighteen-year-old daughter died after taking a single oxycodone pill in 2006, founded Advocates for the Reform of Prescription Opioids, dedicated to ensuring that regulations surrounding prescription narcotics made scientific sense.

Tina Reed, a diminutive woman who worked at a sporting goods store in Broward County, had little money or scientific knowledge. But she possessed a deep and abiding anger, fueled by fear, not grief. She was lucky. Her son was still alive.

The fear and anger had taken over her life one November morning in 2007, when she walked into her son's room and saw him hiding something on his desk, a bill rolled up behind one ear. Her son was twenty-three years old and a marine mechanic. He'd already been arrested two months earlier for possession of oxycodone, which had led to his move back home.

Tina said: Are you snorting coke?

Her son moved his hands away, revealing a tiny pile of blue powder. It was his pain pills, he said. He'd crushed them to make them work faster.

The next five months, Tina watched her son spiral. She confronted his doctor, who refused to stop writing him prescriptions. Her son was caught snorting oxycodone again, and the family staged an intervention. He agreed to go to detox, but didn't follow through. High at work, he accidentally cut off part of two fingers, which made it even easier for him to get oxycodone. Tina researched oxycodone and wrote letters about his doctor to the state board of medicine. Her son went to a detox program, then relapsed a few weeks into it. He disappeared for stretches. He nodded off in front of her. He was arrested for shoplifting cigarettes.

Tina began writing down everything that happened, as well as her frantic thoughts: "Heroin addicts, crack addicts, cocaine addicts, *oxy* addicts? What? What? Why? What is this drug/poison/curse?"

In April 2008, terrified that her son was going to overdose, she went to his probation officer and begged him to have her son arrested. The probation officer met with her son, who failed his drug test. Her son was arrested and put in a rehab program, and Tina felt some small relief. He was safe for the moment.

When she got her son's car back, Tina found pill bottles in his name from a different doctor—a Dr. Enock Joseph from South Florida Pain on Oakland Park Boulevard. Tina filed complaints with the local police and with the Florida Department of Health, but she didn't expect much would come of it.

In July 2008, a week before Tina's son was to get out of rehab, the *Sun-Sentinel* ran a big story and photo about the South Florida Pain Clinic. The article filled Tina with energy and hope. She wasn't alone. Others were upset too. She began calling people named in the article, and, over the next year and a half, Tina Reed became a leading voice against the pill mills. She testified in front of the Broward grand jury investigating pill mills. She called in to Larry Golbom's radio show in Tampa, and Carmel Cafiero featured her on Channel 7. She talked to the White House's drug czar when he came to Broward to learn about the oxycodone trade.

Tina pushed state lawmakers to create a drug database that would prevent patients from doctor shopping. Thirty-two states had databases that tracked prescriptions for controlled substances, and six more states were launching databases soon. Some Florida lawmakers had been trying to create a prescription database since 2002, but pain-management advocates and doctor's groups had repeatedly blocked the legislation, raising concerns about privacy and funding. By 2009, Florida was the largest of the dwindling number of states that lacked a database, which meant that addicts and dealers could seek drugs from multiple doctors with relative ease. No one knew where the pills were going once they got to the pharmacist or doctor's office.

In early 2009, the idea finally began to gather steam, though opponents said it could be a threat to patient privacy. A group of top Florida House Republicans sent Governor Charlie Crist a letter saying they believed the database "would be susceptible to cyber terrorists and criminals who would use such information against the citizens of Florida." Nevertheless, Crist signed the legislation in June 2009, and the database was scheduled to be online within eighteen months.

A *Sun-Sentinel* reporter called Tina Reed to get her reaction.

"I'm thrilled," she said. "It may not be a perfect bill, but the fact is we have a database established that we can work on."

Privately, she wished someone would just swoop in and shut the pill mills down. Surely what the doctors were doing wasn't legal. There had to be some way to stop them.

There were two main ways to take down bad doctors.

One was to charge them with a crime. Like all states, Florida had numerous criminal laws on the books regarding the prescribing and selling and using of controlled substances. It was illegal for patients to doctor-shop—seek prescriptions for narcotics from multiple doctors within the same thirty-day period. It was illegal for patients to lie or deceive a doctor to get controlled substances. It was illegal to forge a signature on a prescription. And of course it was illegal for patients to sell their pills. Local cops spent most of their anti–pill mill efforts harvesting the low-hanging fruit—the doctor shoppers and pill sellers. Those cases were relatively easy to prove. You could catch patients in the act of selling pills, or catch them with a short pill count, or catch them carrying pills without a prescription. It wasn't as easy as busting someone with a categorically illegal substance like cocaine or heroin, but it could be done.

Going after the doctors was tougher. It typically took more time and money and expertise and luck to prove that a doctor had knowingly supplied pills to drug seekers. By state law, it was illegal for a doctor to fraudulently assist a patient in obtaining a controlled substance, or employ a "trick or scheme" to assist a patient in obtaining a controlled substance. It was illegal to knowingly write a scrip for a person who didn't exist. It was illegal to write scrips for no medical necessity.

But what was a medical necessity? On that point, state law was vague: *(A) physician may prescribe or administer any controlled substance . . . for the treatment of intractable pain, provided the physician does so in accordance with that level of care, skill, and treatment recognized by a reasonably prudent physician under similar conditions and circumstances.*

The problem was, it was hard to determine what was going on behind the closed door of a doctor's office, especially if the doctor took a few basic precautions, such as requiring some diagnostic tests (MRIs and drug screens) and maintaining some paperwork.

Only the patients knew for sure whether they were in pain, and pill seekers didn't complain to the cops about doctors who wrote too big.

Despite these challenges, plenty of doctors had been convicted over the years. On its website, the DEA maintains a list of nearly 250 doctors the agency had helped investigate between 2003 and 2009. The charges ranged from distribution of a controlled substance outside the scope of professional practice to conspiracy to launder money. These doctors usually displayed risky behavior. Some had drug problems of their own. Some traded prescriptions for sex. After the investigations, almost all lost their DEA registration that allowed them to prescribe controlled substances, and many also lost their state medical licenses. Their penalties ranged from probation to life sentences.

When investigators turned up dead patients, state or federal prosecutors often threatened to file homicide charges, from first-degree murder to distribution of controlled substances resulting in death. But those cases were tough to win. It was hard to convince a jury that even an egregiously bad doctor should be held responsible for a patient's death when the patient had violated the instructions on the pill bottle. Juries might convict a doctor of other charges, but the defense could usually make a strong case that the death was the drug-seeking patient's own fault.

Pain management advocates protested that such cases were making legitimate doctors afraid to prescribe painkillers. They championed the case of Dr. Frank Fisher, a graduate of Harvard Medical School who opened a pain practice in Northern California. Fisher, a top prescriber of OxyContin, was charged with murder after several patients died. As it turned out, one of the victims had died in a car crash and another had stolen the drugs from one of Fisher's patients. The case fell apart and, four years after

Fisher's arrest in 1999, a state judge dismissed all charges against him. Pain management advocates rallied behind Fisher's case, and the doctor's story was told in sympathetic pieces in the *New York Times* and *Reason* magazine. Pain management advocates said there was a hidden epidemic of pain patients committing suicide after their doctors went to prison. Fisher said one of his patients had driven her car in front of a train.

Nevertheless, by 2009, at least eleven US doctors had been convicted on various charges related to the death of patients. One precedent-setting case involved a Florida Panhandle doctor named James Graves. Four patients died after taking OxyContin he had prescribed, all after either crushing and snorting the pills or dissolving and injecting them. The jury heard evidence that Graves ignored pharmacists and family members of drug-seeking patients who pleaded with him to cut back on his prescriptions. In 2002, Graves was convicted of manslaughter and sentenced to more than sixty years in prison.

But Graves's case was unusual. More typically, prosecutors used overdose deaths as leverage, eventually discarding them in exchange for a guilty plea to a lesser charge.

The other way to stop pill mill doctors was to suspend or terminate their licenses through the Florida Department of Health.

The health department enforced the Florida Administrative Code, which spelled out how doctors should prescribe opioids. The code said doctors should conduct a complete medical history and physical examination, documenting the nature and intensity of the pain and the patient's history of substance abuse. Doctors should write treatment plans and adjust drug therapy according to individual medical needs of the patient. Doctors should tell patients that the drugs are highly addictive. Doctors should periodically review patients' courses of treatment. Doctors should refer the patient to specialists, if appropriate. Doctors should keep thorough medical records.

In other words, doctors who prescribed addictive narcotics should diligently and continuously assess the effects of the drugs on the patients, tweaking the treatments as needed and seeking alternative solutions whenever possible. Mechanically stamping out prescription after prescription for high doses of oxycodone wasn't practicing medicine.

Investigations were usually triggered by complaints, typically from distraught relatives of pill seekers. Compared to many criminal defendants, doctors often had the money to fight or stall cases against them. The Board of Medicine—a panel of physicians that could discipline or suspend medical licenses—was designed to deal with the occasional bad doctor, not a slew of them.

Reporters at the *St. Petersburg Times* reviewed almost two hundred cases of doctors accused by the health department of inappropriately prescribing pain medications. Ninety-nine overdose deaths were linked to the accused doctors. More than a fourth of the doctors who had been disciplined still possessed clear and active licenses, the newspaper discovered, even some who had spent time in prison. Sixty-two doctors had lost their licenses, and usually they had relinquished them voluntarily in exchange for not having to face further board action.

Cases tended to plod through the system, taking eighteen months on average. Larry Golbom, the Clearwater pharmacist/radio host, discovered just how slow the system could be when he complained to the health department about the doctor who'd prescribed drugs that ended up in his son's hands. That case took twenty-seven months and might have gone longer if the doctor had not settled, paying a $12,500 fine and doing some community service. That doctor kept his medical license.

At that time, in 2006, such doctors were still rare. But two years later, a wealthy young felon met a steroid-dealing physician, and through trial and error, created a template for a new industry.

Chris George's personal history and characteristics made him perfectly suited to conquer the oxycodone game. He was capable of straddling two worlds. He looked plausible in a business suit, was good at making calls about zoning bylaws and small-business loans. But he also had none of the straight businessman's qualms about breaking the law when necessary. He possessed both the lubricating influence of money and the reckless aggression of youth. He was an entrepreneur who had few misgivings about selling a deadly product.

Chris George had stumbled into the business, skeptical at first that it would prove lucrative, but over time he learned to exploit three loopholes in Florida law and regulations. The first was the state's lack of a prescription database. Pill seekers and their doctors found it easy to operate in Florida because cops and pharmacists had no way to track the flow of prescription narcotics. Meanwhile, Kentucky and other Appalachian states had developed databases and cracked down on their own pill mills. Drug-running clans began trekking to Florida for pills.

The second loophole: Florida didn't license pain clinics or their owners. The state issued licenses to electrolysis clinics, massage establishments, and optician offices, but anybody who could register a business with the Florida Secretary of State office could own a pain clinic, meaning, basically, anybody. Including Kent A. Murry, a convicted marijuana smuggler who opened Delray Pain Management in February 2009. And Anthony V. Laterza, who opened North Palm Pain Management not long after finishing a five-year stint in federal prison on drug charges. Both clinics modeled their business practices after the George clinics, which had been in operation for a year by that time.

Even if the state possessed the resources to crack down on a thousand new self-proclaimed pain doctors, the clinic owners themselves were largely untouchable, as long as they weren't doctors. Nobody had considered the question: What if a bunch of quick-buck artists and con men and felons decided to hire doctors and open their own pain clinics?

Chris George had discovered the implications of this second loophole early, when Dr. Overstreet died in Panama three weeks after they'd opened South Florida Pain. Yes, sure, he needed a doctor, but any doctor would do. Chris George himself was the hub of the business. This concept was reinforced when Dr. Gittens quit the clinic and again when Dr.

Joseph surrendered his DEA registration.* Dr. Joseph lost his livelihood; Chris George hired *more* doctors, expanding American Pain's full-time physician staff to five.

And doctors who needed work were plentiful in Florida, especially after the stock market crashed in 2008, leaving thousands of retired physicians looking for ways to make some extra money. Some small percentage of them began writing oxy scrips, along with young doctors who needed to pay off crippling student loans and MDs from Caribbean medical schools who couldn't find jobs or earn board certification. And some doctors who simply wanted an easy job and easy money.

The third loophole that led to the oxycodone rush was that Florida law allowed doctors to sell narcotics themselves, no pharmacist needed. Pain clinics that charged for appointments *and* drugs could make a lot of money, and the one-stop shopping concept lured drug-seeking patients who didn't want to pay for prescriptions that might be hard to get filled. Some states allowed this setup; others did not. Some states banned doctors from charging dispensing fees for the drugs. By the height of the state's pill mill rush, Florida doctors were purchasing nine times more oxycodone than doctors in other states. That's nine times more than the other forty-nine states *combined.* In one six-month period, according to DEA records, Florida doctors bought 41.2 million doses while every other physician in the country collectively purchased 4.8 million doses.

Ohio was the second-ranked state in this category of physician purchasers. Its doctors bought about a million doses of oxycodone in 2009. The same year, through his doctors, Chris George bought more than twice as much oxy as every single doctor in Ohio. Four of American Pain's full-time doctors ranked among the top nine physician purchasers of oxycodone in the country.

---

* Dr. Joseph eventually lost his state medical license also. The state said he could potentially recover his license if he paid $15,000 in fines and costs, performed one hundred hours of community service, took some classes, and presented a one-hour seminar on "Falling Prey to Being Employed by Pill Mills." Dr. Joseph did none of the above and let his license lapse permanently.

When Jennifer Turner saw those numbers, she knew she'd found her target.

In the early going, the federal task force had set its sights on ten of the biggest new pain clinics in South Florida. But the DEA numbers made it clear that Florida's oxycodone racket was dominated by a single entity: American Pain. Other agents agreed with Turner that bringing down the biggest, boldest pill mill of them all would be a statement that might do more than any law to deter shady operators from the pain clinic business.

Which is why the task force wanted to take down the entire operation, including Chris George, his staff, doctors and major sponsors, as well as any affiliated pharmacies and key drug wholesalers. Simply arresting doctors or taking their licenses wouldn't erase the problem. Chris George had shown that he would just hire more.

But it was hard enough to build cases against doctors. To take the next step and federally prosecute Chris George and his entire organization would require the use of a tool originally devised as a way to bring down Mafia organizations. RICO—the Racketeer Influenced Corrupt Organizations Act—could allow the government to bring Chris George to trial on the grounds that he operated and managed a criminal enterprise. Chris George's operation had begun with a couple of employees in a single clinic in a shabby bungalow on Oakland Park Boulevard, but it had metastasized to include multiple clinics, pharmacies, dozens of employees, tens of thousands of patients. Throw in his twin brother's two clinics and other illicit activities and you had a sprawling, potentially criminal, organization. Chris George didn't write the prescriptions for controlled substances without a legitimate medical purpose, but he directed the organization that did.

To make its case, the task force needed evidence that Chris George was running the show, and the best evidence would be recordings of his day-to-day phone calls.

To convince a judge to let them wiretap Chris George's cell phone, the task force had to gather evidence of criminal activity. But not so much evidence that the judge would deem a wiretap an unwarranted invasion of privacy. Walking this line wasn't too difficult: 1,891 federal and state wiretap authorizations had been requested in 2008, and 1,891 had been granted. Nevertheless, to avoid having the recordings thrown out in court, the task force had to demonstrate that it had attempted normal investigative techniques, such as surveillance, interrogating participants, and infiltration by undercover agents and informants.

So Turner stationed a surveillance vehicle in the American Pain parking lot. The vehicle contained video cameras, microphones, recording devices, and a Hollywood Police Department detective who knew how to use the equipment. The detective shot video of cars with out-of-state license plates and a trio getting out of one car, one man handing cash to the other two before going inside. The black-tinted windows of the vehicle eventually caught the eye of a security guard, who called Chris George and Derik Nolan to the parking lot to take a look. The detective sat still as George and Nolan tried the doors, speculated about whether it was a news vehicle, and talked about trying to tip it over. Eventually they left.

The task force also began cultivating confidential sources. One early break came when a man was arrested in December 2008 for carrying a concealed weapon. The defendant had a long arrest record and was facing serious time. He told the FBI he could give them information about American Pain. He told them that Chris and Jeff George and Derik Nolan had accused him of stealing hundreds of thousands of dollars from Chris. They'd assaulted and handcuffed him at Jeff's house, and Jeff had fired a handgun next to his head before they let him go. Later, Chris George had given him $10,000 to keep quiet. The story had little to do with American Pain, but Turner was interested. Kidnapping was a predicate crime in RICO cases.

Another break came when Turner talked to Dr. Eddie Sollie, who'd worked at South Florida Pain for a few months in Fall 2008. Sollie said the clinic was a pill mill, that maybe 80 percent of its patients were addicts. The doctor said two of the physicians saw fifty to sixty patients a day, more than twice as many as he believed a doctor could legitimately treat in that amount of time. The doctors rushed through diagnostic paperwork, and the staff didn't care if people were faking their urinalysis tests. Sollie said he'd brought up his concerns to Chris George, who'd dismissed them. Sollie had quit, and now he and George were suing each other. The Sollie interview was Turner's first glimpse inside the operation of American Pain.

Turner wanted more informants. Lucky for her, thousands of American Pain patients were selling pills, and some percentage of them inevitably got busted. Turner's task force eventually interviewed a number of these offenders about what they'd seen inside the clinic. A Boston drug trafficker was arrested with three thousand oxycodone pills from American Pain hidden in his jockstrap. The man told investigators he'd seen Dr. Beau Boshers, who hadn't physically examined him but had made him touch his toes. A Kentucky woman facing drug charges agreed to visit American Pain and report back to the DEA. She saw Dr. Michael Aruta, who instructed her to fill her prescription at a Florida pharmacy, not out of state. A Florida man sold 399 oxycodone pills to an undercover deputy sheriff in the parking lot of a Royal Palm Beach shopping center. Later, he told federal agents that Derik Nolan had sold him the pills. If true, this was excellent evidence for an eventual RICO case—outright drug dealing, mixed in with the more ambiguous illegitimate prescribing. Each of these tidbits was added to the growing pile of circumstantial evidence that would go into the wiretap application. Chris George was not a criminal mastermind, Turner decided, but he did seem to be savvy enough to insulate himself from most of the lawbreaking going on around him.

Brick by brick, the task force built the foundation of evidence needed to get a wiretap authorized. Despite the public furor over pill mills, the FBI investigation moved at its usual methodical pace. Unlike local police, who place a priority on making arrests, the bureau wants to build cases that will withstand the rigors of federal court and actually land targets in prison.

If the feds were going to convict the whole group on racketeering, Turner knew they needed to prove that Chris George was the kingpin, that he was in charge and knew what was going on. They needed to make connections between his various operations and actually see him running the day-to-day business. They needed to go inside the clinic.

Detective Sergio Lopez had been doing undercover work for the police department in Hollywood, Florida, for eight years when an FBI agent called in 2009 and asked him to infiltrate a Boca Raton pain clinic. Meaning, go in and ask for a doctor's appointment. Not your typical street-corner buy-and-bust.

Lopez, a lean, smiley man with merry black eyes and a Hispanic accent, pulled into the crowded American Pain parking lot on a Wednesday in late July. He was wearing audio recording equipment. Inside the clinic, he was amazed to see more than one hundred patients in the waiting room. All the chairs were full, and overflow patients were standing along two walls.

As soon as he walked in, two men approached him. They wore black T-shirts that bore the word Staff. Lopez said he hadn't been there before, and they guided him to the new patient window. Lopez waited in line, studying the room. Signs on the walls instructed patients to turn off their cell phones, to pay attention to staff, to not use cameras.

When he got to the receptionist, Lopez handed over an MRI report and his undercover identification card. Both bore the name "Luis Lopez." The FBI had given Lopez the MRI report; he didn't know where it had come from, but it indicated that his cervical spine showed "no evidence of fracture or dislocation, no prevertebral soft tissue swelling, no degenerative features." In other words, nothing was wrong with "Luis's" spine. Of course, it was intentional. The investigators wanted to see if Lopez could get a prescription with almost no evidence of pain.

The receptionist didn't take the bait. He said he couldn't accept the MRI report. He didn't say why. He didn't look at the report, just handed it back and told Lopez that he would give him a prescription for an MRI. The MRI prescription itself would cost $50. Lopez handed over the cash, and the receptionist gave him a map to the MRI service and began filling out the prescription.

The receptionist said Lopez should pick either neck or back to be scanned because the MRI company charged separately for each. Lopez picked neck.

He left American Pain, rejoined the federal agents, and they headed for the operation, which was in the trailer behind Goldfingers Gentlemen's Club. A man was waiting outside with a clipboard, and he took down Lopez's name and told him to wait in his car to be called. The MRI facility didn't want a line of pain management patients standing around the strip club parking lot. Twenty other people were already waiting, sitting in their cars.

When Lopez's name was called, he went inside the trailer, where a woman took his $250 and said that she could "rush" the MRI results for an extra $200. Lopez paid the extra money. However, there were twenty people ahead of him, so it would be several hours before he could get scanned, she said. Lopez made an appointment to return to the trailer at 1:00 a.m.

When he returned for his middle-of-the-night appointment, the woman instructed him to take off his clothes and put them in a locker. He did so. He was reluctant to lie down on the MRI machine, because the pillow bore a head-shaped shadow of grime from all the people who'd lain on it.

He said: Are you going to change the pillowcase?

She said: Don't worry about it. You'll be done quickly.

Lopez lay down. The scan took forty-five minutes.

The next day, he went back to American Pain and handed the receptionist a computer disc with his MRI scan. The MRI report was already complete, and it reported a small disc protrusion at C5-C6, a mild bulging of the annulus, and mild scoliosis, all of which was news to Lopez, who had no neck pain. He collected a urine sample in a filthy bathroom with an overflowing toilet, filled out some forms, and was eventually called back to see Dr. Beau Boshers.

Boshers asked him to rank his pain level on a scale of one to ten, and Lopez said it was a three or four, intentionally shooting for a low-ish number to see what the doctor would do. Boshers asked him to turn his neck to the right and left, and Lopez flexed his neck vigorously, without hesitating or wincing.

Boshers said: Well, it looks like about an eight or so.

The doctor marked "8" on the document.

Boshers took his blood pressure but didn't otherwise touch Lopez. The doctor jotted swift notes on the pages, wrote prescriptions for 120 oxycodone 30-milligram pills, plus some 15-milligram pills and Xanax. Lopez filled the oxy prescriptions at American Pain, but the pharmacy was out of Xanax.

Lopez returned to American Pain every twenty-eight days for the next five months. He wore a baseball cap and glasses and saw Boshers each time. He recorded each visit and noticed that his appointment times shrank and prescription amounts grew. The first time he was in Boshers's office for thirteen minutes and received 120 30-milligram oxycodone pills. In August, he spent seven minutes in Boshers's office and left with 150 pills. September, five minutes and 180 pills. October, four minutes and 180 pills. November, three minutes and 180 pills. Lopez never asked to be upped.

In September, he covertly videoed Derik Nolan shouting instructions at the patients in the waiting room, telling them to fill their prescriptions in state.

"Florida only!" Nolan bellowed, pacing back and forth in front of the crowd. "If I get a call from outside Florida for verification of a script, you will be discharged, and I'll let you come back next time, and I'm gonna take your money. And then I'm gonna kick you out."

Nolan had a certain presence and seemed to enjoy being the center of attention, the waiting room silent except for his authoritative voice.

"Just follow all the rules, and everything will be fine," he said. "Nobody around here likes you. *I* like you. But nobody else does."

He told the patients to drive carefully and make sure they knew their doctor's name.

"When a cop says, 'Hey, what's your doctor's name?' and he's holding your prescription bottle and you don't know it, you're going to jail."

At one point, Nolan gave the patients a brazen tip.

"Do not be shooting up or snorting in the parking lot!"

Nolan left the waiting room, the babel rising in his wake.

Surreptitiously, Lopez pointed the camera at his own face for a moment, eyebrows raised in jovial astonishment.

"Wow!" he said.

The task force sent a second undercover cop into American Pain. That operation was cut short when the undercover told Dr. Boshers that he drank "a couple beers a day." Boshers didn't like that. American Pain patients usually knew better than to acknowledge that they drank alcohol. The doctor called Chris George to his office, introducing him as "one of our experts," offering the investigators a rare interaction with their primary target.

But Chris George didn't say much at first, as Beau Boshers explained his concerns.

BOSHERS: The thing that bothers me about it though is he drinks every day and you gotta be real real cautious with prescribing these medications to people that drink alcohol cause you can end up you know getting respiratory distress you can go into cardiac arrest, <unintelligible> you can die.

UNDERCOVER: I mean I <unintelligible> I average two beers a day and Friday night I go out and have you know a six-pack with friends. You know I may not drink Monday, Tuesday, Wednesday, Thursday.

BOSHERS: Right.

UNDERCOVER: It's not like . . .

BOSHERS: But that one day that you take a roxicodone and you drink six beers and you die your parents are not gonna blame you they're gonna blame me.

UNDERCOVER: No I know but I'm, I mean, I'm not like a low-life punk, I mean I'm responsible, and . . .

BOSHERS: You don't have to be.

UNDERCOVER: No I know.

BOSHERS: Michael Jackson died from an overdose too, you don't have to be, you can be anybody, anybody can die.

The undercover protested, saying he would stop drinking.

BOSHERS: The thing is that my patients that I treat here they don't drink. You're the only patient that I've talked to that said that. Most of them they don't drink or they drink occasionally, they don't drink.

UNDERCOVER: None of those people (laughs) come on.

BOSHERS: They say they don't drink.

UNDERCOVER: Well I'm telling you I'm not gonna drink if you tell me it's gonna hurt me I mean I'm not, listen Doc I'm not here to kill myself.

Boshers was apologetically firm: He wouldn't write the scrip. Chris George weighed in, saying that he'd give the patient his money back and refer him to a different clinic.

UNDERCOVER: Well are they gonna do the same thing?

GEORGE: (Laughs) No.

Chris George and the undercover left Boshers's office and George gave him directions to Executive Pain and told him to ask for Dianna. She'd get him in front of a doctor within twenty minutes, he said.

GEORGE: If he <unintelligible> doesn't feel comfortable, there's nothing I can do about that.

The undercover left the clinic without drugs, but Turner knew the operation had been a major success. The recording contained evidence that Chris George was in charge of Executive Pain, as well as American Pain. It had also revealed how complex the relationships were at American Pain.

Boshers had seemed apologetic, but he still wouldn't write the scrip, if only because the man had violated an unwritten rule by saying he drank alcohol. And Chris George said he couldn't pressure the doctor into writing it. On the other hand, Boshers had agreed to the boss's plan to send the patient to another clinic that was clearly under Chris George's control. And the doctor was OK with giving the man his money back, even though he'd seen a doctor, which implied that the drugs, not the medical evaluation, were what was being purchased. The recording contained good evidence that Chris George was running an illegal operation.

Everyone on the undercover operation understood the significance of the brush with Chris George. When the undercover rejoined Turner and the other agents after the operation, a cheer erupted.

A year after Turner's watercooler introduction to the pill mill problem, her task force prepared to submit its wiretap application to a federal judge. Pill mills were a front-page problem by now, and Turner's task force meetings were crowded with supervisors from the FBI and DEA. Fifty local police officers had been deputized to work on the federal investigation.

Mike Burt, the DEA special agent, wrote an affidavit that would form the foundation of the wiretap application. It included evidence obtained from the undercover operations, from the various patients who'd been arrested selling pills, from the kidnapping of the friend who the Georges suspected had stolen Chris's money, from surveillance video, and from the doctor who'd formerly worked there. It also included information about Stacy Mason's death in Kentucky.

As expected, on November 6, 2009, the judge granted permission to listen in on Chris George's cell phone calls. They flipped the switch immediately.

The wire room was located in DEA offices, in a big room with a number of computer terminals recording multiple wires simultaneously. In the early days of the Chris George wiretap, the room was crowded. It was exciting to finally hear their target's voice. No one wanted to leave, least of all Jennifer Turner.

Turner felt a certain reverence for the wire. It had taken a year of work to obtain, and it was the greatest privacy intrusion she was allowed by law, except for a search warrant. She'd been thinking about Chris George for months, and now she would hear him conducting his life and work. It was a chance not only to gather evidence but also to learn how his mind worked.

The listeners wore headphones, and the computer screen signaled when there were incoming or outgoing calls or texts. You could hear the phone ringing. They had surveillance vehicles following George much of the time. When George talked with his lawyer, the agents flagged the phone number and marked the call as privileged.

Some of the recordings made the targets seem like frat-boy pranksters, as when Chris George and Derik Nolan discussed what to do about a suspicious vehicle in their parking lot on November 9.

NOLAN: Should I put a mask on and go cover it up or something? (Laughs)

GEORGE: No.

NOLAN: Should I change my clothes and put a mask on and go slash the tires?

GEORGE: The best thing to do is have a slingshot far away and shoot out some of the windows.

NOLAN: You want me to do that? I can go get one. I got a slingshot at my house.

The wiretap didn't yield a smoking-gun statement right away. If George was selling drugs out the back door, or dealing directly with sponsors, or ordering the doctors to prescribe narcotics without a legitimate medical purpose, he was careful enough not to do it on the phone. Turner realized the recordings would have to be mined carefully for more circumstantial evidence that Chris George was in charge and knew what was going on. As when he told the manager of one of his pharmacies that he should "always lie" to inspectors about the percentage of controlled substances the pharmacy distributed. Or when he and Derik Nolan discussed an unpleasant staffer.

NOLAN: I will take care of it. He's just gotta be a little nicer to the patients, right?

GEORGE: Yeah, he never says "hi" or "bye" to anybody. He doesn't welcome them . . .

NOLAN: "Hi . . . Welcome to the dope hole. Can I get you a drink?"

As the days passed in the wire room, the timbre of Chris George's voice began to grate on Turner. He was a mumbler. She speculated that his lack of enunciation was somehow due to heavy steroid usage, but whatever the cause, it was annoying. And many of the conversations were mind-numbingly irrelevant, George musing about the latest thing he was thinking about purchasing: model airplanes, a custom-made swamp buggy, tickets to a fight or game. And breast implants for his girlfriend. Not Dianna, who'd already received hers. His *other* girlfriend. On November 13, after the breast augmentation procedure, Chris talked to that girlfriend's mother.

WOMAN: She's like a zombie . . .

GEORGE: Hey, you know what? She's like one of the patients now.

WOMAN: And why does she take all those pills? She wants to be a drug addict? What happens if she likes that garbage?

GEORGE: I won't let her, don't worry.

Two days later, another conversation between George and his own mother, Denice Haggerty, particularly infuriated Turner. They discussed an article in the *Palm Beach Post* about a patient at one of Jeff's clinics who'd died of an overdose. The article mentioned Jeff's clinics and also

American Pain. George and his mother chuckled about what Jeff had said to the reporter, which was characteristically reckless, including: "Unfortunately, the clinic and the doctor can't control a patient if they go home and do something stupid." And: "I bought my Lamborghini four years ago. If I wreck it, am I going to hold the Lamborghini dealership responsible?" The story also noted that Haggerty was the operator of Executive Pain, but Haggerty didn't sound worried.

HAGGERTY: Oh well. (laughs) I don't think it's going to affect my life very much.

Turner disagreed.

8

The big block-like building was an awesome sight, gleaming white against the Florida sky. At three stories, it was taller and wider than anything else on its stretch of Dixie Highway, and its windowless walls gave it an impregnable, fortress-like look. Chris George and Derik Nolan wanted it bad. They wanted out of shopping plazas and industrial parks, away from restaurants and angry neighbors. They wanted a stronghold.

Chris and Derik checked out the new building the day after the *Palm Beach Post* ran its November 20, 2009, story about the train wreck that killed two patients. It was time to get out of Broward County, which was overrun with clinics. The huge Boca Raton office, where they'd been for almost a year, was feeling cramped. They topped five hundred patients on many days. As had happened everywhere else, the police were stepping up their harassment of patients, and the complaints from neighbors were getting more strident. Chris wanted to find a place with enough of a buffer that the patients wouldn't be constantly disrupting other businesses and residents. He also thought about changing the name again, moving away from calling it a pain clinic. He talked to the property manager for the Boca location about whether he should rename the clinic, using words like "family-oriented" or "general practice." Something innocuous, bland, like "Parkridge Medical Center." Chris had tabled the name change, but he kept looking for a new location.

The bank building was in Lake Worth, just up the road from Boca Raton. The area was populated by antiques shops and high-end home furnishings outlets frequented by the society types just north on Palm Beach. The neighborhood was perfect, all "Mexicans and little houses," as Chris told a friend on the phone. In other words, people who didn't have much pull with the police and wouldn't complain about the clinic.

They talked an employee into letting them inside to look around. The first floor had space for everything they needed to service five-hundred-plus patients a day. There was a second floor for administrative offices and a gangway where security could keep an eye on the waiting room, and an open third floor. Chris and Derik talked it over and decided they would turn the third-floor space into the mother of all man caves. A sweeping wet bar, a giant projection system, and, Derik's big idea, a mixed-martial-arts octagon cage where they could stage private fights. They called the third floor the Fantasy Factory.

But before they could implement any of their plans, the owner had to be convinced to lease the building to Chris, a twenty-nine-year-old felon, for the purposes of opening a pain clinic, at a time when pain clinics were all over the news. Chris researched the owner, who lived in a waterfront estate on Palm Beach.

Chris called the real estate agent, who seemed perplexed by his youthful voice.

"How many square feet are you looking for?" she asked.

"It'll be for the whole thing," Chris said.

She sounded skeptical. Surely he was looking to lease only the small outbuilding where drive-through customers were handled, she suggested. What did he need all that space for?

"Uh . . . medical," Chris said.

"What kind of medical?"

"A doctor's office."

"OK," she said. "Do you have a clinic?"

Chris didn't want to scare her off with the word "clinic."

"Well, I mean . . . just a doctor's office," he said.

He haggled with the agent, doing some quick math out loud regarding square footage and lease prices. He showed her he'd done his homework by saying he knew that the owner owed $2 million on the building. She brought the conversation back to Chris's plans for the property. Chris said he had five doctors, twenty-five employees total, and served four hundred patients a day.

"What kind of practice?" she asked again.

"Oh, we do rehabilitation. We do, um, detox. We do pain management." Chris didn't want to end on those last two words, so he began making up stuff. "We do internal medicine. Um, I have all kinds of doctors. We do laser hair removal."

They talked details, but the agent wondered aloud what kind of doctor's office saw four hundred patients a day.

"That's a pretty big business," she said.

Chris changed the subject, offering her $280,000 a year for the building. She said she'd take it to the owner, and asked for the business's name.

"Uh. American Pain," Chris said, hoping she wouldn't recognize it.

The agent didn't pause.

"OK, and you've been in business longer than two years, correct? How old are you? You sound young."

"I'm twenty-nine," Chris said.

"OK, that's good," the agent said. "An aggressive twenty-nine-year-old. I'm impressed."

"My tax return from last year, I made over a million dollars," Chris said.

This statement was both true and misleading. *This* year, Chris would owe about twice that amount just in federal income taxes. In total, his 2009 take-home would be closer to $9 million, more than the CEOs of Time Warner Cable, Target, and Pfizer.

When Chris mentioned his income, the agent perked up.

"That's wonderful," she said. "And are you a doctor yourself or are you just running the business?"

"No, I'm not a doctor," he said. "I hire doctors to work for me. I just started a few years ago and kept expanding."

"Wow!" she exclaimed.

And just like that, she was on board. Maybe she knew about American Pain and oxycodone, maybe she didn't. But she was no longer skeptical. She would take Chris's offer straight to the building's owner.

The owner met with Chris and Derik at the building. Derik and Chris dressed in expensive suits, covered up the tattoos, tried to speak like educated professionals. Derik could tell from the way the owner spoke and carried himself that he was somebody. He seemed to have reservations at first, said he'd read something about pain clinics. They explained the business to him, leaving out the fact that nearly all their patients were junkies.

The owner barely used the building. He stored paintings in it. They were scattered all over the interior, but the collection was soon going to museums in New York and London. Derik thought this was interesting, especially when the owner said he had one painting locked away in the bank vault that was worth more than $1 million. The owner gave Chris and Derik copies of a book he'd commissioned someone to write about this genre of painting. Derik dealt every day with scumbags who thought of him as a high-level drug dealer. This was a nice contrast. It was a coffee-table book, so Derik took it home and put it on his coffee table, though he never actually opened it.

The owner wanted to see the Boca Raton operation before signing off on the lease. He did a walk-through one day, toured the packed waiting room and the back offices. By that time, Derik and Chris had things running pretty smoothly. The owner seemed impressed and agreed to lease his building to American Pain.

It was a good feeling to have a connection to a businessman of this caliber. Derik believed it meant that he was able to do business with a more legitimate crowd, operate on both sides of the street. Proof that he'd become truly successful despite everything.

On the other hand, Derik knew that the building's owner probably didn't have too many people beating down his door to pay more than

$23,000 a month on a multi-year lease. And when Chris heard those terms, he hadn't blinked an eye.

At the same time Chris and Derik were cultivating the new building's owner, they were also fighting off other pain clinics.

Palm Beach Pain was a clinic run by some guys from North Miami who had several small operations. They had set up shop one mile north of American Pain, on the same side of Federal Highway. It was closer to I-95, which meant it was no doubt siphoning off some patients who were looking for American Pain. Even more provoking, Palm Beach Pain had hired a guy to stand in the middle of Federal Highway and wave a sign, diverting traffic to their clinic.

Derik had sent a staffer to scope out the clinic, but the Palm Beach Pain guys identified him as an American Pain employee and kicked him out. Next, Derik chased off a guy who was handing out Palm Beach Pain cards in the American Pain parking lot. Derik went to the clinic and threw a handful of the cards in the manager's face.

Derik said: Keep it up, and *you're* gonna need pain management.

Derik was proud of the line, thought it was witty, and repeated it to Chris on the phone later in the day. It must have made an impression on the Palm Beach Pain guy too, because he just sat there without saying anything, and then came running out to apologize as Derik was pulling out of his lot.

So Derik was *really* pissed when, a couple hours later, he caught another guy handing out Palm Beach Pain cards one block away from American Pain. Now it was on. Derik stationed an employee in the offending clinic's parking lot, handing out free visits to any patient who switched to American Pain. He called MRI companies and pressured them not to take Palm Beach Pain patients. When he heard about an American Pain patient who had been lured to Palm Beach Pain, Derik promptly called the cops and earnestly explained that he'd found a doctor shopper.

It didn't matter to Derik and Chris that Palm Beach Pain pulled in maybe a couple dozen patients a day, while American Pain was servicing hundreds. The guys from Palm Beach Pain were upstarts and needed to be crushed. If for no other reason than that's what the top dog does.

In late 2009, a patient came in and asked Derik when the new Jacksonville office would be open. Chris and Derik were looking at new locations up north, but it wasn't something that a patient would know about yet, so Derik said he didn't know what the guy was talking about.

The office in Jacksonville, the patient said. The one you called me about.

Derik chalked it up to junkie confusion, until another patient asked him about the Jacksonville office. And another. Everyone saying Derik had called them and said they were opening a new American Pain in Jacksonville.

Derik and Chris started looking into it. They put out word with the staff that they wanted to talk to any patient who mentioned anything about Jacksonville or getting a call from Derik. After quizzing a number of those patients, it turned out that someone posing as Derik had been calling them, telling them about a new branch of American Pain that would be opening in Jacksonville in the middle of December.

Unlike Palm Beach Pain, this was a serious threat. By car, Jacksonville was four hours closer to Kentucky than Boca Raton. If patients believed they could get American Pain service and quantities that much closer to home, they'd go there in droves. Chris and Derik wondered how the new clinic had gotten their patients' names and phone numbers.

They looked up the clinic's state corporate records, and that's when things clicked. They found a connection between the Jacksonville clinic and the MRI service Derik had made a deal with way back at the Oakland Park Boulevard location, the company that had promised (and delivered) twenty-four-hour turnaround on MRI reports. American Pain had made the MRI company a lot of money, and now they believed the company was stabbing them in the back by partnering with a new competing clinic.

Derik got the impostor clinic's phone number from a patient and called it. Someone picked up.

Derik: Can I speak to Derik?

The guy: Hold on.

Pause.

Another guy: Yeah, this is Derik.

Derik: Derik Nolan?

"Derik": Uh huh.

Derik, enjoying himself: That's funny, because I'm Derik Nolan too, asshole.

He caught the guy by surprise for a second, but the guy recovered, barked back at Derik, saying they were going to take the top spot away from American Pain. Guy had a lot of balls.

Derik told Chris: Let me take care of Jacksonville.

The place was set to open December 14. Derik told Chris to give him $5,000, and he'd make sure it didn't stay open long. He'd burn the place down. Literally.

Chris overruled Derik. Go up to Jacksonville, he told Derik, but don't destroy the place. Just check it out, see if someone from the MRI company is there, see how many patients they have. If the new clinic really stole American Pain's patient list, Chris would have grounds to sue.

Derik's first mistake was taking his little brother with him to Jacksonville. His brother was nineteen, a good kid, not someone who should have been involved in this kind of thing. They'd driven up to case the clinic early one morning in mid-December, 2009. The place was called Jacksonville Pain and Urgent Care. It was in a decent location, a thoroughfare one mile off Interstate 10, though Derik knew from experience that the parking lot was too small and the neighbors in the oak-lined residential streets behind the red-brick building would probably cause trouble once the zombies descended.

Derik saw a guy from the MRI company standing outside the clinic, bold as he could be. Derik called Chris and told him about it. Chris said he was coming up to Jacksonville. He wanted to talk to the owner, give him one last chance to cut a deal before he filed a lawsuit. Derik knew Chris's temper, knew a face-to-face was a mistake.

Derik wanted to get a peek inside the place but knew they might recognize him. So at 11:00 a.m., Derik's brother filled out some new-patient paperwork and paid $250. But when his brother returned a couple hours later for his doctor's appointment, the owner, a guy named Zachary Rose, told him he was too young to be a patient. Derik's brother went back outside, got $400 from Derik, came back in and offered it to Rose. But Rose was firm. His doctor wouldn't see a nineteen-year-old.

Derik met Chris and his buddy, and they headed into the clinic. Derik was last inside the door, and they were ready for them. A guy stepped inside right after Derik, and he had a gun. Derik told the guy that if he pointed it at him, he'd better be ready to empty the clip. Rose came out, and Chris was yelling and cursing, saying he wanted 50 percent of the clinic's take or he'd burn the place down. Rose refused, and *another* one of his guys pulled a gun on Chris.

Then the cops showed up. They separated everyone for questioning and searched the American Pain crew's cars.

The cops seemed to know a lot about American Pain, kept dropping hints that made Derik wonder why they knew so much about a pain clinic located three hundred miles away, like when they called Chris the $40 million man, which was a pretty accurate accounting of American Pain's revenue. They also knew Derik's name and what kind of car he drove, even before Derik told them. They asked him whether he'd gone to college, and when he said he'd taken only a few college courses, they made a big deal about that, saying that he couldn't possibly be running a legitimate doctor's office with so little college. They said he was nothing but a thug, driving three hundred miles to extort local businesses.

They arrested the four guys from American Pain on charges of extortion by verbal threat and everybody spent the night in jail. The next morning, a squad of defense lawyers appeared in the courtroom. Derik was surprised to hear that Jeff George, who hadn't been speaking to Chris for a year and a half, had called his attorney, who'd sent the legal reinforcements. High-powered attorneys showing up for an initial court appearance was unusual, something usually reserved for mobsters or the sons of tycoons, and it reinforced Derik's feeling that he'd be able to buy himself out of this mess too.

Dianna drove up, bringing a change of clothing for everybody. She bailed them out and got everybody rooms at the Hyatt Regency on the riverfront. They all went out that night for a nice steak dinner.

The arrests happened on a Monday. The following Saturday, December 19, 2009, everyone went to the clinic's Christmas party at the Breakers resort. Derik wore a $4,000 outfit: a two-toned black custom-tailored suit from Neiman Marcus, black shirt, black shoes—all black, except for the bloodred pocket square and silver skull-shaped cuff links with glittering crimson rubies set in the skull eyes. Underneath his pants, he wore an itchy black ankle monitor, courtesy of the Jacksonville Sheriff's Office. Chris had a matching ankle bracelet.

The Breakers was a 140-acre oceanfront resort in Palm Beach. It looked kind of like a mega-version of the Italianate-Floridian dream homes Derik and Chris had been building for Majestic Homes two years earlier: soaring tawny-hued towers, floodlit palm trees, ornate fountains, vaulted ceilings.

Ethan Baumhoff had arranged the party, and it was a more highbrow affair than Derik's strip-club holiday celebration the year before. If Chris had put *Derik* in charge of the party, he would have just chartered a yacht, hired a herd of hookers, and bought a pile of cocaine.

But Ethan was always trying to legitimize the clinic, with his dress code and policy manuals and "Casual Fridays." So he put his wife in charge of the party planning, and she hired a photographer, and everyone had their pictures taken in front of a snowflake backdrop. Like it was the prom or something, Derik thought. There was a disc jockey, but no one danced, except Derik. The party had a Vegas theme, and Ethan's wife had also hired a gaming company to set up blackjack and roulette tables, which could have been fun, but Derik lost interest when he found out you couldn't win real money. They gave everybody a stack of fake dollar bills to play with. Instead of George Washington's stern-mouthed mug, the bills bore a picture of a grinning Chris George.

They had decided to give employee awards at the Christmas party, including a Doctor of the Year award. The selection process didn't involve secret ballots or patient surveys or anything. Ethan had just told Derik about it one day, and they'd both snickered a bit as they considered the options. Politically, they couldn't go with the elder Dr. Dreszer or Dr. Aruta, since they hated each other, which more or less ruled out the younger Dreszer too. That left Dr. Boshers and Dr. Cadet, and the choice was obvious. Dr. Cadet was consistently nice to everyone, and no one felt threatened by her. She was the one they had new doctors shadow. Most importantly, she was the patient favorite, for her caring manner and enormous scrips.

So Ethan had ordered a small gold-bordered wooden plaque that read:

Recognizing
2009 Doctor of the Year
Dr. Cynthia Cadet
American Pain

Derik gave a cornball speech, thanking everybody for their hard work. Dr. Cadet seemed touched by the honor. Derik couldn't believe she was dumb enough to take the award seriously. But it was always hard to tell with Dr. Cadet. Did she believe she was helping people in pain? Or did she get that it was just a money-for-drugs operation? Sometimes, she seemed to understand that things weren't quite right at American Pain. Like when she asked Derik if she was going to get in trouble for her patient load, which was topping seventy a day. Or was she somewhere in the middle, justifying her actions, grasping at every nugget of favorable evidence, like the doctor-of-the-year plaque, to convince herself that she was still practicing medicine? Derik wasn't sure, and he wasn't going to question her about it. People were entitled to their delusions.

The ankle monitor Derik wore after his Jacksonville arrest was the size of a BlackBerry phone. It was strapped to his ankle, and he was always aware of its presence, which was maybe the point of the thing. It had to be charged like a cell phone, so he would plug it in at night before he went to bed. But he'd thrash around in his sleep, and it sometimes detached from the charger cord, and in the morning, the battery would be low. So then he'd take the charger cord to the clinic and charge it there, sitting at his desk, tethered to the wall outlet like a dog on a leash. Derik was told that his movements weren't actually being monitored, that the device was designed to alert the authorities only if he got close to the pain clinic in Jacksonville. Which was fine. Derik had no desire to go back there.

After Jacksonville, Chris and Derik worried that the police had put listening devices in their cars while they were impounded. They remembered how the police there seemed to know a lot about them, and they wondered if Pedro Martinez had been telling the truth back in October and there really was a big DEA chart somewhere with all of their names and pictures on it. They worried their phones were tapped and their offices bugged. One day, Derik came into the office to find the private investigator who had tried to convince Chris to let him launder his money. Ethan was with him. They had a machine and they said they were using it to sweep the office for bugs. Ethan was enamored with the guy, maybe because he used to be a DEA agent and then had gone bad, just like ex-cop Ethan had done. When the guy left, Chris told Ethan to stop hanging around with him.

Derik's lawyer on the Jacksonville case was making him nervous. The lawyer said if the feds came after them, they would go after the weakest people first, probably the people who were most connected to society and felt they had the most to lose. Derik figured this meant Ethan and the doctors. The feds would scare the weak ones with the threat of long sentences, hard time, hammer them until they agreed to testify. The lawyer said it would be a racketeering case, because that would be the only way to hold Chris and Derik responsible for what the doctors were or were not doing behind their office doors. RICO was probably their best option, unless they could get Chris and Derik on some other charges, like selling pills out the back door, or the Jacksonville extortion charges.

Derik and Chris grew even closer after Jacksonville. They made a pact not to turn on each other. They'd sat in jail together, were both looking at up to fifteen years of prison time on the extortion charges, and those things strengthened their connection. They each knew plenty of damaging evidence about the other one, and they trusted each other not to rat.

After the Jacksonville arrest, Derik once and for all gave up any plans to open his own clinic with Dr. Cadet. He and Chris *couldn't* split up now. They had identical black ankle bracelet monitors strapped to their legs. What could bond two guys more than that?

Their other rival clinic, Palm Beach Pain, wouldn't give up. Derik kept finding flyers and cards from the nearby clinic on tables in American Pain's waiting room.

Finally, Derik summoned his two jumbo-sized Samoan security guards and Chris, and the four of them drove up to Palm Beach Pain. Maybe it was because the Jacksonville criminal charges were hanging over their heads, but the confrontation was all talk and no action. After a while, the Palm Beach Pain guys just called the cops, and the American Pain crew left.

The aggravation continued. The upstart clinic hired people to pose as American Pain patients, sit in the waiting room and talk to people, hand out cards for Palm Beach Pain.

The impostors would say: Look how crowded this place is. Don't wait here, go see this guy. He'll get you in right away.

Late one night that January, 2010, Jeff George called Derik. Jeff said he was bored.

Derik said: Want to go fuck up Palm Beach Pain?

Jeff picked up Derik, who brought along a slingshot and a bag of ball bearings. In the dark parking lot of Palm Beach Pain, they began blasting away at the plate-glass windows with the slingshot. The ball bearings punched holes in the glass until the windows started crashing down in huge jagged sheets. After destroying every window, Derik and Jeff shot up the copy machines. Finally, the slingshot broke, and they took off.

Palm Beach Pain was out of business for a week or so. But Chris couldn't let it go. He was obsessed. He hired a private investigator to put a GPS device on the clinic owners' cars. He'd get up early in the morning and look at the tracker on his computer, see where they'd been promoting the clinic the previous night. Then he and Derik would go there and steal any Palm Beach Pain signs and flyers. Once, they stuck all the clinic signs in front of a police station. None of it made much sense, but that was Chris. He couldn't let anyone else win, not even a little.

By the early months of 2010, as he and Chris prepared for the move to the big bank building on Dixie Highway, Derik was exhausted.

He was overseeing about twenty people, most of whom were funneling parts of their payoffs to him. For the most part, they did what he wanted because he was in charge of them. The hardest part of the job was working with the people who *didn't* directly report to him. And there were more and more of them as the network servicing American Pain patients grew: MRI and labwork companies, pharmacies, the other pain clinics. The largest portion of Derik's income came from kickbacks from MRI companies, so staying on top of that flow of patients was a priority. Chris and Jeff were starting to work together, after their reconciliation in the aftermath of Jacksonville. While a good thing, it meant that Derik had to keep the pain train running between four clinics, working with Executive Pain as well as Jeff's two clinics, East Coast Pain and Hallandale Pain.

Patients who were kicked out of American Pain got a second shot at Executive, maybe a third at East Coast, and so on to Hallandale, and this process had to be coordinated. If things got too busy at American Pain, Derik would send the overflow to the other clinics. In addition to all of that, police departments and pharmacists were constantly calling American Pain, asking for paperwork on doctor shoppers. Derik was always running, trying to keep everyone happy.

The clinic was a beehive of suspicion, patients and employees buzzing with rumors and lies about who was wearing a wire, who'd been arrested, who was selling their pills on the street, who was opening their own clinic, who was stealing patients. Derik had to create and run a network of spies. He'd send a confederate to an MRI company and test its loyalties, try to bribe someone to release the medical records of American Pain patients to a different pain clinic. He'd hire guerrilla marketers to chase down patients leaving other clinics and give them free visits or medication if they switched to American Pain.

Derik was still living with his girlfriend, the pharmacy tech at American Pain. She needed him to take care of her, and she didn't ask a lot of questions, and that was enough. A family dinner with her and her little girl, a nice meal and conversation, or going to Fourth of July fireworks with his little makeshift family—sandwiched between the insanity of a workday at American Pain and a coked-up night at Solid Gold, these little breaks were a chance to pretend he was a normal person.

Derik had a plan to escape the soul-deadening grind. After they moved to the Dixie Highway building, he was going to ask Chris if he could become kind of a roving consultant to the entire empire, leapfrogging from one pharmacy or clinic to the next, making sure things were shipshape. He had to get out of the waiting room.

Derik knew patients were dying. Once, he'd asked Dr. Aruta about oxycodone. Was it easy to overdose on? Was it hard to get off? Derik recalled Aruta saying the detox was no big deal, that oxycodone was the safest painkiller out there. Derik figured Aruta didn't know what he was talking about, because he kept hearing about clinic patients overdosing. A medical examiner had called American Pain the previous summer, looking for records for one of Dr. Cadet's patients who'd died of an overdose. In November, there'd been the front-page story in the *Palm Beach Post* about the guy who'd overdosed earlier in the year on a prescription from Jeff's East Coast Pain Clinic. Then, five days after the Lamborghini story, two women from Tennessee died in a train crash, patients at Executive Pain, though Chris and Derik had never heard from the cops about that one. And in January came a malpractice suit against Jacobo Dreszer, filed by the relative of another patient who died after only one visit to American Pain.

Chris joked to a girlfriend: "First visit. He couldn't handle pain management."

Derik didn't sit around feeling sorry for the patients either. He wasn't holding a gun to their heads, forcing them to crush and snort monster quantities of oxycodone. They sought him out. It was their decision. Though sometimes he wondered if that was strictly true, like the time he saw the little boy grasping the pill bottle filled with candy, the kid wanting to be like his daddy. It made him sick. What chance did that boy have?

The guys kept a close eye on the news. There were stories almost every day about pill mills. Palm Beach County was considering prohibiting cash-only sales and requiring clinics to list the names of clinic owners and operators in state records. Florida lawmakers had proposed four separate bills, each containing different measures. One would require doctors to be in good standing to own or operate a pain clinic. Another would prohibit anyone convicted of a felony from owning or operating a clinic. The toughest bill was one that would prohibit doctors from dispensing more than seventy-two hours' worth of narcotics to a patient, which would cripple the entire Kentucky-to-Florida pipeline. Luckily for Chris and Derik, the Florida Medical Association and pain-management advocates were fighting the seventy-two-hour idea.

Chris and Derik believed they'd be able to operate in Florida for another year, maybe two, before new laws squeezed them out. So Chris was researching the laws in other states, especially Texas, Missouri, and Georgia. They also had staffers making lists of patients' hometowns every day to identify potential locations that already had a concentration of patients. If Florida ever cracked down, he wanted to be ready to move operations. So in February, Chris and Jeff opened a one-doctor clinic called Pain Express in Kennesaw, Georgia. The new clinic was in a suburban strip mall just off Interstate 75 north of Atlanta, nine hours closer to their customer base in Kentucky and Tennessee. Georgia's laws were about as lax as Florida's, and Chris believed the state was a potential gold mine. Georgia didn't license pain clinics either, and nobody was sure how many there were in the state, though the state Drug and Narcotics Agency believed the number to be in the single digits.

But mainly Chris concentrated on preparing American Pain's new home. The first floor of the bank building on Dixie Highway was wide open, so it needed a full build-out—doctor examination rooms, offices for Chris and Derik and Ethan, a large work area for the office staff, and a huge waiting room. Majestic Homes did the work. They built a DMV-like system of patient windows—two for new patients, four for follow-up patients, and one where patients would get their medicine. The staff area had desks and banks of file cabinets and twenty phone lines. They bought two hundred nice leather chairs for the waiting room, six flat-screen TVs, and vending machines. They built a service area so Delray Diagnostics could station someone there to arrange MRI appointments for patients on-site. The biggest problem was that there was only one bathroom on the first floor, but they decided to figure that out later.

Derik loved the second-floor catwalk that would allow him to keep an eye on the waiting room below without actually having to mingle with the zombies all the time. The second floor was connected to an outside porch area with a grill for barbecuing. You could climb up a ladder to the roof from there and survey Dixie Highway and the long flat inland landscape.

Derik put twenty-five plastic chairs outside so patients could catch a smoke. A tall chain-link fence encircled the lot, and he had plastic slats put in it to keep people from seeing what was going on inside. They would finally have the parking spaces and privacy they needed.

A month before the move, the staff began telling patients about the new location, giving them flyers with the new address and directions for their next visit. Derik wanted to get off on the right foot with the neighbors, so he went to the junk shop across the street and introduced himself, dropped a couple grand on a few items. He tried to explain what the business would be, using the phrase he and Chris always used: We're in the medical field. People responded the way they always did, by asking if Derik was a doctor.

Derik would say: Do you know any doctors who own hospitals? No, because they are owned by investors. This is the same thing.

Derik wasn't too sure of these facts, but he gave the spiel many times—to cops, to neighbors, to guys next to him in bars—and people seemed to buy it. Mainly, though, he wanted to prepare the Lake Worth shopkeepers for the deluge without scaring them too much. Derik said if they had problems with traffic or patients, please call him before calling the cops. He would take care of it.

They opened on Dixie Highway on February 1, 2010. Chris continued to pay the lease on the Boca location even though it was empty. He figured if he stopped renting the space, Palm Beach Pain would swoop in there and try to lure patients who were looking for American Pain.

Similar to the previous moves, business was slower for a day or so at the new location, but by the end of the week, Dixie Highway was jammed two blocks south, a line of patients trying to pull into the lot, right-turn blinkers on. Derik hired a team of traffic handlers to flag patients into specific parking spots, like concert venues did. Security guards roved the two-and-a-half-acre lot on golf carts. Derik stationed guards on the roof to keep an eye on the perimeter of the building, looking for cops and media vehicles.

The parking lot exited onto a one-way alley, which then took the traffic through a residential neighborhood. Derik didn't want patients nodding off and running over people. He pondered the problem, then simply took down the one-way signs and had the traffic handlers direct people the other way.

Inside, they taped arrows on the floor to direct the foot traffic. The building worked beautifully, except for the bathroom problem. The single toilet on the first floor was laughably inadequate, especially since they were trying to process dozens of urine tests at any moment. After a week or two, Derik developed a system in which the employees took five or ten patients at a time to the bathrooms on the second floor to produce their urine samples.

Bigger place; same deal. A patient tried to sneak in a bottle full of urine for his drug test, swearing it was Mountain Dew. Derik told him to prove it. The guy grimaced and gulped, and Derik, impressed, moved him to the front of the line. Another patient made the mistake of calling Dianna a bitch. Derik slammed the guy into a wall, grabbed his neck, and started to squeeze. The guy went limp and collapsed, and Derik's 6'4" Finnish bouncer, who looked like the Russian boxer from *Rocky IV*, dragged him out. A couple of patients fished out on the floor, just collapsed and started convulsing, and the staff called 911. The woman who owned the junk store on the other side of Dixie Highway, initially friendly, took to screaming across the street at Derik's security guys. Patients were parking in her small lot, using her restroom to shoot up. Sometimes patients would go into the store and just stand there, glazed over, staring blankly at the same knickknack for five minutes. Once, a middle-aged woman nodded off in her minivan and dropped a lit cigarette in her lap. It burned through her shorts but she didn't wake up until the shopkeeper pounded on her window. Derik and his guys tried to be responsive, zipping across Dixie Highway on a golf cart to talk to her. The shopkeeper told Derik about the problems, showed him blood spurts on the wall of her bathroom. Derik said his guys would take care of things, but the zombies didn't listen, and the shopkeeper started calling tow trucks, as well as the cops.

A doctor at another big pain clinic quit, which sent a flood of new patients to American Pain. That was their biggest day yet. They serviced more than seven hundred patients that day, around $400,000 going into the trash cans and back to the money room.

Derik and Chris liked to climb up to the rooftop to shoot Derik's slingshot at unlucky cars and survey their empire, the flat Florida landscape to the west, the oceanfront condominium towers of Palm Beach to the east. From there, the American Pain employee parking lot glittered in the sun, looking like an exotic car dealership—Maseratis and Porsches and Range Rovers.

On the roof one day, Derik looked across the street and saw a gray sedan parked in the alley next to the junk shop. Two people were in the front seat, a broad-shouldered man and a tall woman with blonde hair. They wore regular street clothes, but Derik could tell they were cops.

Derik said to Chris: Look at those two idiots.

Derik and Chris laughed at the pair, thought about pegging them with the slingshot. They wondered why the cops were even bothering to do surveillance. What were they going to gain? Everyone knew what was going on at American Pain. It was like staking out a Walgreens. They'd been operating out in the open for two years and one month. The cops could stare across the street through binoculars all they wanted, but until Florida changed its laws, American Pain was legal.

One day in February, Chris called Derik and said he could cut off the ankle monitor, he was off the hook on the Jacksonville charges.

Derik said: Huh?

Chris started laughing. The people from the Jacksonville clinic were backing off, not pressing charges. They hadn't shown up for depositions.

Derik was suspicious. Chris would think it was a clever practical joke to trick Derik into cutting off the ankle bracelet, get him in trouble. Derik got off the phone and called his lawyer but didn't reach him. Word got around the clinic, and pretty soon, everyone was urging Derik to cut it off, laughing at his reluctance.

Eventually, Derik got in contact with his lawyer, who told him it was true. He could lose the monitor.

At the end of the day, after the patients were gone, everyone gathered around like Derik was blowing the candles out at an office birthday party. Derik stood in the middle of the work area of the clinic and cut the itchy strap off his leg. He threw it in a box to be mailed back to the bail/bond office. He was free.

At seven in the morning on Wednesday, March 3, 2010, Derik was in the shower in the fancy new house he'd leased two weeks earlier in Black Diamond Estates. His cell phone was already blowing up, ringing again and again. Derik had gotten used to this. There was always some kind of crisis at the clinic. But this was too much. He let it ring until his girlfriend said it was going to wake her little girl.

Derik told her to put the phone on vibrate. He dressed in a suit, the phone still jittering. He finally looked at it. Something like ten missed calls from Chris. Derik called him back.

Chris: What the *fuck*! The FBI is everywhere!

Later, Derik would talk himself down, assure himself that everything would be OK, but he knew right then that the ride was over.

Part III

9

FBI Special Agent Jennifer Turner wanted the takedown of American Pain to be an awesome display of federal power.

According to her plan, more than four hundred officers and agents would hit American Pain and six other locations and fan out across South Florida to track down and interrogate approximately fifty associates of Chris George. The goal of the onslaught would be the immediate shut-down of the nation's largest pain clinic, plus two others, and the seizure of any documents, drugs, and money inside. They also planned to seize Chris George's assets, including multiple cars, houses, and a boat, plus nine bank accounts associated with George or his businesses. Turner hoped this show of force would convince some targets to cooperate immediately. Chris George might hold out, but at least he'd know how serious the feds were about taking him down. She wanted to frighten other pill mills as well. So it wouldn't hurt to attract as much news media attention as possible.

Planning for the raids was already well underway by the time the DEA submitted a search warrant application in late February 2010. Personnel and resources were brought in from FBI divisions around the country. Computer analysis experts stood by. Dogs trained to sniff out drugs and cash were readied. Two days before the raid, participants were briefed at a Boca Raton police facility, where federal agents broke down, step-by-step, how they expected the day to unfold. The task force wasn't planning to make arrests. The search warrants were simply the next step in the investigation. Most participants were assigned to three types of teams: SWAT, search, or interview. The DEA would continue running the wiretap, reporting any relevant calls Chris George made. Supervisors would coordinate from a command post in Miami.

The search warrant targeted the homes of Chris George, Denice Haggerty, and Ethan Baumhoff, as well as South Beach Rejuvenation, East Coast Pain, Executive Pain, and, of course, American Pain.

Turner didn't sleep much the night before the raids. She was too keyed up and had too much to do. She wished she could be at every search location as well as the command post and the wire room. She didn't want to miss anything. But she had decided to join the team searching Ethan Baumhoff's house. After listening to the wiretaps, she believed the former police officer would be the most likely to cooperate, and she wanted to lead that interview. Ethan was the odd man out at American Pain, the only one who wasn't an old friend of Chris or Derik. She'd considered approaching him even before the search warrants, to see if he'd cooperate, but had held off. She knew Chris George kept American Pain money and drugs inside the old bank vaults in the Dixie Highway building, and she assumed Baumhoff would know the vault passcodes. Without the codes, opening those vaults would be difficult, to say the least.

Breaching Chris George's house, on the other hand, would be simple. The feds decided to use a local police SWAT team, equipped with an industrial-strength pry bar to snap the front door deadbolt.

It was crucial to hit all of the locations and targets simultaneously, so nobody would be alerted to destroy evidence or dump assets or fight back. They'd go at first light, just before 7:00 a.m., when everybody would still be at home. When the SWAT team came pouring through his broken front door, Chris George would feel the full weight of the federal government.

Chris wasn't home.

He and Dianna had left the house separately at 6:00 a.m., on one of Chris's obsessive missions to destroy Palm Beach Pain. Chris was still monitoring the GPS tracker he'd put on his rival's car. The clinic operator had been to a fleabag motel the night before, a cheap dump popular with the oxy-tourists. The Palm Beach Pain guys visited motels like this one, putting flyers on cars with out-of-state tags. Then, Chris would wake up at the crack of dawn, check the GPS monitor, and go wherever the guy had been the night before so he could *remove* all the flyers.

Today, Dianna was staking out the motel. On Chris's orders, she was going undercover, planning to catch the Palm Beach Pain guys on video. She would talk to them, posing as a sponsor staying at the motel. Chris wanted some video he could take to the DEA.

At 6:51 a.m., he called Dianna to coach her through the operation. He was following the Palm Beach Pain operator's car.

"Remember, you gotta hold that camera in your hand and not cover it up too much. It's gotta aim at them, you know?" Chris said.

"Yeah," Dianna said. "I'm gonna do my best on that."

"Then say, 'Listen, I bring a lot of people down here. What's the price per pill?' He'll tell you."

Chris hung up. A moment later, his phone rang. The caller said he was a sergeant with the sheriff's office. He said he was in Chris's house, along with the DEA and the FBI, and they had a search warrant. They needed to talk to him. Chris could hear a strangely familiar sound in the background. Like dogs barking. Chris was bewildered. Why were the cops at his house, and why'd they have dogs?

Chris hung up and started calling everyone—Derik, Jeff, his lawyer. Nobody answered. It was 7:00 a.m. He called Dianna back.

"Babe, I'm fucked," he said. "They have a search warrant. The cops are inside the house."

"What?" Dianna shrieked.

"You need to go there and see what's going on," Chris said. "Listen, there's two guns in the garage. You're gonna have to say they are yours, I mean, that you just brought them there. And I wasn't there when you brought them there. Do you have any drugs there?"

"Probably like a little bit of pot, but nothing crazy," Dianna said. "I'll get rid of them."

"Baby, you might have to take the blame for some of this stuff," Chris said.

"That's fine," Dianna said.

"You know, I . . . I think I'm in a lot of trouble," Chris said.

They disconnected, and Dianna gunned her car toward the Talavera house, cutting off other drivers, going up on the curb. Every few minutes, Chris called her back, more upset each time.

"Babe, I'm fucked," Chris said. "I'm not going to deal with it. I'm just gonna kill myself."

"Don't do this," Dianna said. "Don't be stupid. Don't talk shit. You don't know what's going on. Let them do their investigation, OK?"

"Baby, you know I love you," Chris said.

"Yeah, I do," Dianna said. "I know you do. You just need to relax, Chris. And you need to think of a fucking plan. You're smarter than this, OK? Your brain works really hard."

"I don't know why they're there, though," Chris said.

"Think of a plan, Chris. Think of a fucking plan."

"I don't know what to plan for," Chris said.

"You need to think of something," Dianna said. "Killing yourself is not the answer. You cannot leave me here by my fucking self to deal with your dirt."

"Babe, where are you at now?" he said. "Where exactly are you at?"

"I'll be at the house in two minutes," she said.

He was crying.

"Stay on the phone with me," he said. "Stay on the phone, will ya? I'm fucked, babe. They're gonna put me in jail for a long time, babe, a long fucking time."

"I'll take the fall for it," Dianna said. "I'll take the fall for everything, OK?"

"Baby, no matter what happens, if they arrest you for anything illegal at the house, don't worry, I'll get you out," Chris said.

"You promise?"

"Baby, I got a lot of people," Chris said. "I'll get you out, don't worry about that. Let me call you back. Derik's calling me back."

⁓

After prying open Chris George's front door, it took the search team less than a minute to clear the house, room by room. No sign of Chris George or Dianna Pavnick. They did find a sophisticated surveillance system and, in a second-floor bedroom, what looked like explosive materials. They called the bomb squad, not something they had anticipated needing. Agents monitoring the Chris George wiretap said he'd told Dianna Pavnick there were firearms in the house, and this was true. They found two shotguns—a Remington 870 and a Benelli I-12 Diamond—leaning against a refrigerator in the garage, next to a red, white, and black Nazi flag. They also found a loaded Smith & Wesson 9-millimeter pistol in a nightstand in an upper bedroom. And some ammunition that didn't belong to any of the guns, which made the agents wonder if George, wherever he was, had a gun on him. The agents on the wire said George was driving around, crying, talking about killing himself. He was a desperate man, and they hoped he was unarmed.

At 7:24, Dianna Pavnick pulled up to the house, which was still being ransacked by dozens of agents. She seemed terrified. She agreed to talk to three people—the DEA's Mike Burt, a DEA intelligence research specialist, and a local police detective. They put her in an unmarked police vehicle and talked to her, taking notes.

Pavnick said she was the owner of Executive Pain. She said she knew nothing about American Pain. She said patients traveled from so far away because MRIs cost more in those states and doctors there were scared to prescribe controlled substances. Patients traveled together to share costs. She didn't know what a sponsor was. She'd never heard of patients selling their pills in the parking lot. She said Executive Pain provided detox services. When they pressed her on this, she said she could remember only two patients who'd gone through detox. She acknowledged there were two shotguns in the three-car garage and said they belonged to her. The guns were old, she wasn't sure they worked, she'd used them in the past to shoot skeet.

The agents asked if Chris George was making bombs. Pavnick said the materials in the upstairs bedroom were for homemade fireworks, something George and his friends enjoyed.

Then they showed her the pictures of George and another woman in the back of his truck.

Still damp from his morning shower, Derik had called Chris back. Chris was freaking out, saying his home was being raided.

"Dude," Chris said. "It's over, dude. Hear me?"

Derik peeked out of his own window. His street in Black Diamond Estates was quiet, not a cop in sight.

Chris asked Derik to meet him at their usual breakfast spot, a bagel joint next to Walmart.

Derik's first thought: This couldn't have happened at a worse time. He'd loaned some serious money to friends, money he doubted he'd ever see again, and the last two weekends had drained him. Two weeks earlier, he'd taken his girlfriend on a cruise to the Bahamas, bought her diamond earrings, did lots of coke, and dropped probably $20,000 in a Paradise Island casino. The next weekend he spent at the Hard Rock Hotel & Casino in Hollywood, more coke and whiskey, and his losing streak continued. He'd blown maybe $100,000 over the two weekends, and now he felt sick about it. At the very least, he was going to need some serious lawyering, which cost money. He'd probably earned $2 million in the past two years, mostly under the table, and now he was short on cash.

Derik's cousin drove him to Starbucks and then the bagel place, and Chris kept calling Derik with more news, more places getting shut down. Derik said he was thinking about going to American Pain to confront the agents. Chris vetoed the idea. Vehemently.

"They're gonna question you like a motherfucker, dude," Chris said. "About who deals with the money. Who owns the place. Fucking all kinds of shit, dude."

At the same time the SWAT team poured through Chris George's front door, a large truck pulled into the American Pain parking lot. The back doors opened, and a team of police officers with shields and masks poured out.

A staffer who'd gone to high school in upstate New York with Derik was the first American Pain employee to arrive at the clinic that day. The employee was thirty-one, a former Marine who had previously worked for a plumbing company before he started doing paperwork and counting out pills in the American Pain pharmacy. He'd started at $500 a week, but his salary was boosted to about $1,500, plus another $5,000 from patient bribes. At the Christmas party where Dr. Cadet won the "Doctor of the Year" award, this employee had won "Staffer of the Year."

The staffer pulled into the parking lot, then saw a deputy sheriff at the door. Then dozens of agents swarmed him, yelling at him—*get out of the car, do you have a weapon?* They put him in a police car as they ransacked the building. His cell phone rang, over and over, but he didn't answer. A steady stream of early-bird patients pulled into the lot, saw the cluster of police vehicles, then got out of there, looking confused. The cops eventually put a barrier over the parking-lot entrance. Two DEA special agents took the employee inside to grill him in an empty office. He talked about the patients, about the staff, the quirks and reputations of the doctors. Cops and agents were packing patient files into cardboard boxes, studying the surveillance camera system, taking photos of everything.

Outside, neighbors watched from across Dixie Highway as cops wheeled carts and dollies bearing stacks of boxes out of the big white building, loading them into a Broward County Sheriff's Office truck.

At the bagel joint, Chris was flushed and frantic. He told Derik the FBI and DEA and sheriff's office were searching everybody's houses, and they were going to find guns at his house. Derik sent his cousin back to his house in Black Diamond Estates to get the cousin's guns and Derik's money and anything else he could find that would get Derik in trouble if the feds showed up.

Chris and Derik sat in Chris's truck in the parking lot and started calling everybody, doctors and staff, checking in. Derik talked to Dr. Aruta, who said he'd headed in to work as usual that morning, then had seen the police barrier at the clinic and kept on driving.

Derik said: Take off. Go to Costa Rica, go somewhere, just take off.

Everyone Chris talked to was panicked.

Jeff: "The cops come after me, I'm fucked."

Ethan: "Dude, I told you this day was going to come. Remember when I asked you to put some fucking money away in a trust account with an attorney for a defense fund?"

Chris got ahold of Dr. Cadet. They speculated about what the charges might be.

"What did we do wrong that we're racketeering about?" Chris asked.

"I know, right—what?" Cadet said. "Like, we're not . . . We're doing a service and getting money for it."

"I'll try to call you back unless I'm fucking in jail," he said.

"OK," she said.

"If you guys aren't in jail," Chris added.

"Oh, God, I know," Cadet said.

Chris called Dr. Boshers. If any patients or staffers asked him to write a prescription, Chris said, Boshers should treat them like cops. Chris said he'd gone to a gas station and tried to use a debit card linked to his bank account, and it was declined. Then he'd gone to one of his banks; they said his accounts were frozen.

"You gotta get the money out of your account," Chris told Boshers.

"OK," Boshers said. "What are they gonna indict you guys for?"

"Most likely it'll be either conspiracy or racketeering, or something like that," Chris said.

"Yeah, OK, it's just, I don't ever want to go through it, but it looks like I'm in the middle of this crap," Boshers said.

Chris called a representative from a drug wholesaler, just to vent.

"They're taking down every pain clinic, and they're gonna go after the wholesalers afterwards," he said.

"Uh, so what you're giving us is a heads up, you're saying," the rep said.

The feds kept calling Chris, telling him they wanted him to come home, talk to them. Chris had no intention of doing that. For one thing, he knew they'd probably seize his Range Rover the moment he drove up.

Dianna called too, crying. She was still at the Talavera house, talking to the feds, and they were showing her pictures of Chris and another woman in his truck. Everything going on, and she was frantic about Chris and other women.

Under his breath, Chris said: Oh, God.

Then, to Dianna: That's not true.

Eventually, Chris and Derik went to see Chris's attorney, who'd represented him during his 2003 steroid conviction. They met Dianna and Jeff and Jeff's girlfriend there. Chris signed over his new white Range Rover to the lawyer as a retainer fee, since his bank accounts were frozen.

Turner waited outside as the SWAT team invaded Ethan Baumhoff's house. After a few moments, the team reemerged with the clinic manager and led him to a van, where Turner grilled him.

Baumhoff didn't seem surprised about the raid. He was resigned and respectful and, as Turner had suspected, he was an open book. As a former cop who had testified in court many times, he knew that the first person to cooperate was likely to get the biggest break.

Baumhoff gave them the previous day's cash proceeds, the money-counting machine, and the all-important combinations to the clinic safes. He explained the "pain train," how rejected American Pain patients were referred to Executive Pain. He outlined how the doctors wrote scrips for staffers. How Roni Dreszer had a cocaine problem. How Aruta and Boshers carried guns at work. How Baumhoff had tried to institute standards, to inventory pills, to buy a crash cart for patients going into seizures, and how nobody cooperated with his efforts to give the clinic a more legitimate appearance. He said he believed the doctors knew what they were doing, with the possible exception of Cadet. She was naive, the one most likely to have been duped.

Baumhoff talked for hours, a mixture of fact and opinion and rumor. It was like he'd been waiting for months for the feds to arrive.

Derik visited a couple of acquaintances who owed him money. He collected an emergency fund of about $20,000.

People kept calling Derik, asking him what to do, and Derik told them to go to his house, since the cops weren't there. His girlfriend ordered pizza and sandwiches to be brought in.

Derik called Chris with what he knew.

"They got all the doctors and suspended all their licenses," Derik said. "They took Roni in and gave him a piece of paper saying his DEA license was suspended. He's got a hearing in a month. They went to Cynthia's house, gave her a piece of paper, said her license was suspended for a month. Uh, Jacob also."

Derik was thinking the feds might be listening to their calls, so he bought a bunch of burners, cheap cell phones with prepaid minutes, and went back to his house so his girlfriend could activate them. Still no cops in Black Diamond Estates. Derik assumed they didn't know where he lived since he'd moved there only two weeks earlier. A bunch of staffers were waiting at Derik's house, panicked, and Derik gave them all burners.

People kept coming, and Derik's house became an impromptu headquarters, since everywhere else was under siege. Derik was pretty well moved in by that time, a few boxes still unpacked in the garage. Every time the guard at the gate called him to say there was a visitor, Derik figured it was the cops, but they never showed up. The visitors all told their stories. Ethan, with a long tale about how the cops had him in cuffs all day at his house, interrogating him. Another staffer had been getting breakfast at Dunkin Donuts when federal agents walked up to him, wanting to talk.

Another had been at home in the shower when the cops showed up. One was freaking out because agents had seized her Range Rover.

Most of the employees said the cops and agents who'd interviewed them seemed unfamiliar with the details of the case, like they'd been brought in just for the raids. Some of the agents had seemed like they were used to dealing with gangs and cartels and didn't understand why they were interrogating people who worked at a doctor's office.

Chris and Jeff and their women arrived later in Chris's other Range Rover, bringing a bag of steroids they didn't want the feds to find. For some reason, the feds had let Dianna take the black Range Rover, which was a few years older; they were focused on the new white one Chris had signed over to his lawyer.

Late that afternoon, sitting on Derik's couch, Chris and Jeff and Derik watched the local news. The first six and a half minutes of the program were devoted to the raid. The video showed a Palm Beach County Sheriff's Office cruiser parked across the entrance of the American Pain parking-lot gate. The camera peered through slats in the gate to show cops and agents strolling around the parking lot in masks and black jumpsuits.

Derik felt sick to his stomach. Chris and Jeff couldn't believe what was happening either. The feds seemed to think the American Pain crew was equivalent to the Gambino crime family. They couldn't believe the feds could do this, just come in and take everything before they'd been proven guilty. How was that legal? And if they had the power to do that, who knew what else they'd done? Were their phones tapped? Had all the legal advice they'd bought and paid for over the years been completely wrong?

The news anchor cut to a live shot of a reporter standing in front of Chris's house in Talavera. "Neighbors said there was never any cause for alarm," the reporter said, "until the bomb squad showed up." Video showed the street blocked off with a bomb squad truck, orange traffic cones, and fire trucks. A bomb tech in a full military-green armored suit and mask lurched into the house. Derik thought this was overkill. He and

Chris and Jeff liked to build and blow up homemade fireworks. It had nothing to do with American Pain.

Derik's grandmother in Deerfield kept calling. She knew where he worked and was worried he was in trouble.

She said: You're on TV!

Derik said: I'm fine, Grandma. I'm just sitting at my house.

Eventually everyone split. Chris left behind the steroids and older Range Rover and asked Derik to take care of them. Derik wasn't happy about this and wondered if Chris was going to cut him off again, like the time when Derik had gone to jail on the traffic charge and Chris stopped picking up his calls. But Derik did what Chris asked—he hid the vehicle under the covered back porch of a friend's house in Loxahatchee and threw the bag of steroids in a garbage bin behind a McDonalds.

10

The day after the raids, Derik and Chris went back to the big building on Dixie Highway, and reality set in again: It was over.

The clinic, which had bustled with staff and patients just two days earlier, was an echoing ghost town of office furniture. Signs gone from the walls, filing cabinets empty, barely a sheet of paper left. Not a single pill. Nothing in the desk drawers. No computers or mainframes, the security system taken right off the walls. Even the ATM was gone. The feds had taken everything. They'd also seized most everything Chris owned, confiscating more than $7 million in cash and bank accounts, plus his cars.* Chris knew they'd also be going after his three houses in the Talavera development.

A few days later, Derik again visited a lawyer, this time by himself. In the past, lawyers usually made him feel better about his prospects. Not this time. The lawyer basically said Derik needed to prepare himself to go to prison. If the cops came after him, and the lawyer believed they would, Derik needed to think about accepting a plea bargain. If he refused to plead guilty, he would go to trial, which could lead to a life sentence. Derik couldn't believe what he was hearing. Lawyers they'd consulted had always said the clinic was legal, that Derik couldn't be held responsible for what the doctors did behind closed doors. Derik couldn't understand what had changed.

He remembered his weeks in St. Lucie County Jail on the probation violation, how jumpy he'd felt the whole time. No way could he risk a life sentence.

* At Cadet's trial, Chris said he earned about $40 million in revenue from the pain clinics, but less than 25 percent of that was profit. In a November 18, 2009, conversation with his father, Chris agreed to see a contact about a Swiss bank account in Belize. Chris says he never set up the account.

But he also remembered the prosecutors going after his father. He'd learned then that it was wrong to work with the cops, even if your mother had been stabbed to death. He couldn't turn on his friends, couldn't turn rat.

He was trapped.

But the days went by, and nobody was arrested. The cops never even contacted Derik, possibly because they didn't know where he was. His name wasn't in documents filed in federal court.

In optimistic moments, Derik wondered if he was going to squeak by somehow. Maybe nobody knew about him. After all, his name hadn't made the papers. Meanwhile, the George twins had become famous overnight. On Sunday, March 7, the *Palm Beach Post* ran a long front-page profile of Chris and Jeff. Even though American Pain had dwarfed Jeff's clinics and the brothers hadn't been speaking to each other for most of the time the clinics were open, the story made it sound like they were equal partners in a single criminal network.

In the papers, Chris's lawyer played down the case against the Georges.

"These guys may have talked a big game, but they really didn't do anything illegal," he told a reporter.

Privately, the lawyer told Chris that if he married Dianna, it would give them something called spousal privilege, which meant they couldn't be forced to testify against each other. Five days after the raid, Chris and Dianna applied for a marriage license, and four days after that, a deputy clerk of court married them in the Palm Beach County Courthouse. Derik didn't go to the ceremony.

Derik didn't know whom to trust, and he grew suspicious of friends he'd known since he was a kid, hyperaware of the subtleties of every comment or question. He studied phone texts for signs that the sender was being handled by the cops, was trying to catch Derik doing something illegal or saying something that could be used in court. Derik spent a lot of time talking to his former coworkers at American Pain, cajoling everyone to stick together, not to give the feds anything. The fewer people talked, the better.

"I ain't fucking signing nothing, I ain't cooperating, I ain't talking," Derik told Chris. "The only time they're gonna see me is when they put me in handcuffs."

The George brothers' inner circle discussed the situation during dinners at the Bonefish Grill and at their mother's house. During the meetings, they left their cell phones in their cars, because they figured the feds might have the technology to somehow turn on the phones and listen in on their conversations. The guys assured each other they wouldn't break and speculated about who was most likely to cooperate with the feds. Jeff wanted to obtain depositions from everybody so they would all be locked into statements. Everyone agreed they should try to shift all the blame to the doctors.

Another pain clinic owner asked Derik if Chris was willing to sell American Pain's phone number to her. Thousands of American Pain patients were finding out that their oxy supply had suddenly disappeared. They were no doubt panicking, calling the number. Derik asked Chris about it, and Chris said yes. He needed cash. The woman paid $50,000 for it.

Derik also needed money. He was kicking himself for blowing everything. When the clinic owner who bought American Pain's phone number offered him a job doing the same thing he'd done at American Pain, he took it.

He lasted one day. The clinic was depressing. The doctors were low writers, wouldn't prescribe more than 180 oxy 30s a month. They didn't know how to play the game, and everybody was spooked after the American Pain raids.

The feds had not raided Pain Express, the clinic Chris and Jeff had launched a month earlier in Georgia. Nevertheless, it shut down shortly after the raids. The doctor just quit, no doubt alarmed by what had happened in South Florida.

A few weeks after the raid, Derik pulled together a little money and financed another pain clinic in Vero Beach with Dr. Cadet's boyfriend, a doctor who'd worked for a few weeks at American Pain. But Derik couldn't spend much time there because he didn't want to tip off the feds that he'd started another operation. Within two weeks, the doctor quit, saying there weren't enough patients to make it worth the risk. The place just folded, and Derik lost his stake. Derik believed if he could have been present, he could have kept it going. But with a federal investigation hanging over his head, no one respected or feared him any longer. And after the Vero Beach clinic closed, no one wanted to work with him.

Derik waited to get arrested, growing depressed and anxious. He popped more and more Xanax. He barely ventured outside the big house in Black Diamond Estates.

The search warrants changed everything for the American Pain task force too. Information, once so scarce, now threatened to inundate. The raids gave Jennifer Turner and her colleagues a massive document trove to explore, including more than twenty-seven thousand patient files from American Pain alone. They had video from the clinic's surveillance system and photos the agents had taken of all the clinics and homes they'd raided. And then there was everything stored on the hard drives of the computers they'd confiscated. Chris George's money was stashed in nine different bank accounts, but the largest haul had been in several safes in the attic of his mother's house on Primrose Lane, where the search team had found $4,553,400 in cash.

Working ten hours a day for two months, a team of agents and lawyers began combing through the patient files, trying to quantify the scope of the George operation. They reviewed ten thousand files by hand, and found they were all essentially the same. Between July 2008* and the raid, the doctors of South Florida Pain and American Pain wrote 66,871 prescriptions for various medications. Ninety-six percent of the prescriptions were for oxycodone or alprazolam. More than 80 percent of the patients

* South Florida Pain opened in February 2008, but July 2008 was the earliest that any of the doctors under investigation worked at the George clinics. Dr. Gittens and Dr. Joseph left the clinics before the federal investigation began, and they were not targets.

were from out of state.* The five American Pain doctors under investigation wrote prescriptions for fourteen million oxycodone pills. Executive Pain's six doctors wrote for almost four million oxycodone pills. Boshers was the biggest writer, personally responsible for prescribing 3,601,860 oxycodone 30-milligram pills. Altogether, doctors targeted at both clinics had prescribed enough oxycodone to have given every man, woman, and child in Florida a pill.

Then there was the wiretap. The task force had intercepted approximately four thousand of Chris George's cell phone calls between November 2009 and March 2010, plus twice as many text messages. The wiretap recordings had to be mined for exchanges that could be used as evidence that Chris George was in charge of American Pain and understood the clinic's impact. That meant listening to dozens and dozens of phone calls during which Chris George mumbled interminably with a buddy about something stupid. But here and there among the idle chatter, a nugget of conversation illuminated the operation and mind-sets at work, something they could use to show a connection between parties or to establish culpability.

In January 2010, for instance, two months before the raids, Chris George and Ethan Baumhoff had a series of discussions about a questionnaire sent to them by the Harvard Drug Group. The Michigan drug wholesaler—no connection to the university—was one of American Pain's oxycodone suppliers. Baumhoff had lied on the forms about how many patients they saw and what percentage were from out of state. Then he'd asked the doctors to sign the forms.

GEORGE: Was it hard for the doctors to sign those, or did they just sign them right away?

BAUMHOFF: Oh they signed them right away.

GEORGE: Signed them right away. Well, what did you tell them they were?

BAUMHOFF: I told them it was a questionnaire for a wholesaler

* Forty-three percent of the prescriptions went to patients from Kentucky; 20 percent to patients from Florida; 18 percent to patients from Tennessee; and 11 percent to patients from Ohio.

GEORGE: Wholesaler. Did they even read over it?

BAUMHOFF: No. Aruta looked at it and he goes 'this, is this number really accurate?' and I said mmm, probably not.

On January 3, Chris George and a friend discussed a time-share operation that Jeff was running.

FRIEND: But that scam's gonna end. I mean, people are onto that one, that makes the news almost as much as pain clinics.

GEORGE: (unintelligible) it's not killing anybody, though. That's the difference.

The agents also took note of this text-message exchange between Chris George and Dianna Pavnick two months before the raids.

PAVNICK: I'm scared to go away for a long time, but I keep going for you.

GEORGE: Going where?

PAVNICK: Prison.

For a time after the search warrants were executed, the wiretap on Chris George's phone was still operational, though George was suddenly more guarded on the phone. Three weeks afterward, Dr. Cadet sent George a text.

CADET: Hang in there Chris. Let's hope this will all be resolved in time.

GEORGE: Well, it will take time for sure probably while I'm in jail and hopefully no one else with me.

An assistant US attorney named Paul Schwartz was assigned to lead the case. Schwartz was in his mid-fifties and had spent much of his career prosecuting South Florida branches of the Colombo, Lucchese, and Gambino families, leaning hard on alleged *caporegimes* with nicknames like "Fat Tommy" and "Carmine The Snake" and "Ronnie One Arm." He'd used RICO laws to go after a Bloods-affiliated street gang in Miramar. During a Gambino prosecution in 2004, it was alleged that mobsters were planning to murder Schwartz, and that wasn't his first death threat.

Schwartz was hard and foul-mouthed in meetings with defendants but quick to call defense attorneys and apologize afterward. In court, he fired his cross-examination questions in semiautomatic staccato bursts. His Bronx patter was so profuse that even veteran court reporters had to ask him to slow down. A fanatical exerciser, his twice-a-day workouts were legendary in courthouse circles. During trials, he woke at 4:30 a.m. and strapped on a forty-pound weight vest to run one hundred flights of stairs at the courthouse. He said it relieved the stress of his job. He was fit but lacked athletic grace—his movements, like his speech, were herky-jerky, stiff. His diet was as rigid as his workouts: oatmeal and fish and no french fries. He was of average size, but you could see the chest and shoulders under his dress shirts, and his face was lean and creased and hard. He approached his job with a fierce joy, whether he was interrogating wiseguys or studying textbooks. He was always learning something new, and that kept him interested. He was very glad the US Attorney's Office had no mandatory retirement age.

Jennifer Turner believed Schwartz was a perfect fit for this case. Not just because he was a warrior, but because he was willing to stray from his niche. Many prosecutors stuck to cases that fit into their realm of experience. But this case was the first of its kind, in many ways. It called for a prosecutor who was not only willing to learn a new field but one who could think creatively about how to apply old laws to a new kind of crime.

Most of the people who'd worked at the George brothers' clinics had hired lawyers, tying up many of the most prominent criminal attorneys up and down the Gold Coast. Most of the high-level targets weren't talking to the federal agents, including Derik Nolan and Chris George. However, the agents had nabbed early interviews with two doctors. Dr. Michael Aruta had met agents from the FBI and IRS at a restaurant the morning of the raid. Dr. Beau Boshers talked to agents two days later. They both said they weren't aware of illegal activities at the clinic, that they ejected patients they suspected of abusing drugs. Boshers said, yes, Appalachian patients came to the clinic in carloads, but they were just carpooling to save on costs.

The doctors seemed to believe they'd broken no laws. How could they have broken the law by simply prescribing legal medication? That was their job, after all.

Schwartz wasn't accustomed to having to persuade targets that their actions were criminal. Wiseguys knew they were violating the law. For them, lawbreaking was a way of life. They had to be persuaded only that the prosecutors had enough evidence to find them guilty at trial.

These pill mill people, especially the doctors, were another story. The whole idea that they could have broken the law seemed unacceptable to them. Schwartz knew that before he could educate them about their culpability, he needed to educate himself. He needed to know more about pain medicine than the doctors did.

He embarked on a self-guided medical education. He read everything he could find: med-school textbooks, academic journal articles, magazine stories. He flew to New York City to grill leading pain management experts. He learned about pain diagnosing and opioid weaning. Schwartz's colleagues joked that his mother would finally be proud of him, now that he was a doctor.

Schwartz wasn't ready to make arrests yet, but the DEA believed it did have enough evidence to revoke the American Pain doctors' certificates of registration, which allowed them to prescribe controlled substances. All five doctors requested hearings, and the cases were adjudicated in Miami at the same three-day hearing in July 2010.

At the hearing, DEA special agent Mike Burt testified about the deaths of two patients, based on reports he'd received from Barry Adams, the Rockcastle County deputy sheriff. One was Stacy Mason. The other was a forty-five-year-old man, also from Rockcastle, named Timothy York. Early in January 2010, York had seen Dr. Boshers at American Pain. On the way home, he began to overdose in a car somewhere on I-75 in Tennessee. Panicked, the two women in the front seat tried to find a medical center on their GPS device. The device instead routed them to the Williamsburg Police Department, where police found York in the back seat, dead.

The hearing's primary witness was Dr. L. Douglas Kennedy, an expert in pain medicine from the University of Miami. He'd reviewed seventy-eight patient files selected at random, plus the files of Stacy Mason and "Luis Lopez," the undercover pseudonym of Detective Sergio Lopez. Good pain doctors, Kennedy said, conducted thorough medical histories and physical exams, sought past medical records, modified and reviewed initial diagnoses. But the American Pain charts he reviewed, while stuffed with documents, showed no signs that these activities were occurring. The doctors did take cursory histories, but the operation was a prescription assembly line. His report recommended the DEA bar all five doctors from prescribing controlled substances.

"Drug diversion most likely caused a 'mushroom' effect of increased drug abuse, drug addiction, drug overdoses, serious bodily injury and death in those communities spread over several different states," he wrote. "(The doctors') continued ability to prescribe controlled substances will only perpetuate the suffering and be a threat to the public."

The DEA also went after wholesalers, shutting down two distributors that had supplied American Pain with oxycodone: Sunrise Wholesale from Florida and Harvard Drug Group from Michigan. Sunrise surrendered its DEA license. Harvard, one of the ten largest wholesalers of generic drugs in the country, didn't give up so easily and began to work with the DEA to revise its oversight methods.*

* Harvard Drug Group eventually paid a $6 million fine for "failing to have in place an effective system designed to identify suspicious orders of controlled substances, and to report suspicious orders of those substances to the DEA."

Spooked, many other drug wholesalers immediately stopped selling to Florida pain clinics. By July 2010, the amount of oxycodone doses purchased by Florida doctors had fallen from more than eight million per month to around one million.

Out of prospects and almost out of money, Derik packed up the big house in Black Diamond Estates in July 2010 and drove back home to upstate New York. His girlfriend and her daughter moved back in with her parents. Derik and his cousin were going to run a sub shop in Lake George, but that plan went bust, and Derik moved back to the farm where he'd grown up with his aunt and uncle. He put a new roof on the barn, mended some fences, shoveled horse manure, and tried to get his head right, forget what was going on in Florida.

One day, Derik took his aunt to a doctor's appointment and had a revelation: Her doctor's office was a pill mill. It was basically American Pain, just a fraction of the size and without the out-of-state patients. The cars in the parking lot all had New York plates, but they were from counties all over the state. The amount of oxycodone his aunt was taking explained a few things, Derik believed, such as why she'd disconnected from his life over time, and his sister's too, stopped answering the phone or sending birthday cards. She'd been on the meds for years, and Derik had never paid much attention, figured it was OK because a doctor had prescribed it. Like most people, he never questioned it, not until he'd been running American Pain for two years and knew the signs. It made him wonder. How many of these places were out there, doing the same thing as American Pain, just not as aggressively? It would be so easy to fly under the radar, make a lot of money without going all-out like he and Chris had.

A few weeks after Derik moved up to New York, Mike Burt called his cell phone early in the morning. Derik told the DEA agent to speak to his lawyer. Paul Schwartz, the lead prosecutor, called Derik's lawyer, and the news wasn't good. Schwartz said Derik was going to prison for life, that he was a dangerous individual and they had him cold on kidnapping, extortion, and running a drug ring in Loxahatchee. Derik's lawyer said he was, basically, fucked. He said Derik needed to meet with the feds, if only to find out what cards they were holding. Derik returned to Florida.

The feds were pressuring Chris the same way. Derik and Chris agreed to meet with the prosecutors individually. Chris went first. The feds told Chris they had three months of wiretaps of his phone, which was actually kind of a relief, since Chris and Derik had been worried that everybody's phones had been tapped for the past year. Chris refused to give them anything, and they kicked him out.

Derik met with the feds a week later. Before the meeting, he went over to Chris's house. Derik was freaking out, and Dianna gave him a handful of Valium, which he downed.

The meeting was in an eighth-floor conference room in the US Attorney's Office in downtown Fort Lauderdale, palm trees and sunny boulevards visible far below, through the plate-glass windows. A dozen lawyers and agents crowded around a long table. Derik recognized Mike Burt and the tall blonde FBI agent, Jennifer Turner. He'd seen them before—the day he and Chris had been on the roof of American Pain, looking down at an unmarked car across the street. He and Chris had laughed, wondering why the cops were bothering to surveil. That seemed like a long time ago.

Now, Derik was prepared for an interrogation or a negotiation or some kind of offer. But the agents and lawyers didn't ask questions at first. They seemed hostile, like they *hoped* he didn't plead guilty, like they *wanted* him to go to trial, so they could send him away for good.

Schwartz had a close-trimmed beard and an intense stare. He said he was going to quote some lines from the wiretap recordings, some things Derik had said to Chris George. One quote was from one of Derik's lengthy rants about Ethan Baumhoff: "You hate cops. I hate cops. If he was still a cop, he would throw the handcuffs on us." Awkward to hear those words in a roomful of cops.

Then, one of the cops asked: Do you hate cops, Derik?

It didn't seem like a question from someone who wanted to make a deal. Derik shrugged, said something about how, yeah, man, he hated cops.

Schwartz read something else Derik had apparently said to Chris, referring to the large crew of Loxahatchee construction workers who'd become American Pain patients: "Loxahatchee is a gold mine."

Schwartz said: Did someone discover gold in Loxahatchee, Derik?

The Valium was starting to penetrate Derik's brain. The whole scene seemed unreal. He didn't know what to say.

A deputy sheriff from Palm Beach, playing the good cop, said: OK, Derik, you need to tell the truth here. This is your one shot.

Then he started to ask real questions. He wanted Derik to confess to selling pills on the street. They'd heard that Derik had sold a large stash of pills. Derik said he hadn't sold any pills directly, and the cop lost his temper. Derik got up to leave, and Schwartz barked: Sit down! Derik sat down.

They asked about a different pill-selling situation, and Derik said they had the story wrong. Derik said he knew what they were talking about, but someone else had done it. They said he was lying.

The meeting was going in the wrong direction. Derik's lawyer asked for a moment, and they left the room, went down to a parking garage. Derik nervously lit a cigarette and asked the lawyer why he hadn't warned him the feds were going to be so aggressive. The attorney said he hadn't expected it either.

They went back inside, and Schwartz asked the same question in a broader way: Had Derik ever illegally diverted pills from American Pain?

Derik said no.

Schwartz was finished with him. He gave Derik twenty-four hours to get back to him or, he said, they were going to put him away for life. Derik got out of there, feeling wobbly.

Chris was getting the same pressure. Schwartz called Chris's new attorney, a well-known Mob lawyer, and asked if Chris was ready to cooperate. The lawyer said no.

Schwartz said: Well, I'm going to put his ass in jail and see if that will change his mind.

Over the next few weeks, Derik and Chris kept hearing rumors that one person or another had flipped, including Jeff. They went to a tattoo parlor together and got matching leg tattoos: a rat hanging from a noose. Someone took a picture of Chris's rat and sent it to some people.

The feds found out about the rat-tattoo photo, which they believed to be witness tampering, and in mid-October, Schwartz followed through on his threat. The police showed up at Chris's house and arrested him. Apparently, they weren't ready to charge him with anything related to American Pain. They did, however, have him cold on weapons charges, based on the guns they'd found in his home on the day of the raids: the two shotguns Chris had asked Dianna to take the fall for, as well as a pistol found in an upstairs bedroom. As a felon, he wasn't supposed to have guns.

But the raids had taken place seven months ago. Chris knew the feds were arresting him now only to pressure him to cooperate. He seemed unsurprised by the arrest, but he did complain about the cops hauling him to jail in handcuffs instead of just letting him surrender.

Chris said: Why didn't you just call me? I would have come in.

On the west coast of Florida, Larry Golbom told his radio audience about the downfall of the George clinics. The pharmacist was still doing his talk show about prescription narcotics, but he no longer felt like a voice in the wilderness. American Pain and its counterparts had the whole state abuzz with talk about prescription narcotics. The pill mills weren't the root of the problem, Golbom believed, but simply an inevitable side effect of the unleashing of legal opium. Nevertheless, the pill mills were bringing attention to the larger problem, and that was a good thing.

Three years into the show, Golbom had found himself relaxing behind the microphone. He grew looser. Funnier. He stopped channeling the style of other talk radio hosts, stopped shouting. His stomach no longer hurt before shows. He stopped writing out scripts to read aloud. Instead, he went into the studio with a loose outline and a guest lined up. He knew what he believed about the opioid epidemic, and he knew what he wanted to say. Behind the mic, the words just came.

And there was plenty to talk about. The fact that drug deaths had overtaken traffic fatalities as the leading cause of death in the United States, a trend driven by prescription narcotics overdoses. The new Florida law, signed in June 2010, that barred drug felons from operating pain clinics, required pain clinic doctors to undergo special training and allowed them to dispense only three days' worth of medication to patients who paid by cash, check, or credit card, instead of insurance.

Despite the furor, few people paid attention in 2010 when another DEA-approved hike in the oxycodone manufacturing quota took effect, boosting the output from 94,000 kilograms to 105,500 kilograms. This was more than twice the total manufactured in 2005, and almost thirty times the amount manufactured seventeen years earlier. The numbers boggled Golbom's mind. It wasn't as if oxycodone was a new drug. It had been developed almost a century earlier. The basic drug hadn't changed at all, simply the mind-set around how it was prescribed.

Despite the new pressures, many pain clinics simply evolved and continued to operate. The laws limited the amounts physicians could dispense, but many pill mill doctors continued to write large prescriptions to be filled elsewhere. When the laws required pain clinics to register with the state health department, 1,031 applications poured into the department. The department could find no reason to deny most of the applications; 904 pain clinic licenses were approved, including one for the Oakland Plaza Medical Center, registered to Dr. Rachael Gittens, formerly of South Florida Pain.*

Golbom had plenty to talk about in late 2010 and early 2011, when Rick Scott, the governor-elect, decided to shut down the state Office of Drug Control and signed an executive order on the day of his inauguration that froze "all new regulations," which meant that rigorous new pain clinic standards created by the Board of Medicine were shelved.

---

* However, Gittens soon thereafter closed the clinic and returned home to New York, where she went to work for a nonprofit health organization that offered, among other services, treatment for addiction. She did not respond to multiple phone calls and letters asking for an interview for this book.

Then, everyone was astonished when the new governor cut funding to the state's long-awaited prescription drug database. Police, fellow Republicans, and the White House drug czar, among others, urged Scott to reconsider. The database was an ounce of prevention, they said, the best way to keep tabs on excessive prescribing. As Broward County sheriff Al Lamberti put it: "We cannot arrest our way out of this problem." Even pain medicine groups were stunned by Scott's move.

"It's just bizarre," Paul Sloan, president of the Florida Society of Pain Management Providers, told a reporter. "There's nobody in the field of medicine trying to kill (the database). It's the best thing the state has done on pill mills."

Kentucky officials, who'd been asking Florida to implement the database for years, were the most infuriated.

"What they're doing by this is basically setting up billboards across the country saying, 'Come to Florida and get your drugs,'" said Kentucky lieutenant governor Daniel Mongiardo.

For a few days, Scott ducked questions about why he'd killed the database. Then he said it was to save money. Then he said it was simply because a government database was intrusive. He did not elaborate, and the issue was locked in a stalemate.

That's when Purdue Pharma stepped in and offered $1 million to help Florida set up the drug database. The maker of OxyContin was in a transition period. After paying a $600 million fine three years earlier for lying about the drug's risks, Purdue had developed a new type of OxyContin pill that was harder to abuse. The company quietly began distributing the new formulation in August 2010. When addicts tried to powderize or dissolve it, the new pills turned into a gooey mass. Addicts tried filing the pills down to powder, tried cooking them in microwaves. They reported their findings on druggie websites: Nothing worked. Junkies called the new pills "gummies" or "jellynoses" because when they put it in their noses or mouths or needles, the pills caked up. Users who hadn't built a tolerance could still get high by swallowing the pills. But hardcore users could no longer get the full rush at once.

The effects were immediate. Brand-name OxyContin vanished from the streets—few addicts wanted it. In Boston, an addict killed his dealer because he thought the dealer had sold him the new OxyContin. Prescriptions of the popular 80-milligram OxyContin dropped 33.6 percent within two years.

Less of Purdue's product was going to the black market, and the company had transformed into a crusader for abuse-resistant opioids. It lobbied the FDA to deny other companies from making oxycodone pills with an easy-to-beat formulation. Companies like Mallinckrodt and Actavis, who made the oxycodone 30-milligram pills that were the standard fare offered by Florida pill mills.

Then the drug company offered to help fund Florida's prescription database. Governor Scott rejected the offer. Months went by, and the furor grew, and finally, in May 2011, the new governor quietly gave up on his opposition to the drug database and signed off on its funding.

"For almost ten years, at *least* ten years, the citizens of Florida have waited for our Florida state leaders to effectively do something about the drug distribution in our state," Golbom said during the introduction of his next show, "and, finally, Friday night was a historic night for the citizens of Florida."

In the middle of October 2010, Dr. Cynthia Cadet agreed to meet with federal prosecutors. Jennifer Turner and Mike Burt had gone to her house with a subpoena for a handwriting sample and used the opportunity to urge her to come in. She was looking at criminal charges, Burt had said. Cadet brought along a lawyer to the meeting.

Paul Schwartz outlined the case against Cadet with unusual breadth and bluntness. The lead prosecutor said the doctor had been part of a pill mill operation that had unleashed millions of addictive pills into the black market, killing numerous patients. If Cadet didn't cooperate, she would face charges in those deaths. If she cooperated and pleaded guilty to the drug charges, she would likely escape a life sentence. Former coworkers were already cooperating, he said. Cadet had been one of the biggest dispensers of oxycodone in the country, he said, and her former boss, Chris George, was a thug who had Nazi tattoos and a stripper girlfriend-turned-wife. Cadet should have been able to figure out that George was a bad guy and that a pain clinic that kept cash in garbage cans was a pill mill. The prosecutor was indignant and sarcastic, especially when he mentioned how she'd found the job at American Pain.

Schwartz said: What doctor on Earth would apply for a job on Craigslist?

In her soft, airy voice, Cadet told Schwartz she knew nothing about Chris George's private life. Her lawyer added that if Cadet had been a participant, she was an unwitting one. She had a blemish-free legal record. She was a naive and gullible person who had genuinely believed she was acting within the law.

Schwartz said: She may not have known the extent of what her employers were up to, but she enabled the process by prescribing the medication and getting paid a ton of money to do it. So she is not getting out of this case.

The meeting ended in a stalemate.

For Schwartz, one problem was that Chris George had rarely spoken to the doctors on his phone, so the wiretap recordings didn't offer much concrete evidence that tied the doctors into the conspiracy. The most damning piece of conspiracy evidence the prosecutors had against the doctors was that they'd signed the wholesaler questionnaire Ethan Baumhoff had falsified.

Before they could indict the whole group, the prosecutors needed at least one of the American Pain doctors to cooperate, to admit that he or she knew the clinic was a pill mill and to describe the clinic's medical practices. But the doctors still didn't seem to understand they were in real trouble. Schwartz didn't mince words in his meetings with the doctors. He told them he knew they'd gone to medical school, but to him they were drug dealers. He said what they'd done at American Pain wasn't practicing medicine, because *anyone* could have done it, with or without medical training.

Some doctors responded arrogantly, rolled their eyes during the meetings, acted bored. Some meetings ended quietly, others with yelling and F-bombs. Some doctors gave general information about their employment at the clinics, but none were willing to accept the idea that they were criminals, even if Chris George was one. Some of the doctors were so sure they were in the clear that they had taken jobs at other pain clinics. Typically, Jennifer Turner was the second most aggressive person in the room, after Paul Schwartz. She knew the doctors were in denial about their actions, that it would take them time to confront their guilt, but her patience dwindled as the months passed. Sometimes she just took a break, walked out of the room for a while.

The most compelling leverage against the doctors was the threat of death charges. By December 2010, the agents had created a database from the patient records they had seized in the raid of American Pain. The team cross-referenced the names in the patient database with the names of sixteen hundred people who had died of drug overdoses in Florida. More than fifty American Pain patients were on the overdose list. Seven of Roni Dreszer's patients had died in Florida, seven of Aruta's, five of Cadet's, four of Jacobo Dreszer's, and three of Boshers's. Because many patients tended to jump from clinic to clinic, not all the deaths were necessarily due to prescriptions received from American Pain doctors, but it was, nevertheless, a lot of dead bodies. Especially when you considered that 87 percent of the clinic's patients were from out of state. The team wondered how many deaths they would unearth if they began looking in Kentucky and West Virginia.

At long last, almost a year after the raids, two doctors surrendered. Both Dreszers agreed to talk to the feds, and in separate February 2011 meetings the father and son finally acknowledged that they'd known American Pain was a pill mill, though it wasn't something discussed or acknowledged at the clinic. Jacobo Dreszer said 98 percent of the patients were drug dealers or addicts and that Chris George pushed him to prescribe higher amounts. Roni Dreszer said he'd known within a month that the place was illegal, and the other doctors must have known too, even if they didn't speak about it. He'd discussed Carmel Cafiero's news reports about American Pain with other doctors and staff. All the doctors had received state health department complaints about their prescribing habits. Everyone had seen the police repeatedly coming to the clinic to investigate doctor shoppers.

Then, four months later, in June 2011, the investigators got the news they'd been hoping for. The ringleader was coming in. Chris George was ready to talk.

Every Friday, Derik went with Chris's mother to visit Chris in St. Lucie County Jail. He and Chris vowed to each other that they would stay strong and fight the government. But the months wore on, and more and more people flipped. The feds kept calling Derik's lawyer, saying they were going to arrest him any day. Derik just got tired. He stopped urging everybody not to cooperate with the feds. He began telling people to do what they had to do. He just wanted it to be over.

Derik saw Dianna a lot, and even with everything that was happening, she was still obsessing over Chris cheating on her during the American Pain days. She was pregnant with Chris's son. They'd conceived three weeks before his arrest the previous fall.

In jail, Chris spent several hours a day for a couple of months listening to wiretap recordings, accompanied by a law student hired by his attorney. It was strange to hear all those calls, to relive his final days as Florida's oxy king. His attorney asked the federal magistrate judge to quash evidence obtained from the search warrant and wiretap. The wiretap wasn't justified, the lawyer argued, because wiretaps were supposed to be a last resort. In this case, because American Pain was a public business, not a covert organization, normal investigative techniques would have done the trick. And the search warrant wasn't justified because it was largely based on evidence from the wiretap. Chris told Derik that the motions were guaranteed to succeed, and the evidence would be thrown out.

Then, in June 2011, Derik went to visit Chris one Friday, eight months after Chris had gone to jail, and Chris broke the news. Basically everyone was cooperating with the feds, everyone except Dr. Cadet.

Chris said: It's over, man.

Chris had decided to flip, which to Derik seemed like a complete about-face from a few days earlier. Chris told Derik he believed it was his only chance at avoiding a life sentence. They would get long sentences initially, Chris explained, but they could eventually bargain down by testifying against the doctors and drug wholesalers. Factor in time off for good behavior, and, at most, Chris said, they'd do five years.

Derik wasn't so sure, but he knew he had no choice but to flip. If he went to trial and Chris and almost everyone else testified against him, he'd definitely get a life sentence.

Chris met with the prosecutors in early July 2011, just after Dianna gave birth to their son. Derik went in a week later.

The day before his meeting, Derik called Cadet, who was still holding out, insisting she was innocent. Derik said she should meet with the feds too and take a plea bargain. No sense in fighting at this point. He said he would try to explain to them that she hadn't known about his past and the bad things he'd done at the clinic, that he believed she was less to blame than the other doctors. Maybe they'd cut her a break.

At the meeting, Paul Schwartz and the others were much less aggressive. They didn't try to make him cop to selling pills. They said they just wanted a general understanding of the operation. He told them all about it. They seemed to be hoping for more direct evidence to offer about the doctors' culpability. Derik tried to explain: It hadn't been like that. Even he and Chris hadn't talked about it openly most of the time. They thought it was legal, more or less.

Schwartz looked disappointed but seemed to accept Derik's version of events. The only thing that appeared to ruffle him was when Derik tried to explain that Dr. Cadet was probably the least culpable of the doctors. Schwartz said Derik didn't want to finger Cadet because he liked her and she'd been nice to him.

The next day, Derik called Cadet to tell her how it went.

Derik said: They don't like you at all. Once I mentioned your name, they got angry and didn't want to hear it.

11

A month after Chris George and Derik Nolan agreed to cooperate, the US Attorney's Office issued a 123-page indictment that detailed the operation of not only the pain clinics but the steroid clinic and Jeff's timeshare scam.* The indictment named thirty-two people, including thirteen doctors, eleven of whom worked either full- or part-time at either American Pain or Executive Pain. Two of the doctors were in their sixties, four in their seventies.

"The significance of today's takedown is that we have dismantled the nation's largest criminal organization involved in the illegal distribution of painkillers," said John Gilles, special agent in charge for FBI Miami. "Up until today, efforts focused on the demand by targeting individual users. Today, we attacked the source and choked off the supply."

The indictment included Derik Nolan, the George brothers, their mother, and Chris's wife, Dianna. Most of the lower-level employees and part-time doctors at American Pain were not indicted. State officials also charged Jeff George with felony second-degree murder in the overdose death of Joey Bartolucci, the case that prompted Jeff's infamous Lamborghini quote. The state attorney in Palm Beach County said he believed it was the first time a pain clinic owner who wasn't a prescribing doctor had been charged with murder in an overdose case. He'd also threatened to charge Chris George with murder, but backed off when Chris agreed to plead guilty to federal charges.

Schwartz made sure the indictment was longer than usual and full of juicy details. He wanted to bring as much news media attention to the pill

* The charges included racketeering conspiracy, money laundering conspiracy, possession with intent to distribute controlled substances, maintaining drug-involved premises, and wire and mail fraud conspiracy.

mill problem as possible, and the newspapers and TV stations lavished attention on the piles of cash, the doctors carrying guns, the expensive cars. As usual, Jeff captured more than his share of the spotlight. The brothers were portrayed as equal partners, never mind that Jeff's clinics were only a small fraction of the size of American Pain. Though the whole thing had been his idea initially, Jeff was essentially just another of the hundreds of clinic operators who followed in the wake of American Pain.

Those other clinic operators also paid close attention to the indictment. Two Pompano Beach firemen who owned a chain of six pain clinics and one pharmacy studied public records associated with the American Pain case, authorities said, allegedly using details from the indictment to figure out how to run a pill mill without getting busted.*

Only one drug wholesaler was indicted—Steven Goodman, owner of Medical Arts Inc. Goodman had ignored the DEA's warning that American Pain was a pill mill and lied to the DEA about the number of pills he'd sold to the clinic. Other wholesalers who'd supplied American Pain escaped indictment; they hadn't done anything quite that blatant.

Everyone had agreed to cooperate, except for Cadet. The other defendants were allowed to turn themselves in. Cadet was arrested at her home in Parkland and taken to jail in handcuffs. Her lawyer told Paul Schwartz that the doctor was willing to submit to an FBI-administered polygraph examination, but Schwartz refused.

At a detention hearing, Schwartz told a magistrate judge that investigators were still trying to determine how many of Cadet's patients had died.

"There are over fifty-three overdose deaths that we have been able to identify with this case alone, just in Florida," Schwartz said. "Again, we don't know how many kids died behind barns in Tennessee, Ohio, Kentucky, and West Virginia."

---

* It didn't work. In June 2012, the firefighters were charged with state racketeering violations related to their involvement with the clinics.

That fall, an FBI agent named Kurt McKenzie was given the task of tallying Dr. Cadet's death toll. McKenzie had a background in forensic science, and as a former DNA analyst, he understood evidence-handling procedures. McKenzie ran patient names through the Social Security Administration and medical examiners offices in other states and came up with a number. Fifty-one of the four thousand patients Dr. Cadet had seen at American Pain had died.

Probably others had died from drugs she'd prescribed, because many of the pills were sold on the street. But even if McKenzie could have tracked down those deaths, it would have been a stretch to charge the doctor with them, so McKenzie didn't work those cases. Many people also died in pill-related car accidents, but in poor rural jurisdictions in Kentucky, those cases were typically classified as accidents and potential evidence was destroyed.

So McKenzie built a database of the fifty-one deaths and worked to determine how much time had elapsed between when Dr. Cadet wrote the prescription and when the patient died. It wasn't pragmatic to charge the doctor with an overdose death that occurred months after she'd last written that patient a prescription, so he threw those deaths out. He also threw out cases in which the patients had seen other doctors or didn't have lethal amounts of oxycodone in their systems. McKenzie gathered toxicology reports, autopsy reports, and police reports. He and other members of the task force traveled to Kentucky to interview dozens of local police, toxicologists, coroners, and family members. The fast-talking agents and lawyers stood out in rural Kentucky, especially McKenzie, who didn't see another black man during his time in Harlan County.

McKenzie ended up with a list of ten deaths he believed they could take to court, and the prosecutors further narrowed the list to seven: six overdoses and one car crash. The trail of death stretched up the East Coast and into Appalachia.

In Ashland, Kentucky, a fifty-year-old woman's heart stopped in an ambulance headed to King's Daughters Medical Center. She survived for six hours on life support before multiple organs shut down. Two days earlier, Cadet had written her a prescription for oxycodone and Xanax.

At a truck stop in Fort Pierce, Florida, a fifty-year-old woman from Lexington, Kentucky, died in her car. Two days earlier, Cadet had written her prescriptions for oxycodone and Xanax.

In Mount Sterling, Kentucky, a thirty-eight-year-old man died on his couch, an American Pain appointment card in his wallet and a pill bottle with Cadet's name on it next to his body. Two days earlier, Cadet had written him prescriptions for oxycodone and Xanax.

Near Daytona Beach, Florida, a thirty-four-year-old man died on the floor of a house, blood oozing from his mouth. Ten days earlier, Cadet had written him prescriptions for oxycodone and Xanax.

At a Quality Inn in Boca Raton, a forty-two-year-old man from Hamblen County, Tennessee, died, blue-faced, on the floor of Room 265. Pill bottles with Cadet's name were found near the body. Two days earlier, Cadet had written him prescriptions for oxycodone and Xanax.

Just south of Jonesville, North Carolina, a twenty-two-year-old man from Racine, West Virginia, died at 4:45 a.m. when his 1989 Camaro smashed into a pickup truck on Interstate 77.* He was high on oxycodone and no skid marks could be found. Pill bottles bearing Cadet's name were in his pocket. The day before, Cadet had written him prescriptions for oxycodone and Xanax.

And of course there was Stacy Mason, the first Cadet-related death of the group, and the first one they'd unearthed.

In Kentucky, Alice Mason knew nothing of the events unfolding in Florida. It had been almost three years since Stacy had died. People said things would get easier. Alice couldn't say she agreed with that.

She prayed every day that someone would do something about that lady doctor in Florida. During the summers, she kept track of how many

* The crash also killed two passengers, but prosecutors decided it would be too difficult to try Cadet for those deaths.

times she mowed the pasture around Stacy's grave. Each November, on Stacy's birthday, the *Mount Vernon Signal* ran a poem Kevin had written about his brother. When December rolled around, Alice couldn't bear thinking about turning the calendar to January and seeing the date of Stacy's death, so she'd just turn the calendar a couple months ahead. Kevin was the only one Alice could talk to about Stacy. Her husband still barely spoke about his dead son.

In December 2011, Alice was feeding the game roosters when a police cruiser pulled up the long gravel drive of the farm on Hummingbird Lane. Barry Adams was driving. Alice knew who he was, but she'd never met him. Adams had been a deputy sheriff of Rockcastle County, but now he was assistant chief of police in Mount Vernon. There were two others in the car: a tall blonde woman and a broad-shouldered man. Alice couldn't imagine what these strangers wanted with her.

The Mason farm was so remote that even Barry Adams had a hard time finding it. Adams parked the car and turned to speak to Jennifer Turner and Mike Burt.

Adams said: You all just hang out here in the car. I'm going to talk to Ms. Mason, see if she'll agree to talk to you.

He got out. The agents sat in the cruiser, feeling conspicuous, studying the fields, the barn, the tethered roosters. Presently, Adams returned to the cruiser and said Alice Mason had agreed to speak to them. They got out and smiled at the little woman. She was short and round and covered with dirt.

Adams said: Now, Alice, this here is Mike, who is with the DEA, and this is Jennifer, who is with the FBI. They're here to talk with you about Stacy.

Alice invited the agents to come inside the house. Inside the simple house, Alice told the agents how she'd found her son behind the barn, how she'd gone to Florida to speak to the doctor. She cried during the story, and clasped Turner's hand. Turner cried too. Alice took them to the barn, to show them where they'd found his body. She gave them the pill bottles she'd found in Stacy's jacket pocket that day, and said she felt a great relief. Turner said the pill bottles would be great evidence in the case against Dr. Cadet.

Alice said: I knew God would send you.

Turner knew the little country woman would make a compelling and sympathetic witness, even if a South Florida jury couldn't make out everything she said. Turner asked Alice if she'd be willing to come to Florida one more time. If Dr. Cadet went to trial, would Alice come and testify about Stacy's death? Alice said she would.

Chris George pleaded guilty and received a seventeen-and-a-half-year sentence.

Derik did the same and got fourteen years.

The sentence lengths were based upon the number of pills each defendant was deemed responsible for. Because it was a conspiracy case, the ringleaders were considered responsible for all or most of the drugs distributed by the entire network. Thus, Jeff George got fifteen and a half years, and Ethan Baumhoff got eleven years, because he entered the conspiracy later.

The doctors were held responsible only for their own prescriptions. Dr. Beau Boshers got six and a half years. Dr. Roni Dreszer and Dr. Michael Aruta got six. Two of the elderly doctors died before they could be sentenced, one who had worked at Executive Pain and Dr. Jacobo Dreszer.

Chris George told the judge he'd pressured his wife and mother into working at the clinics, but Dianna Pavnick George and Denice Haggerty still received two and a half years each.

Steven Goodman, the drug wholesaler, received two and a half years of home confinement because he weighed 524 pounds and would have been a tremendous burden for any prison to care for. A doctor testified at his sentencing hearing that Goodman was not expected to live much longer anyway.

The defendants were given a few weeks to get their affairs in order before reporting to different federal prisons between April and June of 2012. They all held out hope that they would get their sentences reduced. They'd been given no promises, but they knew if they cooperated at Cadet's trial, Schwartz would likely ask the judge to slash their time.

One defendant who'd initially cooperated with the feds—Dr. Joseph Castronuovo—had second thoughts and refused to sign a plea bargain. Dr. Castronuovo, seventy-two, had worked at Executive Pain for about a year. Before working at the pain clinic, he'd been a prominent specialist in internal and nuclear medicine at several hospitals around New York. When Castronuovo stopped cooperating, the federal team began looking into overdose deaths they could tie to him, as they were doing with Cadet.

In July 2012, a second indictment charged Cadet and Castronuovo with distributing narcotics "outside the scope of professional practice and not for a legitimate medical purpose" that resulted in the death of patients. Seven death charges for Cadet, two for Castronuovo.

Over the next eleven months, the doctors' defense teams pored over 1.2 million documents tied to the case; the documents filled four rooms and the government spent a quarter million dollars on photocopy costs alone. The defendants also exchanged pre-trial blows with the prosecution, claiming the death charges should be thrown out. Schwartz's team had acted vindictively, they said, punishing the two doctors for not accepting plea deals. The judge disagreed.

Both doctors wanted to be tried separately. They'd worked at different clinics and barely knew each other. Dr. Cadet didn't want a jury to associate her with Dr. Castronuovo, who had allegedly told the feds: "This place was illegal, my motivation was financial, and I needed the money." For his part, Dr. Castronuovo didn't want to be tied to a co-defendant who was facing seven death charges. The judge said one trial would suffice.

Dr. Cadet's attorneys outlined her defense in a ninety-page motion. They asked the judge to dismiss the death charges and argued that Cadet had, in fact, complied with Florida's standards for pain treatment. She'd discharged patients who showed signs of illicit drug use or didn't have valid MRIs. If patients lied to her, they were in violation of the Pain Management Agreement they had signed. She said it wasn't illegal to treat out-of-state patients, even if the DEA considered that a red flag for pill mills. She cited e-mails from patients thanking her for getting them back on their feet. She argued that Chris George and Derik Nolan had created a system of paperwork and policies designed to bamboozle the Florida Department of Health, and it was so successful that it had also fooled her. Despite years of work, months of wiretaps, and numerous undercover operations, the government had no concrete evidence that showed she had knowingly engaged in a conspiracy to deal drugs.

The prosecutors said they didn't have to prove that Cadet and Chris George had had a formal agreement to unlawfully prescribe pills together. Circumstantial evidence was enough. The trial brief referred to a 2006 ruling by the US Court of Appeals for the Fourth Circuit that upheld the drug convictions of Ronald McIver, a pain doctor in North Carolina. In that case, the appeals court said federal prosecutors had to prove only that McIver "actually knew of the conspiracy or that he was willfully blind to it by purposely closing his eyes to avoid knowing what was taking place around him."

Flanked by federal marshals, Derik Nolan entered the courtroom and headed for the witness box. It was hard to swagger wearing leg irons, but he managed.

Seated in the box, he leaned back, cocked his head to the side. He tried to be cool, but inside, his heart was thumping hard. He didn't look at Cynthia Cadet, but she was over there to his right, sitting at the defense table, as girlish as ever, a quiet little librarian type, defenseless. He couldn't believe what he was about to do to her, but he had no choice. He'd been behind bars for thirteen months. No way he'd make it thirteen more years. He believed the prosecutors would ask the judge to slash his sentence by a third or even by half, if they approved of his cooperation. He was thirty-five years old. If he could get out by his early forties, he figured he still had a chance to live a semi-normal life, maybe even have a family.

He wore a blue short-sleeved jail-issue shirt that showed off his tattooed arms. He didn't feel remorseful, and he didn't put on a display of it either. The prosecutors wanted Derik to be himself in front of the jury, in all his outlaw glory. During a prep session with the prosecutors, he'd called himself "a wolf in wolf's clothing," and Paul Schwartz had loved it, his eyes rolling to the ceiling in jubilation.

Schwartz had said: *Exactly* like that. Say it exactly like that.

So now, as Schwartz asked him questions, Derik let loose and told the whole grand tale as it deserved to be told, head bobbing and shaking, gesturing with his manacled hands. He explained how he'd gotten to know Chris and Jeff building houses in North Port, how Chris had met Dr. Overstreet, how Derik helped build out the clinic and gradually took on more duties. How they'd played it fast and loose the first six months on Oakland Park Boulevard, then gradually, as the lines outside the clinic grew longer and longer each morning, reined it in. How they'd grown the staff, tried to curb the junkie stunts, hired the hot girls and muscle guys, lost doctors then hired more from Craigslist, including Cadet. His stories rambled on and on, until the defense lawyers were objecting and the court reporter was asking him to *please* slow it down.

Day Two, he was happy to see his sister sitting among the agents and defendants' relatives in the rear of the courtroom. He'd asked her to come. A year earlier, his sister had driven him to Louisiana so he could turn himself in at FCI Oakdale. Derik hadn't been willing to face his last hours of freedom sober, so he'd asked a cab driver where he could get some coke. He'd still been high when he reported to prison.

Now, in the witness box, Derik worked in Schwartz's favorite line when the prosecutor asked him whether everybody—meaning Cadet—had seen him discharging patients, sometimes through threats or manhandling.

"Was it out in the open?" Schwartz asked.

"Yeah, man," Derik said. "I mean, look at me. I'm not a wolf in sheep's clothing. I'm a wolf in wolf's clothing. I mean, I don't hide nothing from nobody."

Derik's sister chuckled, along with a couple of jurors, when Derik told the story about the guy who'd had the MRI that showed a tear in his uterus. Derik really loosened up after that. His voice took on a *no-shit-Sherlock* tone, as if he couldn't understand why Schwartz was asking him all of these questions that he already knew the answers to. He said one of the hot girls was "a whore." Derik's sister winced when he said they'd hired another woman because she had a "nice ass." Schwartz put a picture of the big Dixie Highway building on a screen, and Derik gestured at it proudly, saying, "Look at that building. That's awesome. I mean, that was going to be our headquarters." When they played the wiretaps, Derik in the recording bragging that he was the "fucking underboss" of the organization, Derik in the witness box couldn't help but smile, embarrassed at how full of shit he sounded. He covered his face with his hand, looked at his sister, then away.

His smile faded when Schwartz played a recording in which Derik told Chris that Ethan would be the first to flip. "When the shit goes down, God forbid something happens, where we all get arrested, you know, and the cops come in just to question us or something like that, that little faggot is going to squeal like a fucking pig with a knife in its neck. He's gonna squeal. He knows too much." It wasn't easy to sit in a witness box and listen to himself call someone else a rat.

Schwartz began tying the whole crazy scene to Cadet. Was the doctor in a position to witness the chaos in the waiting room, the patients having seizures, the garbage cans brimming with cash, rival clinic employees handing out cards? Derik answered: Yes.

On cross-examination, Cadet's lawyer focused on the fact that Cadet hadn't started working at American Pain until *after* Chris and Derik had strengthened the clinic's policies and paperwork. Derik agreed that during Cadet's time, patients were regularly discharged for failing drug tests, for being pregnant, for out-of-date MRIs. Derik agreed, the big building on Dixie Highway looked like a legitimate business. After Ethan's dress-policy changes, Derik agreed that even he eventually began wearing conservative office attire, slacks and dress shirts.

The lawyer asked if Derik believed Cadet had been fooled by the clinic's legitimate exterior, but Schwartz objected, since Derik had no way of knowing what Cadet truly believed. The judge sustained it.

But then, Cadet's lawyer asked Derik about the time he called Cadet, right before he'd flipped. Had Derik assured Cadet that he would tell the prosecutors that she hadn't known what was going on at American Pain?

Derik didn't know what to say. He was exhausted. It was after 4:00 p.m.; he'd been answering questions since 9:00 a.m. Schwartz's eyes bored in on him from the prosecutor's table. He felt lost. He rambled, trying to explain how he'd felt when he'd flipped.

"Listen, I was one of the last ones—pretty much the last one to go in there," he said. "I don't want *anybody*, even the people I don't like in this case, in jail. I'll do whatever. It is what it is. I don't remember my exact conversation with the government, you know. I said I like Dr. Cadet. She's an awesome person. She's my friend. I don't want to see anybody hurt, but I wanted Dr. Cadet to take a plea bargain. Everything would be easy, be done with, you know. I feel horrible."

On Derik's third day of testimony, Paul Schwartz was angry on his redirect, and Derik was scared he'd lost any chance of getting out of prison before his late forties. Schwartz's movements were even jerkier than usual, his questions like bullets.

"Sir, yesterday on cross-examination you said the words, 'There was nobody innocent there, everybody knew what was going on,'" Schwartz said. "What were you referring to?"

"Everybody . . . Everybody that I . . ." Derik stuttered, wanting to get this right, correct any damage he'd done to the prosecution's case yesterday. ". . . knew what was going on. Nobody . . ." Then, simply: "There's no children here."

"You say everybody knew what was going on," Schwartz said. "Explain that."

"You've seen the videos," Derik said. "It's hard to comprehend the fact that anybody could *not* know that we were a pill mill."

"Did you tell the government that she was a criminal?"

"I did, but I tried to downsize her role in it because, I don't know, I guess I want to take . . . I'd rather take responsibility than pass it off on somebody else."

"What does that mean?"

"I don't know," Derik said. "I try to be a stand-up guy sometimes when I shouldn't."

"Did you tell the government she was a criminal?" Schwartz barked again.

"I did."

"How did American Pain make its money?"

"Selling pills."

"Was that the plan?"

"That was the plan."

"Did Dr. Cadet participate in that plan?"

"She did."

"Could the plan have been carried out without the doctors?"

"Could not have."

"Were you a drug dealer?"

"I was."

"Was Christopher George a drug dealer?"

"The biggest."

"Was the staff at American Pain drug dealers?"

"We all were."

Extra emphatic: "Were the *doctors* drug dealers?"

"They are."

"Did you ever sit down with any doctor, including defendant Cadet, and say, 'We're operating a pill mill?'"

"No."

"Was it necessary?"

"No."

The Cadet/Castronuovo trial took two months.

The American Pain gang was reunited during that time, having been called back to South Florida from their various federal prisons and camps. They spent the trial on the two floors of the Palm Beach County Jail that housed federal prisoners. They all had prison-life stories by now, especially about the interminable and inexplicable bus and plane rides from one facility to another, fueled only by bologna sandwiches. Dr. Patrick Graham had faced the toughest stretch. He'd been incorrectly assigned to a Mississippi prison for illegal immigrants, and before his transfer could be worked out, a riot broke out, and his neck was grazed by a bullet. After that, he spent six weeks in solitary confinement. The co-defendants spent long days together and they weren't supposed to talk about the trial, so they compared notes about their various sentence lengths, about their different prisons, about their kids. And they talked a lot about the future, where they might live when they got out, what jobs they might pursue. In the evenings, they watched the Miami Heat win the 2013 NBA Finals.

Day by day, different individuals were pulled out to testify. Ethan Baumhoff had gone first, followed by Derik Nolan, then some lower-level guys, then Dianna Pavnick, Roni Dreszer, Chris George, Beau Boshers, and Michael Aruta.

After almost three years behind bars, Chris George's hair was streaked with gray, his build beefier. He looked fifteen years older than the twenty-seven-year-old who'd opened South Florida Pain five years earlier. He was the star witness, of course, and the prosecutors had wanted him to testify earlier. But Ethan Baumhoff had told Jennifer Turner that Chris had had a jailhouse telephone conversation with his father about Ethan's testimony. Turner had seen John George watching the proceedings from the spectator rows, scribbling in a maroon spiral notebook. The prosecution team dug up a recording of the call and everyone listened to it, John George telling his son what questions he could expect on cross-examination. The defense objected to Chris George being called as a witness. He was clearly doing illegal homework, they said. He wanted to provide the most damning possible testimony against Cadet and Castronuovo, they said, in hopes of winning an extra-large sentence reduction. The judge chewed out John George the next day and pondered the mess for a while before deciding to allow Chris George's testimony. Chris testified for most of three days, retelling the story Derik and Ethan had already told. Unlike Derik, whose nervousness in the witness box had made him sprawl out and jabber, Chris turned inward. He sat stock-still, and his voice was even more of a monotone than usual.

Alice Mason testified also, her third real trip outside of Kentucky and the first time she'd ever flown. The federal agents had sent her a plane ticket, and when her husband dropped her off at Blue Grass Airport in Lexington, the attendant asked her for an identification card. She hadn't thought to bring one. She explained that she was going to Florida to testify about her son's death in a big court case, and she just had to get on that flight, no matter what. The Delta officials asked her a lot of questions and finally, reluctantly, let her on board. The shuddering takeoff scared Alice to death—it just wasn't natural to be way up in the air—but it was beautiful up above the clouds. Mike Burt met her at the airport in West Palm Beach, took her to her hotel. In the courtroom, Alice saw Dr. Cadet out of the corner of her eye but wouldn't look right at her. She cried through much of her testimony, which embarrassed her, and the judge didn't let her tell how she'd gone to American Pain to talk to Cadet. She couldn't understand half of what the lawyers said, but at the end, gasping through tears, she said what she'd come to say.

"Me and my husband . . ." She couldn't speak for a moment, then said, simply: "It's hard on us. And I hope there's not nary a family that has to go through what I've had to go through. I don't wish it on my worst enemy. I can't hardly talk about my son without breaking down, and I am so sorry."

Cadet's lawyer just wanted this to end. "Ma'am, I'm very, very, very sorry."

"I know it's been four years, but to me it's just like yesterday," Alice said.

She stumbled climbing down from the witness stand, and Jennifer Turner jumped up to help her. Alice leaned against the tall FBI agent on the way out of the courtroom. Jennifer told Alice she'd done a great job.

Alice was glad to get out of there, away from all those people she didn't know, and go back home.

Paul Schwartz called sixty-four witnesses: ringleaders, staffers, doctors, cops, agents, toxicologists, medical examiners, and pain management experts. By the time the prosecution rested its case, the jury was inundated with details—the important, the trivial, and the lurid—about American Pain and the havoc it had wrought.

The jurors knew a great deal about Cadet's questionable medical practices. They knew she tended to write higher than the other doctors. They knew she saw an average of seventy-three patients a day toward the end, and spent an average of four minutes and forty seconds with each one.* They knew that the staffers who regularly went into her office couldn't remember ever seeing her actually examining a patient. They knew that the doctor never questioned the misspellings and dubious statements on the patient forms she used every day.

What they didn't know for sure was exactly what Cadet knew or believed about what she was doing, whether she was just a bad doctor or a criminal one. The doctor did not testify on her own behalf. And none of the prosecution witnesses offered a smoking gun, a moment when Cadet had said or done something that showed, beyond a reasonable doubt, that she knew she was writing scrips for junkies.

What Cadet did know, according to witnesses, was that American Pain was called out as a pill mill on news reports. She knew that various patients were being investigated for doctor shopping. She knew that patients were ejected on a regular basis for having track marks or dope in their urine. And still she kept seeing more and more patients, pocketing $1,217,125 during her sixteen months at the clinic.

The parts of Derik Nolan's testimony that had directly concerned Cadet were so tortured and conflicted that, despite the ring of truth in much of the rest of his story, it was unclear what he really thought about the doctor's culpability.

* At least on February 24, 2010, a day the FBI chose to analyze American Pain security-camera video of the patient flow into Dr. Cadet's office.

Detective Sergio Lopez testified about his experiences as an undercover patient at American Pain—but he'd seen Boshers, not Cadet.

Aruta, Boshers, and Dreszer testified that it hadn't taken them long to figure out that American Pain was a pill mill. But they also said they'd never had explicit conversations about that subject with Cadet.

The prosecution's pain management expert, Dr. Rafael Miguel, testified that he studied more than three hundred of Cadet's patient files and found them to be clearly the work of a pill mill doctor.

The defense's pain management expert, Dr. Carol Warfield, testified that she'd studied the same randomly selected files, and they looked fine to her.

Paul Schwartz's closing argument, in a nutshell, was this: The doctor *had* to have known that her patients were lying. Everyone else at American Pain had known. There's no way she didn't know. Her actions had directly led to the deaths of seven people, and she deserved a life sentence.

Cadet's lawyer told the jury that in 2010, the government was in a fight for the very soul of Florida. They had to get the prescription drug problem under control, by any means necessary, and Dr. Cadet had been swept into a dragnet prosecution. But, he argued, the case was already over. For all intents and purposes, the government had won, and the real criminals were already behind bars.

The jurors spent twenty hours deliberating. They decided they couldn't see inside the doctor's brain any more than the doctor could see inside her patients' brains.

Whether or not she truly believed her patients were in pain, Dr. Cadet chose to accept the stories her patients told.

And the jurors chose to accept Dr. Cadet's story.

Epilogue

Oakdale, Louisiana

May 31, 2014

The visitation room at the Federal Correctional Institution at Oakdale contains about 150 beige plastic chairs lined up in rows, armrest to armrest. Vending machines and microwave ovens occupy one concrete-block wall, restroom doors and water fountains another. At peak visiting hours, most of the seats are filled with prisoners and their families, and it's hard to hear over the din. It's a self-contained ecosphere, a single room designed to confine inmates for hours at a time. It's weirdly equivalent to the waiting room at American Pain: a handful of guards overseeing dozens of desperate captives. Except, of course, that Derik Nolan was the head warden at American Pain. At Oakdale, he's just another prisoner.

Derik reported to prison more than two years ago, and this is his first time in the visitation room. No friends or family have made the long trip to central Louisiana. We sit across from each other, and he drinks cranberry juice, sipping it slowly so he won't have to ask the CO if he can go to the bathroom. I bought the bottle of juice for him from one of the vending machines. He has no money, of course, so I've brought a prison-approved plastic bag of quarters so we can get something for lunch. He's not allowed to get up and get food for himself, so I buy and heat his double cheeseburger.

Derik has gained weight in prison. The food is crap. Anything decent that comes into the kitchen goes into the inmate black market, and most of what's left is pure starch. So he eats a lot of rice and beans and works out until he can't move. And he reads, hours every day. He barely cracked a book in his first thirty-five years, but now he blows through three or four a week. It's a good way to kill time and stay out of beefs with other inmates. He likes crime stories and historical fiction. It's the only exercise his brain gets, and that, to him, is the worst thing about prison. Out in the world, he had to use his smarts to get by. In prison, he has a roof over his head and three squares a day, and his brain is starting to shrivel.

He and Chris sometimes exchange letters. He doesn't hear much from his other co-defendants, and none of them are in Oakdale. Chris is in Georgia, Ethan in Arkansas, Jeff in Maryland. Dianna Pavnick George and Denice Haggerty are already back home.

Cadet is free, for the moment. Derik follows her case through prison-system e-mails from his sister. After the trial last summer, Cadet and Castronuovo were acquitted of the death charges and drug charges. The jury found them guilty only of money laundering. The *Palm Beach Post* called the verdicts a "stunning defeat" for the prosecutors.

Five months later, the defendants who'd testified or otherwise cooperated in the case against the doctors began to receive their sentence reductions. Paul Schwartz recommended that US District Court judge Kenneth Marra slash sentences by one-third. The defendants asked for more, and the judge cut the sentences roughly in half.

Except for those of two defendants. Chris George got three and a half years off of his seventeen-and-a-half-year sentence, nowhere near half and even less than the one-third that the prosecutors had requested.

And Derik Nolan got nothing. The US Attorney's Office never requested a reduction for Derik, and Judge Marra didn't give him one. Derik's lawyer and sister tried to find out why, but got no answers. Derik figured Paul Schwartz was blaming Cadet's acquittals on his conflicted performance in the witness box. Schwartz, understandably, will not comment. Derik alternated between rage and depression for a while, then gave up hope and settled in for the long haul. If he can stay out of fights and earn his full allotment of twenty-two months off for good behavior, he could be eligible for release in 2024, two years after Chris's earliest possible release date.

In April, Judge Marra dropped another surprise when he sentenced Cadet and Castronuovo. The doctors did not expect lengthy prison sentences on the money-laundering convictions, but Castronuovo got eighteen months and Cadet got six and a half years. Marra didn't buy Cadet's defense that she had been fooled, and he specifically pointed to the undercover video of Derik yelling at the patients to not shoot up in the parking lot.

"All you have to do is look at (that) and see the chaos, the madness that was going on in that facility," Marra said. "It's just not possible to not have known that those people were all drug addicts."

The doctors' lawyers appealed. If Cadet wasn't guilty on the drug charges, her lawyer said, then the money she made was clean. And if the money was clean, how could she have laundered it? The doctors remain free while they pursue appeals, which could take years.

At the FBI, Jennifer Turner and Kurt McKenzie have moved on to other investigations, and neither expects to encounter another case as rewarding or as demanding as American Pain. McKenzie, who led the death probe, says he's worked only one other investigation that took the same toll on him, and that was the terrorist attacks of September 11, 2001.

Larry Golbom ended the Prescription Addiction Radio show in March 2014. He is proud of his seven-and-a-half-year run and believes the show had a positive impact, but it never took off the way he originally hoped. He continues to work for the same major pharmacy, and notes that many Florida pharmacists now refuse to fill opioid narcotic prescriptions. Golbom fills them when he believes the prescription is legitimate and comes from a qualified doctor. He's not anti-opioid; he just wants people to understand the drugs.

Meanwhile, many in the medical profession are beginning to recognize that rampant prescribing of addictive narcotics for chronic pain has proven to be a devastating mistake in many cases. Short-term, the drugs make you feel great. Long-term, many legitimate pain patients are taking the drugs as prescribed and finding it harder and harder to get out of bed in the morning. Take these drugs too long and not under the watchful eye of a doctor who understands the subtleties of opioid pain management, and it may be difficult to regain a normal life. Studies have demonstrated that opioids may actually *increase* pain over the long run and that non-drug treatments are much more effective than opioid therapy. The federal Centers for Disease Control and Prevention has declared that painkiller overdose deaths are an official epidemic.

At the same time, Florida is celebrating having beaten back the pill mill scourge through arrests and legislation. In 2010, ninety of the top one hundred oxycodone-purchasing doctors in the country lived in Florida. By 2014, the DEA said, the state contained only one. The number of oxycodone pills shipped to Florida dropped from 650 million in 2010 to 313 million in 2013. The number of pain clinics dropped from more than one thousand to less than four hundred. Some of the pill mills moved to other states, notably Missouri, home of Mallinckrodt's US headquarters and the last state in the country that lacks a prescription database. Meanwhile, pills grew more scarce and expensive in Kentucky, and hill-country sheriffs began seeing heroin for the first time ever. The same fix, now cheaper.

So the pill mills left Florida, to great fanfare . . . but, unabated and under the radar, the country's appetite for pills has only continued to grow. That much is clear because the manufacturing companies keep asking the DEA for permission to make more pills, and the DEA keeps granting it. All those pills are going *somewhere*. In 2014, even as supplies shipped to Florida were shrinking, the total number of kilograms of oxycodone manufactured took another big leap, from 131,500 to 149,375—almost three times the amount produced a decade earlier, and forty-two times the amount made in 1993.

Any narco cop will tell you, when you kill off one secondary source of narcotics, two more tend to pop up elsewhere. You have to choke off the source, strangulate the fountainhead.

Or, as Derik puts it, junkies gonna get them pills, somehow, someway.

Derik doesn't know what he'll do if he makes it out of prison. Chris's mom sent him magazines not long ago, and the pictures of Ireland made him want to go there. When old friends e-mail him, which is infrequently, he thinks about returning to South Florida. When he hears it's snowing up north, he remembers growing up on the farm near Binghamton, New York, and he longs to go back home.

I've been communicating with Derik almost daily over the phone and e-mail for months, and he shows little remorse about his role in supplying millions of pills and fueling a gigantic wave of addictions up and down the East Coast. He mainly feels sorry for himself.

But he does feel bad about certain things. He feels bad when he thinks about the kids he saw at American Pain. He feels bad when he thinks about how he fired the homeless guy who watched over the parking lot. He feels bad about testifying against Cadet, though he believes she knew what she was doing.

And that's the thing. He wasn't alone. For a few years, in plain view, hard drugs were for sale in Florida, and it seemed to Derik that almost everyone was on the take. He and Chris turned doctors into drug dealers. They turned an ex-cop into a bag man. They turned pharmaceutical wholesalers into accomplices. Politicians and realtors and lawyers and landlords and medical associations and the *New Times* weekly newspaper helped them pull off the scam. And in the end, it was the big boys—Actavis and Mallinckrodt—who made the big money in Florida.

He and Chris were bad guys, no doubt about it. Felons. Violent men. So why did everyone make it so easy for them?

No doubt, this line of thinking is a way for Derik to blame the whole thing on somebody else.

But that doesn't mean it's not true.

"The fucked-up thing isn't that we did this," Derik says. "Of *course* we did it. The fucked-up thing is that we were *allowed* to do it. That they let us do it. Why were two guys like me and Chris allowed to set up a business like this? When we said we wanted to set up a pain clinic, they shoulda been like, 'Umm . . . *No.*' Or, 'Let's see your criminal record.' When we said we wanted to order $100,000 worth of pain medication, they shoulda said no."

He pauses, raising his eyebrows high to emphasize his point.

"They shoulda said, '*Fuck*, no.'"

Sources

This book is a work of reported nonfiction. I changed no names or details. All information in the book was either told to me, observed by me, or found in public records or in journalistic and academic venues.

To report the book, I traveled to Kentucky and Florida numerous times and conducted hundreds of interviews. I researched and visited most of the sites described in the book. I also read numerous books and hundreds of newspaper and magazine articles, as well as dozens upon dozens of scholarly articles and government reports. I attended the 2013 National RX Drug Abuse Summit in Orlando, Florida, where I met many people on the front lines of the prescription opioid epidemic and heard numerous experts speak. I spent two weeks in West Palm Beach observing the federal trial of Dr. Cynthia Cadet. I also reviewed hundreds of court transcripts, pleadings, and investigative documents.

While I did not use a great deal of specific data from the following books and articles, they were key sources nonetheless:

- Barry Meier's books—*Pain Killer: A "Wonder" Drug's Trail of Addiction and Death* from 2003 and *A World of Hurt: Fixing Pain Medicine's Biggest Mistake* from 2013—and his years of coverage in the *New York Times* provided a foundational understanding of the resurgence of opioid narcotics.
- The article "How Florida Brothers' 'Pill Mill' Operation Fueled Painkiller Abuse Epidemic," by Thomas Francis, published on msnbc.com on May 7, 2012, introduced me to the story of American Pain.
- The article "American Pain: The Largest U.S. Pill Mill's Rise and Fall," by Felix Gillette, published in *Businessweek* in June 2012, helped me understand the pharmaceutical opioid manufacturing and sales process.

I read numerous academic journal articles about the opioid epidemic. The following were particularly useful to me:

- "The Prescription Drug Epidemic in the United States: A Perfect Storm," by J. C. Maxwell, *Drug and Alcohol Review*, 2011.
- "Black Beauties, Gorilla Pills, Footballs, and Hillbilly Heroin: Some Reflections on Prescription Drug Abuse and Diversion Research Over the Past 40 Years," by James A. Inciardi and Theodore J. Cicero, *Journal of Drug Issues*, 2009.
- "The OxyContin Epidemic and Crime Panic in Rural Kentucky," by Kenneth D. Tunnell, *Contemporary Drug Problems*, Summer 2005.

I tried, usually more than once, to communicate with every defendant who was affiliated with American Pain. Many chose not to speak to me, including Dr. Cynthia Cadet. Others communicated with me briefly, then cut off contact. Chris George answered many questions over prison e-mail but did not agree to an in-person visit or a phone call. He was concerned that helping with the book would make it look as though he was proud of what he did. However, he said he wanted to tell his story so others would avoid his mistakes, and he asked me to put a note to that effect in the book. Derik Nolan and I communicated for many months, exchanging hundreds of e-mails, speaking on the phone more than a dozen times, and talking for two days in person. Derik paid for many hours of time on the prison computers and phones, and I voluntarily sent him small amounts of money several times (about $100 total) to defray those costs. I also tried repeatedly to contact Dr. Rachael Gittens and Dr. Enock Joseph via e-mail, phone, and letter, and neither responded. Other key interviewees described in the book included Jennifer Turner, Kurt McKenzie, Paul Schwartz, Larry Golbom, Dr. Michael Aruta, Alice Mason, Kevin Mason, and Shelby Durham.

Other people I spoke to did not appear in the book but provided enlightening background information. Pete Jackson of Advocates for the

Reform of Prescription Opioids and Karen Perry of the NOPE Task Force shared information about their organizations and their personal losses. Florida Board of Medicine member Dr. Steven Rosenberg shared information about the height of the Florida pill mill crisis. Mike Fulton of the Asher Agency and Michael Barnes of the Center for Lawful Access and Abuse Deterrence provided useful perspectives on the national opioid crisis. J. E. "Ned" Crisp, director of Fiveco Area Drug Enforcement Task Force in Russell, Kentucky, and Dan Smoot of Operation UNITE provided background about Kentucky's fight against prescription painkillers. Dr. Gary Potter, a criminal justice professor at Eastern Kentucky University, shed light on the current and past drug scene in eastern Kentucky. Dr. Hilary Surratt, director of the Center for Applied Research on Substance Abuse and Health Disparities at Nova Southeastern University in Miami, Florida, provided insight into opioid addiction research. My friend Don Robinson, executive vice president and chief operating officer of MVB Financial Corp., answered my questions about banking and money laundering.

To recreate events, I used a combination of sources, including interviews, personal observation, photographs, videos, wiretap transcripts, court transcripts, and investigative documents. The website www.wunderground.com detailed weather on specific days. When I came across conflicting information, I either left it out or used the version of events I believed was most likely to be accurate. Occasionally, I made minor edits to improve a quote's clarity or brevity, and I took pains to never alter the meaning of the dialogue.

Major sources for specific sections are cited below.

PROLOGUE AND CHAPTER 1

Primary sources of information were interviews with Chris George, Derik Nolan, and Jennifer Turner; courtroom testimony of George, Nolan, and Dianna Pavnick George; and other court documents. Other key sources:

- Articles in the *Sun-Sentinel* and the *Palm Beach Post* and a Florida Traffic Crash Report provided details about the train crash.

- The 2010 National Survey of Drug Use and Health provided the statistics about rates of prescription drug use.
- Stories in the *Middletown Times Herald Record* and the *New York Times* provided details about the murders committed by Derik's father.
- The New York State Office of the Professions provided information about Dr. Rachael Gittens's medical license.
- The website archive.org allowed me to look back at the now-defunct South Florida Pain Clinic/American Pain website at different points in its existence.

CHAPTER 2

Primary sources of information were interviews with Larry Golbom and Carmel Cafiero, the Prescription Addiction Radio show website, http://prescriptionaddictionradio.com/, and the book *Pain Killer*, by Barry Meier. Other key sources:

- Florida Board of Medicine records and the *Tampa Tribune* stories provided information about the case against the doctor who prescribed pills that ended up in the hands of Larry Golbom's son.
- David Morris's 1993 book, *The Culture of Pain*, described the 1950s study that noted differences in the way ethnic background influences how people talk about pain.
- Filings in the lawsuit, *The People of the State of California v. Purdue Pharma L.P. et al*, and stories in *Propublica*'s long-running "Dollars for Doctors: How Industry Money Reaches Physicians" series provided information about the promotion of prescription opioids.
- News stories in the *Lexington Herald-Leader* and the *Huntington Herald-Dispatch* provided details about the Appalachian Pain Foundation.
- "The OxyContin Panic and Crime Panic in Rural Kentucky," by Kenneth D. Tunnell, published in *Contemporary Drug Problems*, Summer 2005, provided information about early OxyContin abuse.
- The Centers for Disease Control and Prevention (CDC) provided information about the rise in drug overdose deaths.

- A Government Accountability Office (GAO) report from 2003 on OxyContin and news stories in the *Chicago Tribune* and *Richmond Times Dispatch* provided details about Purdue's legal fight against personal-injury claims.
- The Federal Register and the Drug Enforcement Administration Office of Diversion Control website, www.deadiversion.usdoj.gov, contained information about oxycodone manufacturing quotas over the years.
- The excellent story by Guy Taylor, "Mills Making the Pills," published in the *St. Petersburg Times* on October 30, 2011, as well as other news stories in the *Lexington Herald-Leader* and the *Weekly Standard* provided information about the DEA's quota-setting process.
- The CDC's Morbidity and Mortality Weekly Report of November 4, 2011, provided the statistic that the United States manufactures enough prescription narcotics for every American adult to take a 5-milligram Vicodin every four hours for nearly a month.
- The 2008 Annual Report of the International Narcotics Control Board provided the statistics about the percentages of the global supply of hydrocodone and oxycodone that are consumed in the United States.
- The 2004 book *The Truth About the Drug Companies*, by Marcia Angell, provided information about the pharmaceutical lobby.

CHAPTERS 3–4

Primary sources of information were interviews with Chris George, Derik Nolan, John Paul George, Carmel Cafiero, and Juan Ortega; courtroom testimony of George, Nolan, Dr. Patrick Graham, Ethan Baumhoff, Dr. Roni Dreszer, and Dianna Pavnick George; and other court documents. Other key sources:

- Florida Board of Medicine records provided information about the Florida Department of Health (FDOH) inspection of South Florida Pain in June 2008.

- The DEA Office of Diversion Control website provided a copy of the 2006 policy statement entitled "Dispensing Controlled Substances for the Treatment of Pain."
- FDOH records provided information about the clinic Dr. Gittens opened in 2008.
- Florida court records, accessed through LexisNexis, provided information about Chris George's arrest in August 2008.
- The Alfred I. duPont Awards channel of Vimeo.com provided the video of Carmel Cafiero's WSVN-TV report about American Pain. WSVN-TV's website, www.wsvn.com, contained more information about Cafiero's interactions with the clinic.
- FDOH records provided information about the administrative complaints against Dr. Gittens and Dr. Joseph.

CHAPTER 5

Primary sources of information were interviews with Alice Mason, Kevin Mason, Shelby Durham, Rockcastle County coroner Billy Dowell, Reverend Tommy Miller, Rockcastle County sheriff Mike Peters, Dr. Gary Potter, Jennifer Turner, and Kurt McKenzie; the courtroom testimony of Alice Mason, Dr. Jennifer Schott, Dr. William Lee Hearn, Dr. George Behonick; and other court documents. Other key sources:

- The "Prescription for Pain" package published by the *Lexington Herald-Leader* on January 19, 2003, provided a great deal of information about prescription drugs and corruption in Kentucky.
- News stories in the *Lexington Herald-Leader* and the *Daily Independent* of Ashland, Kentucky, and court records provided information about the case of Dr. Roger Browne.
- The article "Country Comfort: Vice and Corruption in Rural Settings," by Dr. Gary Potter and Dr. Larry Gaines, published in 1992 in the *Journal of Contemporary Criminal Justice*, provided important details about the drug scene in eastern Kentucky.

- Kentucky Office of Drug Control Policy reports provided statistics about drug overdoses and babies born addicted.
- *Orlando Sentinel* stories provided information about Jewell Padgett.

CHAPTER 6

Primary sources of information were interviews with Chris George, Derik Nolan, and Dr. Michael Aruta; courtroom testimony of George, Nolan, Dr. Aruta, Dr. Patrick Graham, Dr. Roni Dreszer, Dr. Beau Boshers, Ethan Baumhoff, and Dianna Pavnick George; and other court documents. Other key sources:

- A Broward County grand jury report on pill mills issued in November 2009 provided the statistic that a new pain clinic was opening every three days in the county, on average.

CHAPTER 7

Primary sources of information were interviews with Jennifer Turner, Kurt McKenzie, Barry Adams, Florida Board of Medicine member Dr. Steven Rosenberg, Tina Reed, Derik Nolan, and Chris George; the testimony of George, Nolan, Whitney Summitt, and Detective Nicholas Patriarca; and other court records, including DEA records related to the administrative hearings of American Pain doctors.

- An *Orlando Sentinel* news story from March 3, 2011, provided the information about the amount of oxycodone distributed by Florida doctors in 2009.
- A Rockcastle County Court arrest report provided information about the first time Barry Adams saw oxycodone 30-milligram pills in Rockcastle County.
- A July 12, 2012, story in the *Daily Independent* of Ashland, Kentucky, and law enforcement sources provided information about the flights nicknamed "The Oxy Express."

- The Appalachia High Intensity Drug Trafficking Area's Drug Market Analysis 2011 report provided details about the Kentucky/Florida painkiller pipeline.
- News stories in the *Tampa Tribune* and the *Sun-Sentinel* provided information about the fight to create Florida's prescription drug database.
- A September 2010 series in the *St. Petersburg Times* provided information about the analysis of FDOH doctor disciplinary cases.
- The FDOH's annual report of 2008–2009 provided information about the licensing of medical offices.
- A *Palm Beach Post* news story on November 1, 2009, "Painkiller Clinics Use Legal Loopholes," provided information about drug offenders who opened pain clinics.
- A GAO report from August 2011 entitled "Prescription Drug Control" provided the statistic that Florida doctors were purchasing nine times more oxycodone than the other forty-nine states combined.
- A *USA Today* story on February 24, 2011, entitled "Florida Raids Target Sellers of Pain Pills" contained the statistics about how many doses of oxycodone Florida doctors were buying.
- An Ohio Prescription Drug Abuse Task Force report from October 2010 provided information about how much oxycodone Ohio doctors were buying.

CHAPTER 8

Primary sources of information were interviews with Chris George, Derik Nolan, and Nettie Stephens, operator of a store near the final American Pain location; courtroom testimony of George, Nolan, and Dianna Pavnick George; and other court documents. Other key sources:

- An arrest report from the Jacksonville Sheriff's Office provided information about the December 2009 arrests of Chris George and Derik Nolan.

- *Sun-Sentinel* and *Palm Beach Post* news stories provided information about anti–pill mill measures Florida lawmakers were proposing in late 2009 and early 2010.
- A *Wall Street Journal* news story provided information about pill mills moving from Florida to Georgia.

CHAPTERS 9–11 AND EPILOGUE

Primary sources of information were interviews with Jennifer Turner, Kurt McKenzie, Paul Schwartz, Lawrence LaVecchio, Larry Golbom, Chris George, and Derik Nolan; courtroom testimony of George, Nolan, Ethan Baumhoff, Dr. Michael Aruta, and Dianna Pavnick George; and other court records, including DEA records related to the administrative hearings of American Pain doctors. Other key sources:

- A *Palm Beach Post* story provided the quote from Chris George's attorney.
- *Lexington Herald-Leader* stories provided information about the death of Timmy York.
- *Sun-Sentinel* stories provided information about Paul Schwartz's life and career.
- Stories in *Businessweek* and the *Sun-Sentinel* and a 2013 DEA presentation entitled "Prescription Drug Trafficking and Abuse Trends" provided details about the DEA's shutdown of oxycodone wholesalers.
- The Florida Department of Health Annual Report 2009–10 provided information about the number of pain clinics that registered with the state.
- The *Sun-Sentinel* and *Palm Beach Post* provided information about Governor Rick Scott's proposal to kill funding for the prescription drug database.
- Food and Drug Administration records and the *New York Times* provided information about the new formulation of abuse-deterrent OxyContin.
- A DEA press release provided information about the Pompano Beach firemen who allegedly started a chain of pill mills.

Acknowledgments

So many people helped, it's hard to know where to start.

My writing group pals, including Daleen Berry, Dana Coester, and James Harms, read bits and pieces of the story and gave great notes. Special thanks to the group's founders, Alison Bass and Benyamin Cohen, who read even more and provided particularly helpful advice and support. Becky Beaupre Gillespie, April Johnston, and Molly Lyons all read the book proposal and gave incisive feedback and leads; thank you all for your early and enthusiastic support. Josh Fershee and Kendra Huard Fershee read an early draft of the entire manuscript and provided excellent notes, especially regarding legal aspects of the story.

Heartfelt thanks to Ron and Leslie Marcus, who let me use their pleasant condo in Palm Beach County as my reporting headquarters for two weeks in the summer of 2013. Joel and Cheri Schwartz, my mother-in-law and father-in-law, helped make that happen, and I am grateful for that, and for their support. To my sister, Laura Hall, and the rest of her family, thanks for the cheery home and comfortable bed when I visited Louisiana.

I'm grateful to Paula McMahon of the *Sun-Sentinel*, as well as Kevin Nolan and Kim Williams, for helping me track down documents. Many thanks to Kimberly Walker and Christa Currey of the WVU Reed College of Media for their excellent promotional efforts. Thanks to Marlene Fernandez-Karavetsos of the US Attorney's Office of the Southern District of Florida and Jim Marshall of the Miami office of the FBI for helping to arrange interviews in their respective offices. Anne Beagan at FBI headquarters in Washington, DC, cleared the way for me to be granted additional access and documents.

I owe a great deal to everyone listed in the "Sources" section for lending me their time and knowledge. Special thanks to the following:

Alice Mason is one of the most inspiring and courageous people I have ever interviewed. I greatly appreciate her letting me trespass repeatedly on her beautiful farm. Jennifer Turner and Kurt McKenzie spent many hours explaining the FBI investigation of American Pain. Gaining FBI approval for the interviews was a challenge because Dr. Cynthia Cadet's case was still in appeals. But the special agents made the interviews happen because they wanted the story to be known. And so did Derik Nolan, who spent many months answering my endless questions. He witnessed more of the day-to-day operation of American Pain than anyone else, including Chris George. I appreciate Derik's willingness to tell the story and the effort he put into remembering and making sense of it.

As dean of the WVU Reed College of Media, Maryanne Reed has always championed my work and once again helped me find the time and resources to pursue this story. Most crucially, she supported my application for a sabbatical in 2013, and that break gave me time to focus exclusively on understanding the opioid epidemic and the case of American Pain. As my friend, she read drafts at different points and provided her usual excellent notes.

A warm thanks to James Jayo, formerly of Lyons Press, and Joelle Delbourgo of Joelle Delbourgo Associates, for backing the book. The same to Keith Wallman of Lyons Press, whose enthusiasm and thorough edits helped so much in the homestretch. Special gratitude to Shari Smiley of the Gotham Group and to Melisa Wallack, for recognizing the potential and significance of this story.

And none of them would have seen it if it wasn't for Jacqueline Flynn of Joelle Delbourgo Associates, whose cheerful intelligence guided the book from almost the very beginning of the reporting process. Thanks for encouraging me to pursue this story and for always returning my calls!

To my parents, Dan and Loranne Temple, for always being curious about and supportive of my work. To my boys, Gideon and Hank, for reminding me how sweet life can be. And most of all, to my wonderful wife, Hollee Schwartz Temple. You listened so thoughtfully as I rambled for untold hours about my latest problems with this story (even if I did sometimes look over to find you "resting your eyes"). You're a hell of an editor, and I promise not to forget that next time around. Thanks for all the times when I was debating whether I should take another trip to Florida or Kentucky or Louisiana, and you said, simply, "Go."

Index

M

N

P

Q

R

About the Author

John Temple grew up in Chicago, Louisiana, and Pittsburgh. He has worked as a newspaper reporter in Pittsburgh, North Carolina, and Tampa.

Temple is the author of two previous nonfiction books: *The Last Lawyer: The Fight to Save Death Row Inmates* (2009) and *Deadhouse: Life in a Coroner's Office* (2005). In 2010, *The Last Lawyer* won the Scribes Book Award from the American Society of Legal Writers. More information about Temple's books can be found at www.johntemplebooks.com.

Temple is an associate professor of journalism at the West Virginia University Reed College of Media. He lives in Morgantown, West Virginia, with his wife, Hollee Schwartz Temple, and their two boys.